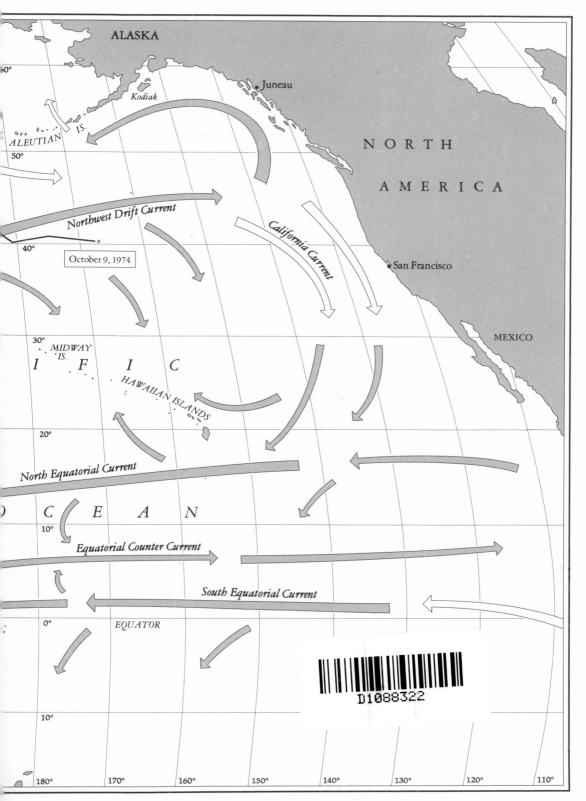

ALASKA

• Juneau

Kodiak

ALEUTIAN IS.

NORTH

AMERICA

Northwest Drift Current

California Current

October 9, 1974

• San Francisco

MIDWAY IS.

P   I   F   I   C

MEXICO

HAWAIIAN ISLANDS

North Equatorial Current

C   E   A   N

Equatorial Counter Current

South Equatorial Current

EQUATOR

Tai Ki

Tai Ki

To the Point of No Return

KUNO KNÖBL
WITH ARNO DENNIG

Translated from the German
by Rita and Robert Kimber

W.H. ALLEN · LONDON
A Howard & Wyndham Company
1976

The initials following the captions refer to the photographers as follows: D, Arno Dennig; G, Carl Grage; K, Bob Kendrick; KK, Kuno Knöbl; P, Hal Price; R, Wolf Werner Rausch; HR, H. Reisl; BM, Bill Martin, Document Associates Inc.; WM, passengers of the *Washington Mail;* MNH, from the Museum of Natural History, New York. The illustrations on page 27 were taken from Wolfgang Marschall's book *Transpazifische Kulturbeziehungen* and appear here with the permission of the Verlag Klaus Renner, Munich. We are also grateful to the Holle-Verlag, Baden-Baden, for permission to use the photographs of the terra-cotta portraits that first appeared in Alexander von Wuthenau's book *Altamerikanische Tonplastik.*

The first two photographs following page 214 are by Arno Denning.

Designed by Susan Windheim

To follow the dream, and again to follow the dream — and so
— always — *usque ad finem*. . . .

— JOSEPH CONRAD, *Lord Jim*

Foreword

KUNO KNÖBL AND ARNO DENNIG WERE THE INITIATORS OF THE
Tai Ki expedition. They were later joined by Carl Frederik Grage,
who built the ship and acted as the nautical adviser for the entire expedition.

Our publisher, Fritz Molden, financed the expedition. Other
persons and organizations to whom we are indebted for help are
listed in the Afterword.

The book is based on the personal notes of the author and
of Arno Dennig. Supplementary material was drawn from Carl
Frederik Grage's journal and from the journals of the other crew
members.

The crew of the *Tai Ki* was a small community formed for
the purpose of realizing a common goal. Every member of the
crew had his work to do and his burden to bear, both in the storms
of the Pacific and in the days thereafter.

Contents

Tai Ki

CHAPTER ONE

"To Follow the Dream . . ."

NIGHT HAS FALLEN WITHOUT WARNING, AS IF A DARK CURTAIN had dropped, covering a blood-red sun burning among flaming clouds. The Pacific lies motionless and heavy as molten lead. Dead calm.

Two hours later the first gusts are whistling through the rigging of the *Tai Ki,* and waves are thudding against the broad bow of our junk. The sea begins to writhe under the lash of the storm.

The sky is black, devoid of stars. Heavy cloud banks hang low over the sea, enveloping us in total darkness as our ship begins her battle. The helmsman takes a firmer hold on the steering ropes, throws his weight against their pull. As the waves swell higher, he can no longer remain seated on the helmsman's bench. He leans against it, spreads his legs, braces himself to take the sudden gusts that can send him flying if he is not prepared for them. It's his job to keep the boat on course. Winds have reached gale proportions.

Carl emerges from his cabin. Arno heaves himself up from his air mattress. Bill comes in from his lookout post on deck. Two or three sections of sail have to be reefed. Carl and Arno feel their way along the safety lines and stumble out onto the forward deck, make their unsteady way to the mast and the wooden crank that lowers the rattan sail.

Wind whips at their faces. The storm is mixing salt and water, water and air into a new element that makes breathing difficult. Water rains down on the forward deck. Waves strike the catwalk, rush off, tumble over the gunwales, scurry across the decks.

The *Tai Ki* groans as she plunges through seas growing heavier by the minute. The waves rise to twenty feet and more. They are barely visible to us in the darkness, but we feel what we can't see as the small, keelless boat dives from the crest of a wave and drops two stories on this seemingly endless roller coaster.

Waves roll toward the ship in a dark, foaming, implacable phalanx. One assault follows another. The bow rises, hovers in midair, dives into the valley between the waves with a roar, the flat belly of the ship slapping onto the water below.

The barometer plunges from 30.7 to 29.7. The air is still warm, but the spray, driven by the force of the wind, slashes at the hands and face like hail, and the men working at the mast shiver with cold. They have developed a routine by now: Bill hauls on the sheet; Arno jams a foot against the mast, leans into the crank; Carl guides the sail. Everyone staggers, struggles to keep his footing. The sail drops, but the *Tai Ki* does not slacken her pace. The storm is driving her to the east, driving her toward her goal. But the Pacific — seven thousand miles of water — lies between her and her destination. No chance of sighting land, not even an island. Water, nothing but water.

By morning the faces of the crew are gray with fatigue. Sleep is out of the question. The best one can hope for is a chance to lean against a wall and doze for a few minutes. We're too tired and tense to be able to sleep. And the waves keep tumbling over the bow, slapping onto the deck. Water pours down on the cabin, leaks inside.

How many storms have we been through? No one has counted them. Nor has anyone counted the quiet days at sea, days of breathtaking stillness when our thoughts could take flight.

We started with nothing but an idea, a crazy, impractical, harebrained idea, perhaps, but one that haunted us, kept after us, one we refused to give up no matter where it led us. And it has led us a long way. It has forced us to transcend our limitations, mentally at first, then in the world of fact.

Now our idea has become reality. It is concrete and tangible, like the timbers, the rigging, the instruments of our ship, like the water beneath her. It is the wind, the rhythm of night and day, the course of the stars, the expanse of the sea, the sense of motionlessness. It is all around us — visible, palpable, audible — the steady creaking of the mast in its tabernacle, the hum of the rigging, the groaning of the rudder, a thousand sounds we have never heard before, a thousand sounds we are coming to know.

A hand stretches out toward the rattan matting of the cabin wall, touches rough wood, bamboo, reaches for the floor. There are sea bags piled up toward the bow. One of the crew lies sleeping on a mat. He just came from his watch. Jasmin tea spills from a jug.

A naked, bearded man is sitting motionless at the rudder. The steering lines are twisted around his wrists. He looks at the sail through the cabin window. Than he glances at the compass beside him. His face is serious, intent. He is learning.

Water. Waves slapping against the hull. The same sound again and again. The rocking of the boat and the hollow thump of the bow plunging into the water. Two men forward are shortening stays, talking, cursing when something goes wrong.

There are no more new smells. But there is no end to the new sights. We still can't believe we are here. We are still not convinced our idea has indeed become reality. We still do not laugh freely with each other; we have still not become "a crew." The long days in Hong Kong — and the long days before that — have told on us all. But now we are underway, finally underway.

Logbook:

Friday, June 28, 1974. Wind out of the southwest, partially cloudy, temperature 80 to 85°, light sea, becoming heavier in the course of the day. Barometer: 29.7 and steady. Our course is 110°, our speed, 4.5 knots per hour. The *Tai Ki* set her own sail yesterday at 2330. The sail is half reefed, but we are still making good time. Heavier seas in the afternoon, waves from nine to twelve feet. Wind, fresh to strong (5 to 6 Beaufort).

The *Tai Ki* will cover at least a hundred nautical miles today. One hundred nautical miles! We start making calculations despite ourselves. How long will it take if . . . ? If.

Saturday, June 29, 1974. Gentle wind out of the northwest at about ten miles per hour. Cloudy. The *Tai Ki* is making between one knot (0000 to 0300) and three knots (1100). Course 120 to 140°. The night watch was remarkably quiet. Nothing worth noting occurred.

We are in historic waters, the scene of the Pacific campaign thirty years ago. Who can imagine what those men thought and felt? How many died here? Yaeyama Retto, Miyako Retto, Miyako Shima are the names of the islands around us. Okinawa is about 250 nautical miles away. A bloody sea.

The *Tai Ki* is alone. We saw a ship glide by far off on the horizon today. The vast expanse of the sea comes home to us when we consider that we are in a relatively "heavily traveled area" here. How inadequate, indeed, how incorrect, concepts drawn from our everyday world seem when we apply them to this world.

Flying fish leap from the water in elegant play. Small schools of them, small playful schools. A moment of reflection shows us how dominated by clichés our thinking is. Those fish aren't at play. They take to the air in fear of their lives, rise from the water to escape an enemy invisible to us.

Our first swim in the warm, dark blue water and one of our first dramatic moments of the trip: Bob Kendrick plunked himself down on a life raft, picked up scissors and razor, and began to cut off his magnificently long and wavy hair, which reached down to his shoulders and had evoked giggling admiration from the girls in Kao-hsiung. We were taken completely by surprise. Bill raced for his camera so that he could record the event. A half-hour's work and Bob sat bald and grinning before us. As Hal remarked sarcastically, he looked more like a galley slave than a ship's doctor.

Sunday, June 30, 1974.

Weather: Blue skies, calm sea (we could be somewhere in the Aegean). Temperature at 0900: 88°. Barometer: 29.7. Wind: 6 miles per hour. Course: 160 to 170°.

The mood of the crew remains difficult to ascertain. Everyone is feeling the others out. It's a good day for swimming once the chores are taken care of. The currents are taking us somewhat off course to the north. During the night, Allan contacted Sweden on the radio and was interviewed by the Swedish Broadcasting Company. Interviews with German, Danish, and Austrian radio stations are planned.

The weather reports from Hong Kong are still coming in clearly. They are a great help to us.

Two weeks later. Hardly a breeze stirring. The *Tai Ki* seems to lie motionless on the water. Bob and I have KP. He is the cook, I the dishwasher. He is staring at the water. Then he points to the plankton drifting by. No, it is not drifting by; it lies immobile next to the boat.

"Our progress is breathtaking," he grumbles. "At this rate we should arrive sometime next May."

"Maybe as early as March," Wolf throws in.

"A leisurely stroll across the Pacific," says Hal. "Who else would ever come up with the crazy idea of walking across an ocean?"

A closer look at the plankton shows Hal's assessment to be inaccurate. The plankton is moving past us so slowly that a pedestrian could easily outstrip us.

"Goddam!" It is Arno. He races to the stern and dives into the

7

water, surfaces a few seconds later next to our life buoy. It had fallen off its hook and into the water. "A bad omen," Wolf says loudly.

"Bullshit," Arno counters as he climbs on deck.

"We'll have to lash that ring down better," Carl suggests. A few days later it fell into the water again and, rocking gently on the waves, slowly drifted away from the ship. This time we were unable to retrieve it.

Bill and Wolf are putting on their life jackets. Wolf sets a blue Mao cap on his head: the future pastor from Hamburg as a young and somewhat outsized member of the Red Guard. Our rubber dinghy is launched. Cameras hang from Bill's neck. The *Tai Ki* is to be filmed for the first time as she moves slowly across trackless seas. I'm envious. If I didn't have to wash up, I could go with them. But work comes before play; I stick by my plates and pots and pans, scrub them, wash them, dry them. Bob is sitting behind me kneading dough. Yes, we are baking our own bread. Arno showed us how, and since the first samples turned out well, we decided that every KP team had to make at least one loaf. Bob kneads furiously and keeps getting up to look out at the dinghy rocking in the waves several hundred yards away. He would like to be out there, too.

Bill and Wolf come back beaming all over.

"It was fantastic," Bill says. "We suddenly had a sense of freedom out there that we didn't think was possible anymore."

"We were tempted to cut the safety line," Wolf says.

"Idiotic as it sounds, we could hardly resist cutting loose from the boat," Bill adds as he packs away his camera gear.

"We'll keep that in mind," our ship's doctor notes. "If anybody throws a tantrum, we can stick him in the dinghy and drag him along behind."

"We really considered cutting the line," Wolf says. "Your imagination can play some nasty tricks on you."

Arno snorts something about "stupid talk" and continues working on a piece of rope he is splicing. Hal and Carl are silent.

At supper Carl takes out his logbook. "I'd just like to tell you how far we've gone," he says and chews on his corncob pipe. "According to our log, we had covered 1,278 nautical miles by July 13. But the log isn't right. Geographically, we're 1,520 nautical miles from Hong Kong. Because of currents and errors in our log, our data have an overall factor of error of about 20 percent."

"Not half bad," Wolf comments.

I feel a certain sense of pride. The figures are, I suppose, trivial and insignificant. But for the first time we can see in concrete terms what we've accomplished. There it is in black and white. Our cigar box of a boat has ambled over 1,520 nautical miles of Pacific Ocean. All at once the fit of depression we experienced when we saw the plankton moving by us at a snail's pace has disappeared. We've moving after all. Amazing.

Later that night Bob, Arno, Bill, and I are standing at the bow. The sky is filled with stars. Our conversation turns to what Carl told us at supper.

"It's hard to imagine," Bill says, "that Japan is more than 500 nautical miles away. I have the feeling that there's land right behind the horizon, some destination or another."

"Don't waste your energy imagining something out there," Bob says. "There's nothing but water. And beyond that, there's more water."

"And below us there's nothing but water, eighteen thousand feet of it," Arno adds.

Absolute silence surrounds our boat, and conversation falls off. Long pauses follow our occasional words. There is nothing to break the silence but the light creaking of the sail, the rigging, the planking of our hull. The sea is motionless, the mirror of the water smooth under a faint veil of mist. Still, the night is clear, illuminated by the light of the stars. Bob has gotten up and is

9

leaning against the small arched cabin near the bow. He stretches out his hand, searching for the stars. Vega. Bill looks in the charts. He has a flashlight clamped between his teeth, and he mumbles a nearly unintelligible confirmation. "Right. There it is." Bob continues to search the sky. Draco, Sagittarius, Aquila. Bill continues to search the charts.

It is 2200. Time for a new watch. Carl takes over the lookout post on the forward deck, and I relieve Allan at the helm.

Under the gable roof of the helmsman's cabin, there is a long, wide bench. Two ropes that control the rudder run through pulleys fastened on the left- and right-hand walls of the cabin. From his place on the bench, the helmsman can see the entire interior of the ship. The barometer, a brass clock that rings ship's bells, the log, and the duty roster, from which everyone learns what he is supposed to do when and with whom, all hang on a long bamboo screen about three feet high. Above this screen there is a triangular opening that gives the helmsman a view of the sail with the Tai Ki emblem painted on it in black.

The compass is screwed onto the helmsman's bench. In a corner to its left stands a radio that sometimes produced tremulous music, sometimes startling news. For the most part it didn't offer much more than a backdrop of noise. A wave put it out of commission; then Allan repaired it, and there was music again. But at that point the junk was too far from land to be able to pull in any news.

The rudder itself is mounted behind the helmsman's bench, and on the rudder housing are a life preserver, Allan's antennas, and the red, white, and red Austrian flag. We can claim with reasonable assurance that we are the only representatives of the Austrian Navy currently afloat in the mid-Pacific.

I feel my way below deck and wake Bill. It's time for his watch. He rolls over on his side as though he were going back to sleep. Then he jumps to his feet and asks, "What's the course?"

"Sixty degrees."

"Anything else I should know?"

"No."

"O.K."

Now I could sleep . . . sleep? Who can sleep after a watch under tropical skies in the Pacific? Anyone who thinks sleep comes quickly under those circumstances is seriously mistaken. The mind is much too busy sorting through impressions of the day, memories of the past, expectations for the future. The brain keeps churning out thoughts; the worries and questions of the past come up for review, and with them comes the most basic question of all: how did this voyage come about? When did this journey from Asia to Central America actually begin?

It began in 1966 in Vietnam. To be more precise, it began in Hue, the ancient imperial city of Annam. I had been in Vietnam for several months gathering information for a book on the NLF, months filled with jungle heat, the steady thunder of artillery, the crackle of machine-gun fire, months of misery, blood, death. Now, all of a sudden, I was in the museum in Hue, accompanied by a frail student who, for the price of a few piasters, was acting as my guide.

The halls of the museum were hot and empty. The present had driven out the past. I saw only one other visitor, a U.S. Army major. He stood, completely absorbed, before a row of Buddha heads carved in ivory. He mumbled, "Hi!" and continued staring at the smiling faces that radiated a tranquility incongruous with the world outside.

A brass-framed showcase stood in one corner of the hall. The glass in it was dirty, greasy, dotted with fingerprints. There seemed to be nothing under the cloudy glass but threadbare rags torn from dark cloth. They were tied in knots that produced peculiar shapes, gewgaws in cloth. There were cords as well — blackened by many hands or by age — delicate strands forming a strange net and woven together with the strips of cloth into a bizarre web.

The apparent absurdity of this web prompted me to look more

closely. I stared at it with amazement, strangely affected by this odd something, these senseless shapes in cloth and cord. My guide enlightened me in halting French. I was looking at a code in knots, legible only to the initiated. It had been used at some time or other to keep secret records, to make notes, to pass down information that had to be kept hidden from official eyes. It was a secret script.

This explanation did not lead me any farther at the moment. I did, of course, make the connection with a similar South American phenomenon, the quipus or knotted cords of the Incas. I also recalled that similar cords are still in use today on the Ryukyu Islands east of Taiwan. But here the chain of association broke off abruptly, and I didn't follow it any farther, didn't draw the obvious conclusions. I simply noted what I had heard. That was all.

Later that night, as I was working in a tent the U.S. Army had set up for war correspondents, putting my impressions of the day down on paper, the parallel between what I had seen in the Hue museum and the knotted cords of pre-Columbian America not only came home to me but also prompted me to speculations that seemed to follow from it. This is what I wrote in my journal:

Camp DOG, February 23, 1966. Visited Hue museum. Saw something of great potential interest. Knotted cords. If we assume that the basically simple process of using knots as aids to memory was developed into a complex system and if we assume further that historically — as far as I can establish now — there are no other instances of these knot codes occurring anywhere else but in East Asia and South America, then I would think it at least possible that this complicated system of writing, if we may call it that, was transmitted from Asia to America sometime in the past. The truly astonishing similarity of some buildings in Indochina (those I saw in Angkor, for instance) with Central American ruins I have seen in pictures lends support to this idea. . . . But how little I really know. And how little we all know about ancient intercontinental migrations, migrations that are conceivable and that perhaps actually took place.

The mystery of these knotted cords in the Hue museum haunted me. I kept thinking about them after I had returned to Europe, and my mind continued to dwell on the many similarities between ancient American cultures and those of Southeast Asia. Was that really all just a matter of coincidence? Prompted by these thoughts, I began to read everything available on cultural contacts between Asia and America.

I told friends in Graz about my reading and speculations. Together with Arno Dennig and Johannes Koren, I began to develop some concrete plans. If a bamboo raft or a junk built to ancient specifications could manage to cross the Pacific from Asia to America, then the possibility of cultural contacts during the golden age of the early American civilizations would be established. In the course of my efforts to provide what was still a castle in the air with some solid foundations, I soon came across the name of a scholar who was regarded as the major authority in the field of intercultural relations: Robert Heine-Geldern, professor emeritus of ethnology at the University of Vienna. His theory of cultural diffusion had evoked massive controversy among scholars in the field, and I decided to call on him.

I found myself facing a man eighty-two years old. The near-transparent skin of old age revealed the veins in his hands as he shuffled through the carefully ordered papers on his desk. His eyes looked at me expectantly, sometimes ironically. His head was bent forward, not with age but with the effort of concentration.

My superficial introductory remarks must have struck this man as peculiar indeed, ridiculous perhaps. I was a layman, not even a student, and here I appeared out of the blue and made all sorts of claims. I had crashed into this scholar's inner sanctum and was sitting there regaling him with platitudes as eagerly as if I had been revealing great discoveries. Indeed, much of what I had to say I presented as if I actually were dealing in discoveries. And in fact I was, but my discoveries were discoveries for me alone, not for Heine-Geldern.

The absurdity of this situation did not dawn on me for quite a while, but then it did, instantaneously, when Heine-Geldern interrupted me and said, "You don't have to convince me, you know." Then he added softly, "No, not me." Only now, many years after that first meeting with him, have I finally become aware of the patience he showed in letting me recount to him all manner of things he already knew. And only now can I understand, too, his nearly rude, irritated reaction when I touched on the idea of using a boat of ancient Asian construction to demonstrate at least the nautical possibility of transpacific contact in the ancient world. Ideas that had to be followed up in the realm of action were alien to him. They probably always had been. He didn't need any "simple, concrete" evidence to prove the thoughts he had developed over the course of decades.

"Essentially there is very little that you will be able to prove or show probable," he said. "We already have some of the scientific evidence we need; and in the coming years, further research will turn up more and more material to prove that contact between Asia and America did take place." Then he added, "It's a long journey."

But Heine-Geldern was ready to help, even though our thinking was alien to his. He was no longer interested in new information, but sought only to consolidate the old. Still, he was intrigued by our project despite himself. He had too little time left to help us, but he helped nonetheless. He gave me a comprehensive list of titles essential for my preparatory studies, and he provided me with introductions to Dr. Gordon Ekholm of the Museum of Natural History in New York, Dr. Pedro Bosch Gimpera at the University of Mexico, Dr. Betty Meggers and Dr. Clifford Evans of the Smithsonian Institution in Washington, and many others as well.

Heine-Geldern regretted that the archives in the People's Republic of China were closed to foreigners. Our own experience proved him correct. When Dr. Kirchschläger, the Austrian foreign minister, later attempted to enlist Peking's support for our project, he met with refusal and an almost total lack of interest.

"The Asians' discovery of America and their influence on early cultures there," Heine-Geldern emphasized, "have never been subjects of much interest, or of any interest at all, to the general public or even to the scholarly world. Despite the fact that first-rate scholars are working in this field, it still remains unpopular and — unfashionable." Heine-Geldern uttered this last statement, which is the last note I have from my talks with him, in a tone of bitterness and resignation.

A start had been made.

I had a notebook full of material drawn from my conversations with Heine-Geldern. Two points seemed particularly important for us in the initial phase of our planning.

One of these was the problem of the ship itself. Heine-Geldern thought it would be very difficult to reconstruct an ancient Asiatic ship exactly enough so that it could lay claim to being an authentic replica. Boats and junks are pictured, of course, on Chinese temples and in the reliefs at Angkor. Descriptions of them also occur in writings of the Dong Son civilization, which was located in the area around Tonkin. But these representations are either highly stylized or come from a late period. Furthermore, with very few exceptions, these representations are of river boats; and there is no evidence that these river junks also made extensive sea voyages.

The Chinese junk is the most ancient and at the same time the most modern of all sailing vessels. Its design is timeless, and it is more than likely that the world's first seagoing ship was a junk, a box made of wooden boards.

In its structural concept, the junk is simply a raft with upswept ends and with side walls that raise it above the surface of the water. Just when and where the first junk was built is unknown. In Chinese myth, it is reported to be a gift of the gods.

Of all sailing ships, the junk has the shallowest draft proportional to its sail area. "It does not cut through the water but skims across its surface," Paul Laechler and Hans Wirz write of it. "It is modeled after water birds, and its stern resembles their upswept tails in form."

A junk can be built quickly and easily, but despite this ease of construction, a system of watertight compartments makes it capable of withstanding just about any punishment dealt out to it.

The junk's rigging, the simplest and handiest ever invented, is a masterpiece of design, too. Horizontal spars divide the sail into several panels that fold and unfold like those of a Venetian blind. The spars are attached individually to the mast and thus divide the wind pressure evenly along its entire length rather than concentrating the pressure at one point, as the rigging design of our sailboats does.

We meant to build a ship of this kind, following the oldest available plans, and we soon had a name for the junk that was to carry us across the Pacific: *Tai Ki.*

In Chinese, Tai Ki (also spelled Tai Chi) is a term invented by ancient philosophers to describe the origin or cause of the cosmos. It means something like the Great Ultimate or the Great All. An insigne associated with the term is a circle divided in half by an *s*-shaped line, an ideogram that the French amateur archaeologist E. T. Hamy came upon in the ruins of Copán in Central America.

Was the occurrence of the Tai Ki symbol in Copán a matter of pure coincidence? Or is the symbol in fact a key to one of many unsolved mysteries the ancient American civilizations have handed down to us? The Tai Ki emblem is far from being the only clue of its kind in Copán.

Copán, one of the most important sites of Mayan culture, is located in Honduras only six miles from the border of Guatemala. The Spaniard Don Diego García de Palacio was the first to discover these completely overgrown ruins on the banks of the Copán River, and he described them to King Philip II in a letter of

March 8, 1576. It was not until 1834 that the first actual expedition was sent to Copán. This expedition was made under the leadership of the Irishman John Gallagher, who took the name of Juan Galindo while in the service of Spain. But this Irish Spaniard's reports and publications went unnoticed, and Copán lay forgotten until John Lloyd Stephens, an American diplomat, businessman, amateur archaeologist, world traveler, and later president of the Panama Railroad, came along and "discovered" it. In his book *Travels in Central America and Yucatan,* published in 1842, he publicized the existence of the previously neglected Mayan culture and initiated modern research on pre-Columbian America. Stephen's traveling companion, the English painter and architect Frederick Catherwood, made numerous drawings of the exotic structures he found hidden in the tropical jungle. We are indebted to him for the first — and often the only — representations we have of art works from this site.

The Englishman Alfred Percival Maudslay was the first to undertake a systematic, scientific study of the Copán ruins. Among the many objects he studied and photographed was Stela B, which later became renowned as the "elephant stela" and prompted speculation and violent discussions among scholars. This heavily ornamented stone column stands in the middle of what has been designated as the Main Square. A dignified male figure is portrayed on the front of the column. The face displays clearly Mongolian features: slanted eyes, a short beard, high cheekbones. The figure is wearing an oriental turban, as are a number of other small decorative figures to the right and left of it on the stela. Even then archaeologists were quick to point out the possibility of Asian influence. N. Arnold wrote: "The carvings are so clearly oriental that they admit no doubt as to their origin. The face of the figure is one that could easily occur in sculptures from Cambodia or Siam. The clothing, the ornamentation, and the turbanlike headdress, found nowhere else in the world, are purely Indo-Chinese in character."

Stela B has other interesting features as well. Stephens was

the first to note one of the most striking of these: ". . . Two ornaments on the upper part of the column look like elephant trunks,
but the elephant is unknown in this part of the world." Furthermore, many observers identified the figures squatting on what
are presumably elephant heads as turbaned mahouts or elephant
drivers. A heated debate arose. Where did these elephants come
from and how did they get to the Americas? With the exception of
the mammoths of the Ice Age, nothing of this kind had ever
existed in the Western Hemisphere. The opponents of the elephant theory chose to identify the mysterious ornaments as representations of bird bills or of tapir snouts or merely as abstract
decorative designs.

Arnold's statement poured oil on the already glowing coals of
scholarly controversy, and the Englishman G. Elliot Smith added
fuel to the fire with his book *Elephants and Ethnologists*. Archaeologists, he wrote, seemed reluctant to challenge accepted
dogmas and therefore overlooked obvious facts. He went further
with his theories than any previous scholars had, claiming that
the long-nosed Mayan divinities and the Mayan rain god Chac
were descendants of Ganeśa, the elephant-headed god of fortune,
son of Shiva and Parvati, the major Hindu divinities.

In the Englishman D. A. MacKenzie, Smith found an ally
more radical in defense of the "elephant theory" than he himself
had been. MacKenzie launched a violent attack on the narrow-
mindedness prevalent among scholars in the field and declared
that the Copán elephants were not only elephants beyond any
shadow of a doubt but were also Indian elephants as well. The
shape of their ears showed that they belonged to the Indian
species, not to the "large-eared African variety." MacKenzie's
statement was directed at the theory of some archaeologists that
the elephant heads on Stela B were of African origin.

The Copán elephants are no longer a subject of scholarly debate. Dr. Betty Meggers, who is herself convinced of transpacific
cultural contact, spoke with considerable restraint when she

called the elephants of Copán an unsolved but "fascinating mystery of our time." The mystery is all the more fascinating because only portions of the carvings remain. Sometime after Maudslay had photographed the heads, the small figures seen as if riding on top of the elephant heads were destroyed, but not the elephant heads themselves. We will never know whether vandals or, just possibly, enraged opponents of the "elephant theory" were responsible.

But it was clear to Arno and me when we were in Copán that Stela B is not the only piece of evidence to be found there. Directly across from it stands Stela C, guarded, so to speak, by a huge turtle with two heads. Of all the statuary on the Main Square in Copán the figure on Stela C is most clearly Asiatic in character. It has an oriental face with narrow, slanted eyes; a long, flowing beard; and even more prominent cheekbones than those of the Stela B figure. If the figure were not so heavily laden with intricate ancient American ornamentation, it could easily have come from Asia, possibly Indochina or even China. The turtle that guards this stela also suggests transpacific contacts, for a myth common to both the Mayan and the Zapotec cultures of southern Mexico tells of a giant turtle that crept out of the Pacific long ago, bringing many strangers who came as teachers. . . .

We could have used that giant turtle with his teachers from the Orient on board the *Tai Ki*.

We had agreed to set up a study program for our "leisure hours." Subjects ranged from nautical skills to an investigation of the motives that had brought us all together on the *Tai Ki*. Spare time on board ship is not so easy to come by as it would seem. We had only occasional evening hours free and nowhere near as many as we had imagined we would have.

Those of us who had been studying the subject of cultural ties between Asia and pre-Columbian America for years now had the task of introducing the new members of the crew to the field.

"Marco Polo," I said during one of our talks, "was ridiculed when he returned to Venice from the Far East and told 'the truth' about China and the other exotic countries he had visited. Nobody believed him, but everybody believed the 'travel writers' who told about men with four heads and sea monsters that could swallow ships whole. Nobody was ready to believe that the Chinese were a highly civilized people with a culture superior to that of the West. Even the well-traveled patricians of Venice refused to believe Marco Polo. They laughed at him and considered him a liar and teller of tall tales. Yet he was the first man to provide accurate reports about the Far East."

"What does that have to do with our thesis — I mean with your thesis?" Hal asked.

"It doesn't have anything to do with my thesis but with the thesis of a great many eminent scholars. Their theories meet with disbelief or, at best, grudging acceptance, while everybody is ready to believe stories about UFO's from outer space."

Our discussion was interrupted by a loud summons from Bill. "Dinner is served, lads! Come and get it, the finest Hungarian goulash ever prepared in the galley of a junk." As the crew members started sampling the evening meal, someone came up with the theory that the goulash might have been prepared from "Copanese elephant trunks." I could do nothing but shrug my shoulders and mumble something along the line of "A prophet is not without honor, save in his own country, and in his own house."

But despite the skepticism my talk of diffusion theory evoked in the crew, our discussions of this subject continued because we were, after all, out to rewrite the discovery of America and its first inhabitants. Confusion about this land and its people originated with Columbus himself, for Columbus thought he had landed in India and therefore identified the people there as Indians. Once it had become clear that the native Americans were a "new" and independent race, speculation about their origins soon ran rife.

No one was willing to accept the most obvious possibility that these people were simply the original inhabitants of the new continent. America and the Americans had to be assimilated into the Christian view of history. The prevalent theory — but one that admitted of a few other possibilities — claimed that the American Indians could be traced back to Noah, if not to Adam and Eve.

While the Inquisition was smashing Mexico's temples, stone tablets, and statuary and sending up in flames the sacred books and historical documents that might have revealed the true past and origins of the Indians, the first violent debates about their origins were well underway. The wildest theories were proposed. One that still has its adherents today is that the Indians are descended from the lost tribes of Israel. Another traces them back to the tower of Babel, still another to the crews of King Solomon's Ophir fleet.

In the seventeenth century, hypotheses began to come closer to the truth. The astronomer Edward Berewood suggested that the Indians were descendants of the Tatars. The Dutchman Johan de Laet argued that the Scythians, a Central Asian nomadic tribe, were the ancestors of the North American Indians. Hugo Grotius, a historian, offered a more complex theory. He thought all the Indians located north of Panama had originally come from northern Europe, those of Yucatán from Ethiopia, the Peruvian tribes from China, and the remaining South American tribes from the islands of the South Pacific. De Laet concurred with him in this last point but categorically denied that Peruvian settlers could have come from China. "The long, extremely difficult and dangerous sea voyage," he thought, would have made this impossible.

In 1677, the Englishman Matthew Hale presented the view that is still accepted, with some modifications, today. Hale claimed that Asians had migrated to the Americas by way of a land bridge that crossed what is now the Bering Strait, and that there had been several migratory waves occurring in different periods.

North America and northern Asia experienced several ice ages, just as Europe did. Geologists believe that the ice masses were extensive enough to lower the water level of both the Arctic Ocean and the Bering Strait, thus creating an isthmus between Alaska and Siberia. The Bering Strait is about one hundred and fifty feet deep, and the water in it probably dropped far enough at least twice to permit game animals and their pursuers to pass between the two continents. This presumably happened once in the period between 45,000 and 25,000 B.C. and again some twelve thousand years ago.

And even if the sea did not drop far enough to form a land bridge, ice bridges, passable by men and herds of game animals, must have spanned the Bering Strait. The strait is only a little over sixty miles wide today, and it was no doubt considerably narrower in earlier eras. In the course of time, the migrating hunters spread out through all of North, Central, and South America.

By the time the high civilizations of Central and South America arose, the Americas were settled from Alaska to Patagonia. The fact that they had been settled in a number of migratory waves partially explains why there were so many striking differences among the various Indian tribes of the New World. There seems to be little doubt, too, that several Indian tribes and nations, particularly those in Mexico and on the Pacific coast of South America, had already achieved a relatively high level of culture before later waves of immigration from the Old World reached the Americas.

But what distinguished the peoples of Mesoamerica and the Andes so clearly from all others in the New World is the fact that they were able to achieve in the course of a few centuries a level of civilization that other cultures had taken thousands of years to reach. While most of the tribes in both North and South America remained on the relatively primitive level of hunter-gatherers, their neighbors in Central America, on the Pacific coast of South America, and, to some extent, in British Columbia developed high cultures at a speed that can only be called breathtaking when seen in the context of that era. It is this amazing phenomenon that suggests the possibility of cultural influence from the outside.

Despite the fact that none of the American Indians had emerged from the Stone Age, some high cultures had quickly and inexplicably taken shape among them. The advanced tribes developed complex political systems and showed other achievements that command our respect today. The Mayans, for instance, had a calendar far superior to the one in use in Europe. Methods of dyeing and metal-working known in Peru, Colombia, and Ecuador were every bit as sophisticated as those of the Old World. While many tribes have remained incapable to the present day of constructing anything more complex than a tent or wooden hut, their neighbors built temples, streets, and cities and created works of art the equal of anything known in the Old World. How did this all come about?

The predominant view among historians always has been and continues to be that the world's high cultures developed independently of each other and by mutation, as it were. Without exerting or receiving any influence, they slowly grew from primitive cultures. The British historian Arnold Toynbee sees this as the logical consequence of similarity among human beings. Similar in nature, they will necessarily be similar in their achievements. Whether Toynbee is correct or whether all cultures have developed from a common origin and by means of more or less regular contacts with each other remains a question of fundamental importance for historical research.

Central to the growth of cultures and their later advancement to high cultures is the transition from a hunter-gatherer economy to an agricultural one. The earliest agricultural civilizations of the Neolithic period arose in the eastern Mediterranean region sometime between 7000 and 5000 B.C. The crucial point here is that the Neolithic Age began later everywhere else in the world. This fact would suggest that all other civilizations were influenced by the original ones of the Near East.

The first advanced civilizations arose in the Near East, just as the first Neolithic cultures had before them. There is more or less general agreement now that the Mesopotamian culture dating from 3000 B.C. was the world's first advanced civilization. It was followed a few centuries later by ancient Egypt, by Minoan Crete, by the culture of the Indus Valley, then, around 2000 B.C., by China, and, another thousand years later, by the Olmec and Chavin cultures of South America.

Only a detailed account would allow us to draw a sharp line between the last "semirural" village cultures already caught up in the process of urbanization and the earliest cultures we could designate as "advanced." They are both transitional stages in one and the same general development. Toynbee has suggested that early advanced cultures evolved independently through a process of "challenge and response": that is, the challenge of a not overharsh environment and man's response to it. But Toynbee's theory leaves too much unexplained. It seems inevitable that early man, in his intercontinental and transoceanic wanderings, must have carried his previous knowledge and skills with him.

The cultures of the Near East were approaching their decline before their achievements began to reach other parts of the world. Sometime before 2000 B.C., for example, some Neolithic ceramics whose origins in eastern Europe and Iran have been established made their way to the Far East. The Lung-Shan civilization evolved from this encounter of an invading culture with the already existing ones in what is now China.

The Lung-Shan culture, which Heine-Geldern has designated as a "near-advanced culture," was overrun by a new wave of immigration from the West. China's new masters, the Shangs, were not bearers of a highly developed culture, but they did bring with them much that had been unknown in China before: techniques of bronze casting, the use of bronze weapons, certain tools, and the chariot. We can assume that the Shangs of northern China had received this knowledge from the early advanced cultures of the Near East. The fusion of the Shang and Lung-Shan cultures produced the high culture of ancient China, and recorded Chinese history dates from this period around 1650 B.C. It is thus impossible to speak of a completely independent and isolated evolution of advanced civilization in ancient China.

Nor did the earliest advanced cultures in the Western Hemisphere, that of Chavin in South America and of the Olmecs in Central America, arise independently either. One hundred and fifty years ago, Alexander von Humboldt was convinced that early American civilizations had been influenced by Asian cultures. But since Humboldt's time, the view that the American cultures developed independently has hardened into historical and archaeological dogma. Toynbee's theory of "human similarity" and other theories like it were invoked to explain similarities of cultural features in the Old and New Worlds.

This simplistic assumption forced historians into a paradoxical and self-contradictory position. No one contests the crucial influence of early Near Eastern cultures on European civilization. No one would argue that each civilization can claim the wheel, the skills of pottery, weaving, and bronze casting, or the construction of religious and political systems as independent inventions. No one assumes that the cultures of the Far East could arrive at more or less the same level of civilization at more or less the same time as the earlier advanced cultures if there had been no contact whatsoever. But for some reason, none of this should apply to America. For the New World there should presumably be new rules.

For one reason or another, the smelting of tin, the amalgamation of copper and tin into bronze, the chemical treatment of gold, and various techniques of weaving and dyeing are all supposed to have been discovered independently in a number of different places. But these are not the only areas in which astonishing parallels occur. Why do we find similar symbols of rank in Asia and America? On both continents the parasol is an emblem of dignity. And why is it that the same colors are used in both Asia and America to designate points of the compass, blue for the east, red for the south? And why is it that many games follow the same rules and have similar sounding names? What is known as *patolli* in Mexico is called *pachisi* in India.

While studying the so-called Valdivia culture of Ecuador, the archaeologists Betty Meggers and Clifford Evans found figures, pottery fragments, and ornaments that revealed striking similarities with artifacts from the Jō-Mon culture of Japan. When Meggers and Evans pooled artifacts from both cultures together and asked specialists in the field to separate them out again, not one scholar was able to establish significant differences between objects made on two continents separated by the Pacific Ocean.

In 1942, Dr. Gordon Ekholm was making excavations in the Huastec region of Mexico. The Huastecs spoke a Mayan language and lived in an area surrounding the present city of Tampico on the northern Gulf coast of Mexico. In the course of his work, Ekholm found a remarkable clay figure near Panuco. It was intended to represent some kind of animal, but it was so crudely modeled that identification of the intended animal was impossible. It was simply a four-footed animal whose feet took the form of axle bearings. Axles passed through these bearings, and on the ends of both axles were wheels. "When I described this figure in an article," Ekholm recalled later, "all I did was call attention to its special feature, i.e., that it stood on wheels that could actually turn."

Ekholm's find was astonishing indeed, for the wheel was unknown in pre-Columbian America, and to this day archaeologists have still not discovered any evidence that the wheel was in use for any kind of transport in the Western Hemisphere. The figure

Animal figurines on wheels. Since the wheel was unknown in pre-Columbian America, Gordon Ekholm's discovery of animal figures mounted on wheels (1, 2) caused considerable astonishment. These figures, modeled in clay, are complete with axles and axle bearings as well as wheels, and their similarity to wheeled figures from China and India (3, 4) is striking.

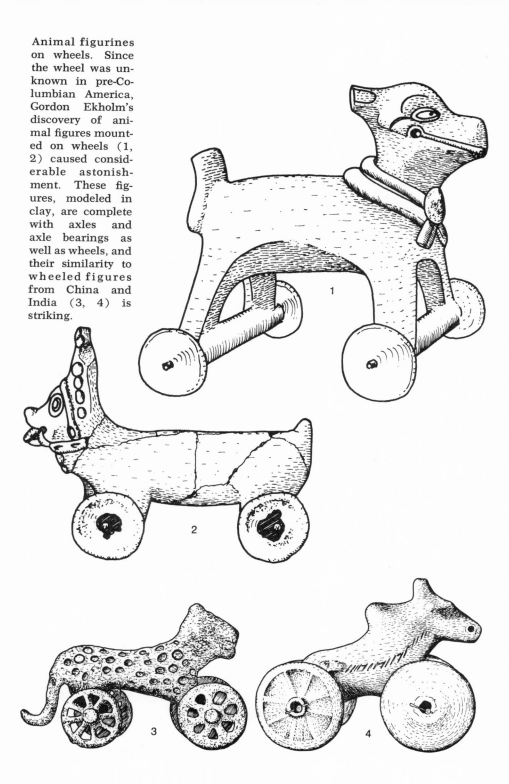

demonstrated that the Indian who created this "toy" was familiar with the principle of the wheel and capable of constructing wheels, axles, and bearings. The thirty-three-year-old Ekholm could therefore not help wondering why the wheel never came into use among the Indians. Ekholm was more puzzled still when he found on closer examination that the wheels and axles on his figure had never been moved, despite the fact that they could be moved. The wheel bearings did not show the slightest trace of wear. But Ekholm's surprises were still not at an end. He learned later that similar figures had been common in eastern Asia and are still made in India today. Practically any shop in Europe that deals in wares from India will carry these small wheeled figures.

Ekholm wondered why the Indians would have made these figures at all, why they constructed a figure with a clear function but at the same time did not even grasp what that function was.

The wheel is, of course, one of the most significant of all human inventions, and the advanced cultures of pre-Columbian America differ from all other advanced civilizations of the ancient world in being the only ones in which the wheel was not in use. Considering the technical sophistication these cultures achieved in other fields, it is highly unlikely that the Indians discovered the principle of the wheel and were then unable to make practical application of it.

There are remarkable parallels in mythology, too. The Aztec god Quetzalcoatl takes the form of a plumed serpent, a motif that also figures prominently in Chinese art. In no other cultures of the world has the plumed serpent occurred in this particular form and with the particular mythological significance it has both in Chinese art and in the art of pre-Columbian America, the serpent symbolizing the earth, the bird symbolizing the heavens.

At a convention of American archaeologists held in Mexico in September 1974, Gordon and Marguerite Ekholm presented a paper, "The Scroll-Wing Motif in Ancient China and Mesoamerica." The Ekholms' study focused on the use of this motif in the Shang dynasty (1520–1030 B.C.) and in the Chou period (up to

221 B.C.) as well as in the first and second Han dynasties (through 220 A.D.). A year earlier, Ekholm had said to me, "I am concentrating on ornamental detail now because many questions in this field are open to concrete proof and because so little has actually been done in it." In his comparisons of artistic motifs and, even more important, of their symbolic significance, Ekholm has been able to point out truly astonishing similarities. If a motif as used in two cultures shows a total correspondence down to the finest detail and in all its stylistic variations, then the possibility of simultaneous but completely separate evolutions of this motif on two continents thousands of miles apart seems remote indeed.

Twenty-five years ago a *finquero* on the cattle ranch of Monte Alto near La Democracia in Guatemala stumbled upon some strangely carved stones. He began digging and uncovered massive stone heads. The Archaeological Institute in Guatemala City was informed of the find, and excavations turned up other heads whose origins were unclear at first and whose exact age has still not been determined. But in the meantime archaeologists have been able to assign these heads to the Olmec culture. Unfortunately, we have no written historical knowledge of any kind concerning the ancient Olmecs. Who they were, where they came from, and what language they spoke all remain unclear. Massive Olmec heads have been discovered at La Venta and Tres Zapotes on the Gulf coast of Mexico, and further Olmec artworks have been found in Monte Alban near Oaxaca. The Olmec culture, too, seems to have sprung up out of nowhere, yet it had a written language and left behind works of sculpture that demonstrate a high level of artistic proficiency. Archaeologists have come to regard the Olmec culture as the primal ancestor of all other Central American civilizations. Dominant motifs in Olmec art often seem to resemble those from Asia: temple niches with sitting figures in them, scroll-wings, massive heads portraying broad Asiatic faces with thick lips, slanted eyes, and flaring nostrils.

One of these massive statues stands in front of the museum

The lotus motifs pictured above (1, 2) occur in reliefs from Amaravati in India. Reliefs found in Palenque, one of the major sites of Mayan culture in Yucatan, reflect this same motif (3, 4).

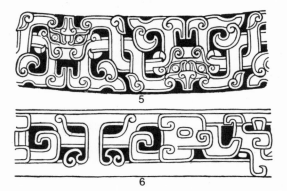

Archaeologists found the upper ornamental band (5) in China, the lower one (6) in Mexico. The similarities cannot fail to impress even the most determined opponent of diffusion theory.

in La Democracia. The face is that of an old man, a sage perhaps, with deep lines in his cheeks, lowered eyelids, nearly closed eyes. The figure radiates tranquility as it faces a small park in which other gigantic figures are on display. These other figures, weighing several tons each, are weathered portraits, some with the folded hands of men in prayer. The employees of the museum in La Democracia have given the figure in front of the museum the same name that its discoverer gave it: Buddha.

In September 1949, the exhibition "Across the Pacific" was presented in New York at the American Museum of Natural History and lent tremendous impetus to the study of cultural ties between Asia and America. The exhibits had been prepared especially for the meeting of the International Congress of Americanists. Two men were primarily responsible: Gordon Ekholm, the forty-year-old scholar whose first findings had just aroused considerable interest, and Robert Heine-Geldern, a Viennese refugee from Nazi-dominated Europe who was working as a research associate in anthropology at the Museum of Natural History. As Heine-Geldern expressed it, this exhibition was to make the possibility, indeed the probability, of cultural contact between East Asia and America "an acceptable subject for research."

Time magazine remarked that this exhibition of New World cultural materials that apparently had their origins in Asia struck "like a bombshell."

Ekholm's comment on the exhibition was one of deliberate understatement. "I only wanted to see," he said, "if we could present our case convincingly."

The case was convincing. The ethnologist Dr. Pedro Bosch Gimpera recalled his impressions. "The exhibition did in fact strike the scholarly world like a bombshell. I was so deeply impressed and so thoroughly convinced by it that I began working on diffusion theory myself." Bosch Gimpera became a passionate advocate of diffusion theory and published his own study of the subject in 1970 under the title *Transpacific Parallels and Their Chronology in Pre-Columbian Cultures.*

With their exhibition in New York, Ekholm and Heine-Gel-dern had taken an important first step. The subject of cultural contacts between Asia and America remained controversial, but it had been made respectable and was no longer condemned to a second-class existence on the fringe of scholarship. The parallels the exhibit had brought into focus could no longer be overlooked.

One archaeologist wrote: "As one piece of evidence to support his theory, Ekholm presented a relief from Amaravati in India dating from about 200 A.D. On the ends of the relief are animal heads with fish-like bodies. Lotus flowers are growing from the mouths of the heads. . . . A relief from a Mayan temple at Chichén Itzá in Yucatán contains a similar figure. The figure is damaged, but there is no doubt as to what it represents. In the Mayan version, the fish does not have an animal head, but the fish is in the same position, as if eating the lotus flower. Since the lotus flower is a symbol of Buddhism, Ekholm concludes that Buddhist missionaries may have brought this lotus symbol to Yucatán.

"He also displayed an Indian carving of Buddha sitting on a lotus flower. Alongside this figure, he placed a stylized lotus flower from Yucatán. In this flower, a Mayan god replaces Buddha."

The *Tai Ki* was holding to her course. Log, July 11, 1974:

The weather is improving. Both the wind and the waves are abating, and our speed is dropping accordingly. We were making 4.5 knots per hour yesterday. Today 3 is the best we can do, and we may slow down to as little as 2 in the course of the day. The barometer is rising and read 29.8 at 0900. Since 0200 our course has been 70°. Position: 132° 21' east longitude, 24° 28' north latitude.

As we expected, the wind is dropping even more in the afternoon, but seas are still relatively heavy, with foam rolling on the crests of the waves.

Water is leaking into the third compartment behind the mast.

What's wrong? Was the planking laid improperly, or did we damage the hull in Kao-hsiung? Arno climbs below with Wolf and emerges cursing and sweating ten minutes later. The pump detail will have to be reinforced and more carefully organized.

1600: The wind picks up suddenly. We're at its command. We set more sail, and soon we're making four knots again. The mood of the crew improves. A fair wind is blowing, and we're moving along. We've left the first thousand miles behind us. Bob is sitting on his air mattress and reading Heine-Geldern.

CHAPTER TWO

One-Way Ticket to America

JANUARY 1971. COPENHAGEN. CHARLOTTENLUND, TO BE exact, a few miles outside the city. A gray dawn, the sun hidden behind mother-of-pearl clouds. The sea lead-colored and rough. The horizon, framed between the cables of the short mast, wandered up and down erratically. The deck of the boat, together with its few low superstructures, rose and sank, a dark mass on the reflecting surface of the water. Gulls. Torn by the wind, their cries came raggedly to our ears.

The small North Sea cutter pulled at its mooring ropes. Dampness. Every line dripped with the dampness of the night. The wheelhouse rose up on the afterdeck like a sentry's hut. Gray wood, cracked paint, misted windows. Awkward, hesitating steps across the slick deck. A hand on the door. We entered the small wheelhouse. Quiet. The insistent whistling of the wind and its painful touch were shut out.

With practiced motions and a few words of explanation, Carl Frederik started up the diesel engine. The pistons throbbed with a slow, hollow beat. Their strokes sounded short and weak. The engine was struggling against the cold, too. We could hear it searching for heat and the strength heat could bring.

Carl opened the wheelhouse door and went forward on steady sea legs to untie the mooring rope from a rusted iron ring in the cracked wall. One rope fell away, then another.

"Can I help?"

"No, stay inside." He was only thirty feet away from me, but I could hardly hear what he said. The wind tore the words away as he spoke them.

Carl Frederik came back to the wheelhouse. He was wearing a blue pea jacket and a blue cap. Crow's-feet at the corners of sparkling eyes. He reached for a shiny brass lever, threw switches. His hands were steady on the wheel. A black, oily chain ran down from it into the bowels of the cutter. The hollow strokes of the diesel picked up speed. The hull trembled, began to move, ran out backward into the middle of the harbor.

For the first time I was with him on a ship, my legs spread wide, braced against the rolling of the deck.

"Rough sea," Carl Frederik shouted into my ear. "We'll have to see what it looks like when we get out a little farther."

I can't remember what I said to him. All I can remember is the immense joy I felt. I think I just laughed, for here I was, standing next to the man who was going to build our junk. Here I was with the man who would skipper our ship across the Pacific Ocean, sailing out with him into a gray sea that suddenly seemed aglow with light. In Carl Frederik, Arno and I had found the key man we needed to realize our plan. We may have considered ourselves capable of just about anything we cared to take on, but in one point we had no illusions about ourselves. We were hardly experts in occidental, much less oriental, seamanship. None of our past adventures had provided us with the knowledge we needed, nor had a number of cruises on the often far from gentle Mediterranean. We needed a seaman, a real captain who would also be capable of building our ship. Arno held a master's license for coastal vessels, but we needed someone with even more knowledge and know-how than he possessed. We needed a man with experience on oceangoing ships, a man who had grown up with the sea and had it in his blood, a man for whom both the theory and practice of navigation and shipbuilding were second nature.

35

Arno knew just the man, his brother-in-law, Carl Frederik Grage, a forty-two-year-old Danish engineer. Arno had already spoken with him, and the Dane had been interested. Now I had come to speak with him.

Lean, weathered, and bony, he seemed taller that he actually was. He had a blond mustache, able hands. A porcelain pipe — "a gift from my father" — was stuck between his teeth. He was taciturn, his eyes distant, his face strangely immobile. His expression rarely changed, as if experience had taught him not to reveal his feelings in his features. Or was this impassivity innate? Silent and apparently unresponsive, he listened as others spoke, then spoke himself, very slowly and softly, radiating a quiet self-confidence. Or he would burst out in loud, roaring laughter. Some might call it a barroom laugh, the kind of laugh men sometimes laugh when they mean to be jolly.

He loved hunting and enjoyed talking about it. He loved the sea, too; but he spoke less of that love, probably because there was no need to speak of the obvious. His understatements often seemed to be a mode of exaggeration. Nautical instruments, compasses, sextants, old spyglasses, charts, and model ships lined the walls of his study. In one corner he had a radio he used to contact ships passing by his house. His thoughts were always out on the sea, even if he happened to be ashore.

With quick, nervous movements of his hands he demonstrated the use of an old pocket sextant from England and showed me how his radio worked. He pulled out some charts and told me what preliminary work he had done, pointing out the tentative course he had worked out for our expedition. His notations of latitude and longitude marked the points we would someday pass, perhaps.

Now I was standing next to him on his boat. We were approaching the breakwater that still sheltered us from the open sea. The diesel engine pounded hollowly in its struggle against the inrushing waves. The roar of the sea and the breakers smashing against the harbor wall penetrated to us in the wheelhouse. The swells, crowned with foam, were short and frequent, leaping nervously in the grayness of the morning. We cleared the breakwater, and the sea took hold of us, tossing the bow and letting it fall again with a thud. The windowpanes of the wheelhouse rattled in the wind. The boat tossed beneath my feet, its motions strange and unfamiliar to me.

Carl Frederik stood at the helm. How would I see him a year from now or two years from now somewhere in the Pacific? How would we weather storms together somewhere off Japan or near the date line or south of the Aleutians? What was waiting for us out there? This sea off the Danish coast suddenly struck me as insignificant, just as its grayness seemed dull in comparison with the brilliant sunlight and blue waters of tropical seas.

We had been underway half an hour, perhaps, when Carl Frederik spun the wheel and headed his bow back to port.

"We're going back in," he yelled at me.

"Why?"

"Too dangerous. If the engine gave out in these seas, we'd be smashed against the shore in no time."

Carl Frederik, I thought to myself, seems to be a man who knows his own limits. But his decision surprised me nonetheless. Had I in fact just seen a demonstration of clear thinking and responsible seamanship? I was too ignorant of nautical affairs to pass judgment on what Carl Frederik had done; but with all due allowance for my own incompetence, his action still left me slightly uneasy.

In my preparations for the expedition I had hunted through the archives and libraries of Europe in search of descriptions and drawings of ancient Asiatic ships. I was looking for a junk that might have been in use at the time of Christ's birth. I discovered to my astonishment that there was hardly any literature available on early Asian shipbuilding.

In the Prince Hendrik Maritime Museum in Rotterdam, I

finally found what I needed: *Les Jonques chinoises,* an eleven-volume work by Louis Audemard, a retired French frigate captain. I had a copy of this work with me when I visited Carl Frederik in Copenhagen.

Audemard, born in 1865, was a French naval officer who first traveled to East Asia as a nineteen-year-old cadet. He returned to China in 1902 as the commander of a gunboat on the upper Yangtze River. For two years he navigated the dangerous rapids of the Yangtze and made a name for himself as a designer and builder of boats that made use of both European nautical technology and his experience on Asian rivers. He was appointed to the Legion of Honor and later retired to a castle in Brittany, where he established a museum, devoted himself to study, and wrote his monumental work, which was published in 1957, two years after his death.

In 1948 the Maritime Museum in Rotterdam became aware of Audemard's writings, of which only excerpts had appeared at that time. The museum in Rotterdam recognized that Audemard's work was a crucial one for the understanding of Chinese seafaring. Audemard attempted to give not only a precise description of different types of junks, showing, for example, just how the junks of the Yangtze differed from coastal junks, but also a precise description of how they were outfitted. He also attempted — on the basis of sources available to him — to trace the history of Chinese navigation and shipbuilding back to their earliest origins.

For this reason, Audemard's work was a much more important source for us than that of George R. Worcester, a British naval officer who served as river inspector on the Yangtze for thirty years and opened 1,700 miles of it to steamer service. Worcester, too, traced the history of Chinese shipbuilding, but Audemard went several steps further. He gave considerable thought to the likelihood that Chinese mariners undertook transoceanic voyages and did not exclude the possibility that they had crossed the Pacific.

"The Chinese were certainly capable of long sea voyages," Audemard notes, and he assumes that "the Chinese reached America at least a thousand years before Christopher Columbus landed on the island of San Salvador." Among other evidence he marshals to support his assumption, Audemard points to one archaeological discovery in particular, a stone carving in Copán, Honduras, "that has on it the Tai Ki ideogram, one of the oldest of Chinese symbols." According to Audemard, the Tai Ki symbol was often displayed on the bows of junks as "a good-luck charm and a talisman to drive away demons."

Audemard's statement that the Chinese were capable of long sea voyages and actually undertook them requires no further proof than we already have. We know that the Chinese reached East Africa and Madagascar sometime during the reign of the Tang dynasty, that is, sometime around the seventh century A.D., and it is more than likely that they made such voyages much earlier than that. Between 1402 and 1421, the Chinese eunuch Cheng Ho traveled to the African coast several times. A few years later, Prince Henry the Navigator thought it quite an achievement to have sailed to the Azores from Portugal. Coins and pottery fragments found on the East African coast prove that the Chinese did in fact reach Africa and therefore had made voyages of at least 6,000 nautical miles.

Under the Tang dynasty, around 900 A.D., merchants from Canton maintained regular trade with Ceylon, and Chinese seafarers reached Arabia, the Gulf of Persia, and traveled down the African coast to the Cape of Good Hope. Chronicles report that as many as four hundred Chinese ships "carrying valuable and expensive cargoes" were plying the Gulf of Persia. Marco Polo recounts traveling from China to India by junk, then returning to China by land. The fleet he traveled with included forty ships of varying sizes, which carried fifteen hundred seamen and their provisions for two years. The fleet reached Sumatra after a voyage of three months, then sailed farther, eventually circling back to its home port after another eighteen months at sea.

I mention this voyage for two reasons. First, it proves that the Chinese were capable of planning, equipping, and carrying out a nautical undertaking of these proportions; and, second, it demonstrates the existence of a strong nautical tradition in ancient China. For without this tradition, without the knowledge and experience it handed down, the Chinese would not have been able to conceive of such an expedition and bring it to a successful conclusion.

We know, too, that the Chinese reached Australia and probably New Zealand as well. And we know that there was lively sea trade in Indonesia, where not only junks were used but other kinds of sailing ships that can still be seen in this part of the world today. Asian waters have always been the scene of remarkable nautical achievements. Sailors and merchants from India traveled to East Asia as much as East Asians did to India. The Vietnamese city of Da Nang was once an Indian colonial town.

Most of us are familiar with the nautical accomplishments of the Arabs, but those of the Polynesians are less well known. Their voyages were made considerably later, but they serve as still another example of the seafaring skills the people of the Far East and the South Pacific possessed.

Natives of the Marquesas Islands reached Hawaii and, by way of Tahiti, New Zealand sometime around 1000 B.C. Without compasses and navigating only by the stars, they traveled distances of 3,300 miles. Archaeological findings in New Zealand, Hawaii, and the Marquesas prove that these contacts took place.

A Polynesian saga tells of a daring voyage the seafarer Cupe made when he set out to capture a huge octopus. In his pursuit of the octopus, Cupe discovered New Zealand, the largest land mass in Polynesia. He than followed the octopus into what is now the Cook Strait off North Island, killed his prey, and finally returned home. This is reported to have happened in 900 B.C. Other sailors followed the route Cupe had discovered and colonized the new lands he had seen.

Sea and land contacts existed between the Far East and Persia as well as between the Far East and Byzantium. But active as the ancient Chinese land and seafarers may have been, we soon learned to our sorrow that they had passed down discouragingly little information about themselves. We could not find any precise descriptions of ancient Asiatic ships in the museums of London or Paris, nor were we any more successful in the Netherlands, in Scandinavia, or anywhere in the German-speaking countries. Audemard's work was the most detailed we could find, and, equipped with that as well as with some of his own materials, Carl Frederik began his preliminary work.

In the meantime, I continued my search, for it seemed incomprehensible to me that no reports whatsoever — neither descriptions of voyages nor plans of ships — had come down to us from ancient China. We had to locate a ship used around the time of Christ's birth yet built with a degree of sophistication that could only have been the product of several centuries of experience on the high seas. We were not looking for what could be called an "archetypal" boat but rather for one that showed signs of considerable skill in shipbuilding without being a mere copy of nearly contemporary junks. "The evolution of Chinese shipbuilding," Audemard writes, "shows variety as well as a strong adherence to tradition. It is a simple enough matter to identify differences of detail in different types of ships in different periods. It is by no means so simple to grasp fundamental differences of construction." At the beginning of 1971, the oldest plans for a junk that we had were taken from Audemard's work, and they dated from the fifteenth century.

At the same time that we were trying to locate plans for our ship, we were also trying to find records that would help us establish the route that ancient Asiatic sailors had probably followed across the Pacific. Two possibilities seemed likely. The first lay close to the land masses and islands of the North Pacific. Beginning somewhere near Canton, it led through the Formosa Strait and along the coast of Japan and the Kuril Islands until it reached the southernmost tip of the Kamchatka Peninsula at about 160° east longitude and 50° north latitude. It then turned eastward south of the Aleutians, reaching Kodiak Island off the coast of Alaska before it swung southeast and followed the coast of North America down to Mexico. This route exposed the sailor to the storms and cold of the North Pacific, but only at first glance did it seem forbiddingly difficult. The major advantage this route offered was the constant closeness of land, for this made it possible to interrupt the trip at any time and to extend it over a long period. Furthermore, it seemed likely that the first travelers from Asia to America may well have hopped from island to island rather than taking a direct route across the Pacific. Time was clearly of no importance to them, and if we tentatively put aside the idea that the first Asians to reach Central America sometime between 1000 B.C. and Christ's birth were castaways, then the Aleutian route would seem to be the most logical one. And we actually found Chinese sources that told of voyages along this route, voyages to the legendary land of Fu Sang.

One of these reports is attributed to Hui-shen, a monk, merchant, and missionary who returned from such a voyage in 499 A.D. after a forty-year absence from China. This oral account has been recorded in the official histories of China. The first European translation of Hui-shen's story appeared in French in 1761, and a version of Hui-shen's report occupies a prominent place in Charles G. Leland's book, *Fu Sang and the Discovery of America,* published in 1875. Unfortunately, neither of these renderings accurately reflects the Chinese original. In his book, Leland deals with the early history of Central America, with similarities he claims to have found between Asian and American languages, and with possible routes across the Pacific.

Freely translated, the name Hui-shen means "The Wise One." He apparently came from Afghanistan and was a Buddhist monk, possibly even a priest. When he arrived in China as a young missionary in 450, Buddhism was expanding rapidly, and extensive missionary journeys both by land and sea were quite common. Hui-shen left China again soon, accompanied by four other young priests or monks. These young missionaries put out to sea in a junk to travel to distant and unknown lands and convert the inhabitants of those new territories. There obviously must have been more than five men on board the junk, but Hui-shen seems to have regarded only his fellow missionaries as full-fledged members of the expedition. He describes sailing northeast of Japan to the Land of Ta Han, the Kamchatka Peninsula, and from there another 20,000 *li*, or 6,600 nautical miles, eastward to the Land of Fu Sang.

The distances and directions involved indicate that Hui-shen sailed up the Asian coast, followed the chain of the Aleutian Islands to Alaska, and then turned south down the North American coast to Mexico. He and his companions stayed there for forty years, teaching and learning. When he returned to China as an old man, he brought Emperor Wu Ti gifts from this newly discovered land and presented a detailed journal of his expedition.

The name Fu Sang was by no means unknown to the ruler of China. Long before Hui-shen set off on his journey, many a tale had been told of the mythical land of Fu Sang, an Asian Atlantis on the far side of the great ocean, a paradise where herbs of eternal youth could be found. Everything was said to be bigger and more beautiful in this fabulous land. Silkworms there supposedly grew six feet long. Even in present-day China the name Fu Sang retains some of the magical aura it had in the past. When modern merchants offer "Fu Sang silk" or "Fu Sang porcelain" for sale, they are suggesting that their wares are particularly valuable and possess qualities of an almost otherworldly nature.

Unlike most legendary figures, Hui-shen seems to have been a real historical personage, and the fact that Prince Yao Ssu-lien, a member of the royal family, was commissioned to record the monk's accounts and incorporate them into the royal archives

43

suggests that Hui-shen's reports were taken quite seriously. About a hundred years later, the historian Li Yan Chu reworked the account of Hui-shen's journey again, and from that point on his story appeared repeatedly in the works of later scholars, all of whom represented Hui-shen's story as fact, not fiction.

The objective tone and the clear, precise descriptions contained in Hui-shen's report also speak for its authenticity. The route he allegedly took via Japan, the Kamchatka Peninsula, the Aleutians, Alaska, and the west coast of North America is clearly possible even for a relatively primitive ship, and it is no doubt much less dangerous than a direct route across open seas. The northern route is essentially a matter of island-hopping, and only the stretch from Komandorskie Island just east of the Kamchatka Peninsula to the first of the Aleutian Islands at about 171° west longitude and 58° north latitude takes the sailor into relatively open seas. On this leg of the journey there is no land for about two hundred nautical miles, but on all the other legs a ship can always remain within a hundred miles of land. Almost the entire journey can be made in sight of one island or another, and this is the very route the Buddhist explorer Hui-shen describes in great detail.

In addition to a careful description of the route traveled, Hui-shen provides precise sketches of the countries and people he encountered on his journey. "The Land of the Tattooed People," he said, "lies about 7,000 *li* northeast of Japan. The inhabitants there have drawings and stripes on their bodies suggestive of wild animals . . . if these stripes are long, wide, and straight, then the person in question belongs to the upper classes. But if the markings are small and curly in form, that person will be a member of a lower class. . . ." We know today that in some Alaskan tribes different forms and styles of tattooing are used to indicate rank in the tribal hierarchy.

Many of the tales Hui-shen told about the inhabitants of Central America struck his first readers as remarkable indeed. "They have a system of writing," he reported, "but no walled or fortified cities, no weapons, and no soldiers. War is unknown in this kingdom." In his book *Mexico before Cortes*, Ignacio Bernal designates the period in which Hui-shen's stay in Central America might have fallen as the "Golden Age." Other writers speak of it as the classical period. The art of writing was widespread, and mathematical skills were developed to a high level. The concept and use of zero was known in Central America long before it was in Europe, and the magnificent cities of the Mayans or of the still unidentified people who built the temple city of Teotihuacan were in fact completely without fortifications.

"There is no iron ore there," Hui-shen reported, "but copper is available. The people place no great value on gold or silver." Lodes of iron ore did exist, but they were never exploited before the Spanish conquest. "Metals never had any great significance in early American cultures," Ignacio Bernal writes. "They were used primarily in luxury items rather than in practical implements."

Hui-shen provides us with information on the social hierarchy, on slavery, crime, law courts, weddings, customs, funeral rites, and on many other things as well. Unfortunately, our knowledge of ancient American cultures is still too spotty to allow verification of many of his statements. Teotihuacan has, of course, been restored and made into a major tourist attraction of the Mexico City area. But research has still not been able to determine the origins of the people who were able to construct, seemingly out of nothing, a temple city of this order. Even the Aztecs did not know who had built Teotihuacan. They called the complex of ruins "the place where the gods lived" and told the Spaniards that giants had once lived there.

Scholars have differed in their views of Hui-shen's reports. Some claimed that Fu Sang did not lie to the east but to the west and that Fu Sang might well have been Madagascar. The route Hui-shen describes, however, would speak against this theory.

45

Others have identified Fu Sang with Japan, but the evidence against this theory is even more overpowering. First, the Chinese had detailed knowledge of Japanese history by 297 A.D. at the latest. Second, the use of iron was known in Japan. And, third, the Japanese, who carried out an invasion of Korea during Hui-shen's lifetime, were far from being a peaceful people.

It is possible that Fu Sang is comparable to Atlantis, a legendary land of plenty, and that Hui-shen's story is simply one more poetic rendering of this myth. But a close study of his work makes this conclusion seem doubtful. His reports are transcribed in the clear, laconic style characteristic of ancient Chinese "travel literature," a style that differs radically from the style of fictional writings of that time.

Charles Chapman, an American historian who has done considerable research on the subject of Fu Sang, comes to the following conclusion: "Either Fu Sang was located in the Americas, most likely in Mexico, or the entire story is a falsification. But if there were some truth to it, we would have to revise our thinking drastically."

Fu Sang is no longer a subject of heated controversy, but it is perhaps worth recalling that scholars smiled condescendingly when Schliemann set out to find Troy, using Homer as his guide. Yet Schliemann did find Troy. In any case, Joseph Needham, perhaps the most eminent Western authority on China, was "deeply impressed" during an extended visit to Mexico "by the obvious similarities . . . in basic features of Central American cultures and those of East and Southeast Asia."

Needham also studied the possibility of transpacific contacts, and in this connection he tried to establish when the Chinese first became aware of the Kuroshio Current, which flows west to east across the Pacific from Japan to the Americas. He learned that the current was known under the name of Wei Lu as early as the epoch of the Warring States (481–221 B.C.). Wei Lu means something like "the cosmic cloaca," and it was said to move toward "a world in the east from which no man has ever returned."

The Kuroshio Current, the Gulf Stream of Asia, is not as wide as the Gulf Stream, but it is still one of the major ocean currents of the world. Because of its deep blue color the Japanese call it "the black stream." It is not as warm as the Gulf Stream, either, but is generally ten to fifteen degrees warmer than the waters south of Japan. Also, its course is more erratic than that of the Gulf Stream. The much heavier storms of the Pacific probably account for this, for it has often been observed that winds out of the northeast have halted the west-to-east movement of the current for days on end.

No matter how poetic or legendary many of the ancient Chinese descriptions of the sea, its currents, and the land beyond it may seem, the fact remains that ocean routes to the east were known before the birth of Christ.

Hui-shen's account of his journey is not the only one of its kind. In 219 B.C., the Taoist, scholar, and alchemist Hsu Fu told the Emperor Shih Huang Ti of three islands in the middle of the Pacific that were inhabited by immortal beings. The emperor had an expedition organized, and though he soon complained bitterly about the costs of the expedition and the burden it imposed on his research budget, he still gave Hsu Fu permission to go ahead. Chinese literature abounds with accounts of this journey, but the most informative is contained in the biography of Prince Huai Nan. The text reads as follows:

Shih Huang Ti sent Hsu Fu across the sea to search out wondrous things and creatures. This is what Hsu Fu told us on his return.

On an island in the middle of the ocean I met a great magician who asked me if I had been sent by the Emperor of the West. I answered him that I had. Why have you come? he asked, and I replied that I was searching for herbs that could prolong life. The gifts from your king that you offer in exchange are paltry things, he said. You may look at these plants, but you may not take any with you.

Then we traveled farther toward the southeast and came to P'eng-lai, and there I saw the gates of the Chih-Cheng Palace, and before them stood a guard with a metallic complexion and a shape like a dragon. His radiance illuminated the heavens. Here I paid homage twice to the magician of the sea and asked him what gifts we should bring him.

Bring me young men of noble lineage and education. Bring suitable maidens with them and bring artisans from all the trades. Then you will receive the magic herbs you want.

Shih Huang Ti was pleased to hear this, and he gathered together three thousand young men and women for Hsu Fu, gave him an adequate supply of seeds for the five types of grain, and selected artisans of every trade for him. Then the fleet set sail.

Hsu Fu must have found a peaceful and fruitful plain somewhere, surrounded by forests and rich marshland, and become a king himself. In any case, he never returned to China.

He had disappeared into that land "from which no man returns." But it seems possible that behind this story of Hsu Fu's disappearance across the great sea to the east lies the actual story of a sea journey to America. It is striking that a definite number of young men and women is mentioned, that grain seeds were taken along, and — perhaps most important — that all kinds of artisans were included in the expedition. Among them there surely must have been a number of artists. All these people that accompanied Hsu Fu might well represent a wave of immigration that could help to explain a number of phenomena hitherto unexplained. They would account for the sudden appearance in America of cultural and technical achievements of a high level. One thing is clear: if there was an immigration from Asia to America, these newcomers in the New World must have had knowledge that was worth passing along. It is unlikely that shipwrecked fishermen would have had such knowledge, but artisans and artists certainly would. What they brought with them from their homeland would have enabled them to impart significant new impulses to the cultures they found already established in America.

Probably no one will ever be able to verify these stories and many others like them that tell of journeys across the great sea to the east. We will probably never know to what countries Hui-shen and Hsu Fu sailed or if they even sailed at all. The reports of these journeys may never be regarded as valid research sources, but they do suggest how early the Chinese were capable of making long voyages and that by the third century B.C. they knew of a fabled land far to the east. We can also learn from these stories what kinds of ships and sails these legendary mariners probably used.

While our search for a suitable model for our ship continued, so did our search for a suitable route. Hui-shen's island-hopping technique did not strike us as practicable for our expedition. Climatic conditions along the extreme northerly route would not permit us to make the entire journey in one sweep, and we could not take time for the layovers ashore that Hui-shen and other early mariners must have made. Furthermore, we assumed that if contact between Asia and America had existed on a regular basis, efforts must have been made to find a route across the open sea.

During our early considerations of routes, Arno and I had thought of utilizing the Equatorial Current to cross the Pacific. The first European to make use of this route was the Spaniard Alvaro de Saavedra. In 1527, he sailed from the Pacific coast of Mexico to the Philippines without sighting a single island. His attempts to return by the same route failed, and we soon realized that we, too, would encounter formidable difficulties if we attempted to use the equatorial currents in a crossing from Asia to America.

That left us two possibilities: the southern route or a northerly route across the open sea. In either case we would be following currents. In the south a current flows from Tasmania past the South Island of New Zealand and finally reaches Chile. But this current moves through the "Roaring Forties," an area extending over the fortieth parallel, and makes this route dangerous, if not nearly suicidal. Ice floes and violent storms plague the southern

49

route all year long. The Frenchman Eric de Bisschop tried to travel it and failed. Then, too, it seemed most unlikely that the ancient navigators had used this route both because of its inhospitable nature and because the approach to the southern current from Indonesia or southern China is in itself a highly complicated venture in navigation. Whatever the drawbacks of a northerly route across the open sea, it now remained as the only conceivable possibility.

Carl Frederik had holed up in Denmark for a few weeks; then he turned up again with rolls of sea charts under his arm. On a U.S. Navy pilot chart of the Pacific, he had sketched in our route and, on the basis of known currents and wind velocities, our expected positions at different times during the voyage. This plan projected that we would leave the Chinese coast near Hong Kong or Canton on May 25. At this point, we were still expecting support from the government in Peking. "If we leave any later than that, we'll run into the typhoon season, and that wouldn't be much fun," Carl said.

On May 31 we were scheduled to pass the southern tip of Taiwan. By the beginning of July, after a little more than a month at sea, we would be 1,000 nautical miles east of Japan on a latitude with Tokyo, and on July 20 we should cross the international date line. We would reach the coast of North America near San Francisco after a little more than three months, and on October 10 we would reach Tehuantepec, Mexico, our first destination in Central America.

"I'd guess we'll be underway something like five months, maybe six," Carl told us. "Things will be a little more difficult if we want to head on to South America. The Humboldt Current will be against us there, and we'll need more time."

"How much?" I asked.

"Two, maybe three months. Nobody can predict too accurately how the winds and currents will behave." Carl was silent for a long time; then he went on. "I've run all the data through a computer. We ought to come out right with this course and the time we're allowing for it."

That conversation took place in midyear of 1972. We would obviously need more detailed information on the route Carl Frederik had suggested, but we at least knew what our route would be.

The ocean currents of the Pacific make up a circular system flowing clockwise between Asia and America (see endpaper map). The Kuroshio Current makes itself felt just to the east of Taiwan and moves eastward away from Japan along the fortieth parallel, eventually joining the North Pacific Current. This in turn unites with the California Current off the American coast between San Francisco and Eureka, on the Oregon-California border. Near Seattle, the California Current splits into two branches, the northern one flowing northwest into the Gulf of Alaska. The southern branch flows southeast along the California coast to Mexico. But just off the southernmost tip of Baja California at about 20° north latitude and 110° west longitude, this current joins the North Equatorial Current, which flows from east to west. Here, within sight of his goal, the mariner is in danger of being swept back toward Asia. But if he sails close to the coast, the southern branch of the California Current will continue to take him southeast. Assuming that we would be able to follow this route exactly, we would have no difficulty in reaching the peninsula of Baja California. From there, we would sail in sight of the Mexican coast, touching it at the ports of Mazatlán, Puerto Vallarta, Acapulco, and, finally, Salina Cruz in the isthmus of Tehuantepec.

Of all these ports, Salina Cruz was probably the easiest to approach and the most important in terms of our purpose, for the Tehuantepec isthmus presents an advantageous point for possible immigration from the west. The Gulf coast of Mexico can be reached with relative ease from here, and the valleys that extend to the north and northeast provide natural travel routes into the Oaxaca region. In determining our landing points on the Mexican coast, we were guided not only by practical nautical considerations but also by the crucial question of what points could have offered pre-Columbian mariners from Asia the best land routes into the interior.

Five sites seemed possible to us. The first was near the mouth of the Rio Santiago. The valley system of this river and its tributaries would have made immigration to the area around Guadalajara possible, and it was in this area that miniature houses resembling those of the Han period were found in tombs.

The second site was at the mouth of the Rio Balsas. The central plateau of Mexico can be reached through the valley system of this area, and cultural influence could easily have spread by this route to what is now the state of Guerrero. Guerrero could also have been reached by way of Acapulco, which we considered as a third possible landing site. A number of remarkable terracotta figures have been found in Guerrero. Dating from the pre-classical period, these figures are clearly reminiscent of Japanese terra-cottas of the Jō-Mon and Haniwa cultures. The Museum of Natural History in New York has a terra-cotta head from the Rio Balsas region that portrays a man with bushy eyebrows and a long beard. Although long beards are hardly characteristic of American Indians, a number of figures with clearly identifiable beards have been found in Guerrero.

The fourth landing site, and the one I considered most significant, was Salina Cruz. In addition to immigration routes to the Gulf coast and Yucatán and those to Oaxaca and the central plateau, travel along the Pacific coast to Guatemala, San Salvador, and Honduras was also possible from Salina Cruz. Archaeological findings indicate that the earliest advanced civilizations of Central America were located on the isthmus of Tehuantepec, and it is possible that the Olmec culture spread from this area to Oaxaca, Guatemala, and the Mexican Gulf coast.

A fifth possible landing point was the area around the port town of San José on the coast of Guatemala. Here, too, there are clear routes leading from the tropical coast to the highlands of Guatemala, where noteworthy finds have also been made. One example is the "Buddha" of Monte Alto, which now stands in front of the museum in La Democracia.

Finally we knew where our journey would begin, what route we would follow, and what our destination was. The northerly route we had chosen was first charted by the Spaniard Andrés de Urdaneta. He had set sail from Mexico in 1564 with four caravels and reached the Philippines without incident. On the return journey, he sailed north of Japan until he reached about 45° north latitude, then traveled east, striking the coast of North America somewhere near Eureka. Sailing down the coast, he reached Mexico again in 1565. On this trip, which he described precisely in his log, the Spaniard opened what would remain for centuries the only shipway between America and Asia.

We had planned our route, but we still lacked plans for constructing our ship. We finally found what we needed in a ship's model that had been uncovered in excavations near Canton in 1952 and that is now in the Canton Museum. The British sinologist Joseph Needham was probably the first Western scholar to see the model, and he described it in great detail in his *Science and Civilization in China*.

The model, a funeral gift discovered in a tomb, is about fifteen inches long. Chinese archaeologists believe it dates from the Later Han dynasty and was built sometime around 100 A.D. "The model seems to be so precise in its detail," Carl Frederik wrote, "that it could be copied from photographs. I'm having all available Chinese literature about it translated. Wish me luck."

At last we knew what we wanted to build, but when, where, and how we would build it was still unclear. We waited for news from Carl, hoping he would be able to find a shipbuilder with the knowledge and experience to construct our junk on the basis of this ancient model. Carl made preliminary sketches, studied junks, their sails, their maneuverability. He poked about in libraries, translated, read, bargained with shipbuilders and lumber dealers. He analyzed the construction of modern junks and observed the huge sailing junks from the People's Republic of China as they plied the waters off Hong Kong. Before long we heard from him again. "My time in Hong Kong has been more useful than I'd imagined it would be. I've found a shipbuilder. Now I'm coming home to Europe to put together what I've learned and to draw up the blueprints."

That was early in March 1973. Carl came home glowing. He had been victorious, this time around anyhow. We spoke with him a few times briefly in Austria, then he flew home to Denmark, armed with sketches, plans, and data from the Royal Observatory, the British Navy, the U.S. Navy. He had Japanese, Chinese, and English books on shipbuilding, a notebook stuffed with addresses, and a sack full of various woods and fibers, samples of shipbuilding materials whose quality and durability he wanted to test at the Polytechnical Institute in Copenhagen. He also wanted to build a detailed model according to the specifications he had gathered. He could then run this model through a series of experiments to see how both hull and sail would stand up to actual conditions of wind and water. "I'd rather see a few models capsize or go down in the test tank than have us try the same tricks in the middle of the Pacific," he said just before he boarded his plane.

While Carl was at work in Copenhagen, preliminary work was also being done at the shipbuilding wharf in Hong Kong's Ap Lei Chau (Aberdeen Island) district. Carl would soon be spending days, weeks, and months there.

Filthy alleys, streets barely wide enough for a man to walk through. Everything that has to do with ships is made on Ap Lei Chau: ropes, motors, sailcloth. Fishing nets are knotted in dark rooms. The whole district seems like a Hollywood set for a film that will never be made.

A gray school building made of cement blocks that started

Overleaf: The *Tai Ki* in heavy seas. All
but two panels of the sail are reefed. (ᴋᴋ)

Our ship, the *Tai Ki*, measured just over sixty feet from bow to stern. She was our home for 114 days on the vast expanse of the Pacific.

On the far left, the Austrian flag is visible above the helmsman's cabin. The structure with the mushroom-shaped roof houses the kitchen and living quarters. In front of it, under the low, rounded roof, are our sleeping quarters. Toward the starboard bow, a leeboard, raised to its horizontal position, stands out light gray against the dark hull of the ship. The rattan sail on its 48-foot mast displays the Tai Ki symbol. (D)

The six-nation crew:
Right: Kuno Knöbl, Austria,
leader of the expedition. (BM)
Below: Allan Kartin, our quiet
radio operator from Denmark.
(BM)

Above: Wolf Werner Rausch, student of
theology from Hamburg, former
member of the German Merchant
Marine. (BM)
Left: Hal Prince, Ireland, English
teacher and sailing enthusiast. (BM)

Left: Carl Frederik Grage, Denmark, captain of the *Tai Ki*. (BM)

Below: Bill Martin, U.S.A., cameraman. He shot the film of the expedition. (BM)

Above: Bob Kendrick, England, ship's doctor and world traveler. (BM)

Left: Arno Dennig, Austria. Together with Kuno Knöbl he planned and carried out the expedition. (BM)

The sea is still calm, but the cloud formations on the horizon indicate that a storm is approaching. Preparations include reefing the sail. (BM)

Overleaf: The inside of the cabin at breakfast time. Sitting on the spare mast are (left to right) Carl, Hal, Allan, and Bob. On the opposite side of the cabin are Bill, who is cook for this meal, and Wolf, with his back to the camera. (D)

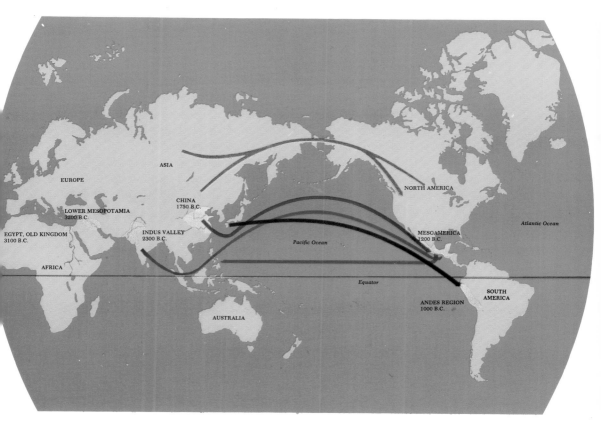

Above: Transpacific contacts between Asia and the Americas. This map, which was on display in a Mexico exhibit in 1974 at the Museum of Natural History in New York, is based on Gordon Ekholm's sketches and shows possible routes Asian travelers may have followed to the Americas. (MNH)

Below: Found near Canton in a tomb dating from the Han period (100 A.D.), this clay model of a junk provided the basic design for the *Tai Ki*. This photograph was taken in the museum in Canton. (G)

Elephants in America? In the jungles of Honduras there are the ruins of Copán, a center of
Mayan culture in the 5th century A.D. One column, or stela, has carved on it what seems to
be an elephant complete with ears, trunk, and even mahouts. But the elephant was
unknown in the Western Hemisphere. Its primitive ancestor, the mammoth, became
extinct there at the end of the Ice Age. Is this "elephant stela" therefore proof of cultural
contact between Asia and pre-Columbian American cultures? The above drawing (*left*) and
photograph (*right*) were made by the Englishman A. P. Maudsley. (Both KK private archive)
The photograph on the right-hand page shows the stela in its present mutilated state. (D)

The "Chinese stela" of Copán presents still another mystery to scholars. This column stands opposite the "elephant stela" and portrays what could well be the face of an ancient mandarin. This relief shows a striking resemblance to Chinese sculptures and paintings. American Indians didn't have beards, but the above figure clearly is bearded. The headdress also suggests Asian influence. In front of this stela there is a giant turtle carved in stone. An Indian myth tells of an immense turtle that came out of the sea to the west, carrying many strangers, who brought new knowledge and happiness to the land. (D)

Architecture also offers startling clues. This niche pyramid in Angkor Wat, the Khmer temple city in the Cambodian jungle (*right*) (HR) bears a striking resemblance to the pyramid of Tajin in Central America (*below*). (D)

This amazing series of terracotta heads found in Mexico and dating back to pre-Columbian times would seem to provide positive proof of contact with the Old World. The variation of facial types is astonishing. All races from the Far East to the Mediterranean and Black

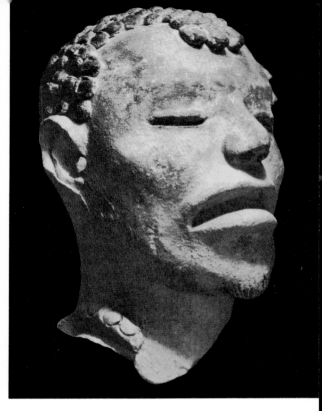

Africa are represented. Can these lifelike, realistic faces be nothing more than the product of an anonymous Indian artist's fancy? (From Alexander von Wuthenau)

Copán is an archaeologist's paradise, abounding with artifacts that challenge the imagination. The stone shown above is one of them. Its surface displays the Tai Ki sign or ideogram, the Chinese symbol for "the Great Ultimate," that also graced the sail of our junk. (D)

crumbling as soon as they came out of the mold, a soccer field next to the school, steel plate being welded on oily ground across the street, a woman with white gloves weaving soft bamboo fibers into a mat. Then a brightly colored sign: "So Brothers Shipyard."

A small house with low-ceilinged bedrooms upstairs. A kitchen, dining room, office, and "construction hall" were all housed in one large room at ground level. A squeaking fan spun about overhead, but barely stirred the sticky, humid air. The ground around the house and the paths to it were slick with oil. A broken stairway and the image of a god stood opposite the entrance, which was always open and always illuminated by a red neon light.

The way to the wharf lay over planking, boards, barrels, and ropes. The distance is not great, but you stumble at every step. Your feet sink into sawdust sodden with oil and dirt. Mangy dogs sniff through garbage. There is a shed near the water, just a wooden roof resting on poles, no walls. That's the work area. Next to it some oil-soaked planks lie half-buried in mud: the dry dock. The short ramp leading up to it would be a challenge to anyone but a tightrope walker. Scrapped junks. A motorboat awaiting repair. An unfinished fiberglass hull. Similar establishments lie to either side of the So Brothers Shipyard. Ap Lei Chau is a world unto itself, a world the rest of the world has left behind.

This was where our junk would be built. The So brothers, who had agreed to take on the job, came from a long line of shipbuilders. The eldest brother, Rocky So, was Carl's first partner. In Chinese, he had the melodious name of So Hawk Sum, which means "the All-Knowing One."

He proudly showed Carl his books: a work on Chinese junks in several volumes, written by a European who turned out to be none other than Louis Audemard. Rocky, Carl wrote, planned to start building our ship in May 1973, and the tentative delivery date was October of the same year. "But we had better leave ourselves a margin of safety," Carl added. "I wouldn't count on getting the boat until the end of December."

Rocky had promised to go to Taiwan and find a couple of shipbuilders who were used to working with Chinese pine and bamboo, who knew the techniques of all-wood construction, and who still had the necessary traditional skills our project demanded. Most of this knowledge was available in Hong Kong, but certain old-fashioned details of construction had gotten lost. These two men were to fill in the gaps.

In the meantime we signed a contract with a publisher, made up timetables and schedules, changed them, threw them out, started all over several times. I got a leave of absence from my job at Austrian Television, and Carl returned to Hong Kong. Everything was going along as planned. Then we received a telex from him: "We're working out the details now and waiting for the building materials."

Carl was fighting daily battles in Hong Kong, trying to hold to schedules, keep delays to a minimum, secure manpower and materials. Suddenly the wood needed for the hull was unavailable. "Red China isn't going to supply us now," Rocky So explained with a shrug. Maybe Taiwan could help out. No, Taiwan had declared an export embargo. Perhaps our whole operation should be moved to Taiwan. We decided to stick with Hong Kong. By this time it was early September and we were four months behind schedule. Building should have begun in May, and we had hoped to have the ship finished by December. What was wrong? The interminable bargaining of the Chinese was wearing on Carl. Time was a matter of complete indifference to them; to us it was precious and the waste of it intolerable. "This business with the wood has been frustrating, but it seems to be coming clear now," Carl reassured us. He continued his negotiations with the shipbuilders. Prices had gone up. Carl could save us some money by importing the wood from Taiwan himself. But when would the builders lay the keel? When would they finally get around to building the ship? Carl had constructed some new models, experimented some more with draft and steerage, made some slight changes in the dimensions of the hull.

Arno and I were on pins and needles. Our deadlines drew closer and closer. Would we be able to meet them? We revised our schedule once again. Our situation was critical. If work on the ship were not begun by mid-September, we would be in serious trouble. And the building of the ship was not the only problem we had to contend with.

More time passed, and our anxiety grew. If we had not received any favorable news from Hong Kong by the end of September, if we did not have a firm schedule and projected date of completion for the ship, we might well have to call off the entire project.

Then, at last, a letter from Carl. Photographs, too. Among those pictures there was one in particular that let us breathe more easily: it showed a drawing of the framework on a scale of 1:1. The builders would use this drawing to construct templates for the ship's frame. It seemed that work on the ship had begun. The date was September 21, 1973.

CHAPTER THREE

The Great Ultimate

ANYONE WHO HAS EVER BUILT A HOUSE KNOWS WHAT KINDS OF difficulty, both major and minor, such a project involves: the struggle for a building permit, disagreements with the architect, trouble with the workmen. Anyone who has waited in impotent rage for the plumbers to arrive, only to hear that they will not begin work now but three weeks from now; anyone who has seen a carpenter stroll up and announce that he cannot possibly have the roof closed in before winter; anyone who has caved in helplessly before the electrician's quiet yet convincing argument that this fresh wallpaper will have to be torn down or that newly plastered wall cracked open because the code requires him to run his wiring this way and not that way; anyone who has experienced all this will perhaps be able to understand our feelings as we waited in Europe, in America, and in Asia for our ship, our elegant *Tai Ki,* the first junk ever to be built according to ancient specifications, waited for this ship we had dreamed about for years, a ship that had already been completed months ago in our imaginations and now lay rocking elegantly in the waves of the Pacific, waited for this ship to get off the drawing board and become reality, waited for it to be done, finished, completed. *Tai Ki* — the Great Ultimate. We were sitting at the great poker table of the Pacific and had put all our money on this hand. Our opponent, time, might just call our bluff and send us home without a nickel between us.

Arno, Carl, and I were not the only ones to grow uneasy. Our publisher, Fritz Molden, was getting nervous, too, and with good reason. Our project was costing nearly half a million dollars, and now, after a seemingly endless number of changes in our plans, he was more than ready to see some results.

We showed him wooden pins that would be used to secure the planking to the framework of the hull. These were not the actual wooden nails that would be used, but only samples. The little shop in Hong Kong that would supply the nails had not yet begun to produce them. But it would soon, very soon.

We showed him samples of our rattan matting, quoted data on it that the engineers at the Polytechnical Institute in Copenhagen had established and that proved it to be ideal for our purposes. Our sail and matting would be woven from this material that could neither tear nor splinter, but the firm in Hong Kong responsible for it . . .

Carl initiated us into the mysterious functions of a junk's sail, explained how our sail would be set in different winds and why, explained how the rudder and the steering lines worked. We ran around with samples of wood and explained why billian was better for our purposes than teak, why Chinese pine was better than oak, what we were doing to impregnate and preserve the hull. We displayed documents, sketches, plans. But when it came to the ship itself, our lovely *Tai Ki,* we still did not have much more to show than some drawings and some photographs taken at the shipyard of the All-Knowing One on Ap Lei Chau.

But Carl had other problems to deal with in Hong Kong besides the beginning of work on the ship. He still had to sign our contract with the shipyard. Only then, we realized, would work actually get underway. But this all-important piece of paper did not even exist as yet. We had commissioned a lawyer in Hong Kong to complete the contract as quickly as possible. But clocks in Asia seem to run as slowly for lawyers as they do for ship-builders.

On October 9, we received some news that afforded us some encouragement: two thirds of the wood needed for the ship had been delivered. Carl had measured it and inspected it. All the details related to construction of the boat had been cleared up with the shipyard, and as soon as the contract was signed — this was to happen within the next few days — work on the junk could begin. The new date set for completion was May 15. Carl thought that would still give us ample time before departure to distribute ballast in the vessel, inspect the ship carefully, test it at sea, and generally prepare it for the voyage. May 25, 1974, still remained firm as our departure date. The mast would be imported from Taiwan, and the rest of the wood we needed was scheduled to arrive in good time. "Things are going well now," Carl wrote us, "and I'm feeling much relieved."

The contract was signed, and work began. We were far behind our original schedule, but we could at least be grateful for the fact that we had made as much allowance for delays as we had. We had reason to be optimistic. Carl set to work in Hong Kong, and the hull of the ship was completed in December.

During this period, Arno and I had been traveling in the United States, Central America, and South America. We had crept around in libraries, consulted with scholars, and made photographs. At the end of the year I returned to Europe to meet with Carl and take stock.

One problem that had been on our minds from the beginning but that we had put off as long as we were still in the planning stage was the crew of the *Tai Ki*. How many crew members would we need? The answer to that question would be dictated by the size of our ship, living space both above and below deck, safety requirements, the amount of provisions we could carry, and the amount of work that would have to be done on board. We finally arrived at the number eight; that is to say, Carl arrived at that number, for as captain and nautical leader of the expedition, the decision rested with him. Besides Carl, Arno, and me, we needed five more men. We agreed quickly on criteria for selection and, more important still, on who would make the selection. All three of us would keep an eye out for suitable candidates, and we would have to agree unanimously on the final choice of the crew. We had already made some tentative choices. One of them was a German mountain climber and chief instructor at a skiing school in Alaska. Arno had been with him on several expeditions. Another was a sailing companion of Carl's, a small blond Dane by the name of Allan Kartin. He was twenty-nine, had a ship of his own, captain's papers, and — what might prove particularly useful to us — a pilot's license as well. "But even more important," Carl said, "is that he's a first-rate radio man." Arno had had a meeting with this talented ham radio operator. Kartin had not proved especially communicative. He listened to Arno's explanation of our plan but said neither yes nor no. He said nothing at all. We hoped he would join us but did not know if he would.

When the first notices about the expedition appeared in the press, we began to receive inquiries from prospective crew members and soon had thirty applications.

A fifteen-year-old schoolboy wanted to join us because he found school "dumb" but thought our expedition sounded "keen." An inventor offered to provide us with one-man life rafts of a "completely new" design. "I've tried them out in the pond near our village," he wrote. A peace activist asked us to christen the expedition an "Action against the A-Bomb." A "scholar" sent us a long letter about "mariners from other worlds." But we also received letters from a doctor, two sailors, two sports teachers, and a psychologist who wanted to study group dynamics aboard the *Tai Ki*. A German cameraman in Hong Kong wanted to shoot a documentary on the construction of the junk.

It had become clear meanwhile that at least one crew member would have to be a cameraman. We had decided to make a film of the expedition, and Phil Hobel, our American producer, had already suggested one or two possible cameramen. As of early 1974, the crew consisted of Carl as captain, Arno, myself, and Allan Kartin, the taciturn radioman from Denmark. Allan had still not given us a clear affirmative answer, but the fact that he was already at work on radio equipment for the *Tai Ki* led us to believe he was a sure thing. Arno's friend in Alaska remained undecided. Four berths were filled, and we had to assume that two more would be filled by cameramen. What we needed to round out the crew was another experienced deep-sea sailor and a doctor.

A doctor was particularly important. It would have been nothing short of irresponsible to set out on a voyage of six months without a trained medical man on board. Quite apart from injuries that could befall us at any time, disease could endanger the entire expedition. Klaus Hehner, who had participated in the first regatta to sail from San Francisco to Yokohama with one-man crews, described in his book (and in a conversation with Arno) the dangers Pacific crossings of this kind could encounter. A French competitor in this regatta was struck on the head by a boom and suffered a fracture of the skull. If circumstances had not been as fortunate as they were at the time, the man could never have been saved. Even if a ship's doctor could not be expected to handle injuries of that magnitude, his presence would at least guarantee that lesser fractures and wounds would receive prompt treatment and heal properly.

It was obvious that we would have no trouble recruiting our crew of eight, but we began at this point to consider again a question we had dealt with at some length in our early planning but then put aside: how could we bring eight individuals together to form a genuine crew, a closely knit unit that would be able to take the stresses of several months adrift on the Pacific? We wondered if it were not foolhardy even to consider setting out with a crew that had been recruited more or less by chance. Ideally, each crew member should know the others well. The crew should be a trained team accustomed to living and working together.

That would have been the ideal solution, but there was little chance of realizing it. The time factor was against us. We would have had to assemble our crew at a point in time when we were not at all sure ourselves whether our project would ever become a reality or not. Then, too, all three of us in the original team had professional obligations that made advance training impossible. Arno was fully occupied running his agricultural and quarrying enterprises, and I was working full time as a program director for Austrian Television. Only Carl was relatively free. And it was likely that prospective *Tai Ki* crew members would have similar professional commitments. No one could possibly have afforded the time or money for training ventures that might have welded us together into a team. Now, four months before we planned to set out, considerations of this kind were completely idle.

Carl argued that if we could not go to sea with a fully trained team, then we would be better off with one we had assembled willy-nilly. He felt the latter choice was far better than having crew members who were only half-trained and only partially acquainted with each other. With such a group, sympathies and antipathies would have formed but would not have had a chance to be neutralized by a long period of working together toward a common goal. Arno and I found Carl's case convincing. Indeed, it would probably be best if some crew members did not know each other at all beforehand. The danger of conflict on board would still exist, but where no prejudices either for or against another crew member had had a chance to form, this danger would be somewhat easier to overcome. The prime loyalty would be to the expedition as a whole, not to any individuals in it. And then again, the press of time left us no other choice.

I had spoken with Richard Friedmann of NASA in Washington as early as 1973. There were two things I wanted to find out from him: first, whether some, or even all, of our crew members could take part in a training course for astronauts, and, second, whether NASA could provide us with any of its records that dealt with problems of group psychology. We were interested in test results and actual experience, anything that would tell us how men isolated in small groups behave under extreme duress, what they feel, how they react, when and why crises are likely to occur.

The *Tai Ki* expedition seemed to me comparable in many ways to the exploratory flights of the space age. The astronauts are completely isolated in space, with radio and TV their only links to the world behind them. They are alone and can depend on no one but themselves. The much touted "red button" that is supposed to bring help in case of extreme danger may well set concrete rescue mechanisms in motion, but in reality it offers little more than moral support.

There was no possibility of our taking part in a training session. American astronauts not only learn what they have to know to complete their mission in space successfully, but they also learn survival techniques for the jungle, the desert, and the open sea. Only an ignorant man will give up the struggle to survive. Even a little knowledge and a slight acquaintance with the environment lend a sense of strength and confidence. This holds true for anyone likely to encounter extraordinary circumstances: the mountain climber or the deep-sea sailor, the jungle explorer or the astronaut. Survival training of this kind would have made sense for us only if the whole crew had been able to take part. And since the whole crew did not even exist, that was clearly impossible. But we were grateful in any case for all the information NASA made available to us.

We simply had to take the chance of going to sea with a crew of "unknowns." None of us was happy about this, not even Carl. But we had no choice. Our crew would have to become a crew as best it could. Once we had achieved some clarity on this point in our own minds, our worries about it faded somewhat, though they hardly disappeared entirely.

Then a novelty of quite another sort came up during a visit I made with Dr. Betty Meggers and Dr. Clifford Evans of the Smithsonian Institution in Washington. Dr. Meggers showed great interest and enthusiasm for the topic of transpacific contact in general and for our project in particular. "It's a subject that simply begs for more research," she said, beaming. "We are deeply involved in it, and other scholars are, too." Then she went on to add: "Not long ago there was a young man here who told me he was planning an expedition very similar to yours. He, too, had noticed striking similarities between the cultures of Indochina and Central America, and he's been making preparations for his expedition for the last few years."

If Betty Meggers had only known what was racing through my mind as she spoke. . . . A year earlier in New York, I had heard that some Americans were planning an expedition like ours. I had followed up this chance lead but not been able to learn anything more. Now the rumor had been confirmed. "Yes," Betty Meggers continued, "they've organized a research corporation just as you have. I think there are four men involved. Their home office is somewhere in Texas. . . . Let me find the address for you. Their plans and route are identical with yours."

Perhaps we should have been pleased to hear that someone else wanted to prove what we wanted to prove and by the same methods. If our hypothesis could be confirmed twice, then our case would stand on even firmer ground. But we still wanted to be the first to deliver the proof.

I finally found an article in an issue of the Honolulu *Star Bulletin* dating from October 1972. The headline read: "Adventurer Plans to Sail Route of Ancient Explorers." Accompanying the article was a map of the Pacific with the intended route sketched on it. It was nearly identical with ours. Hong Kong was the point of departure. There would be a stop in Japan, and the first landing in the Americas would be San Francisco, followed by Manzanillo and Acapulco. Our competitors were planning to sail in a ship of North Chinese design, an Antung freighter, and they

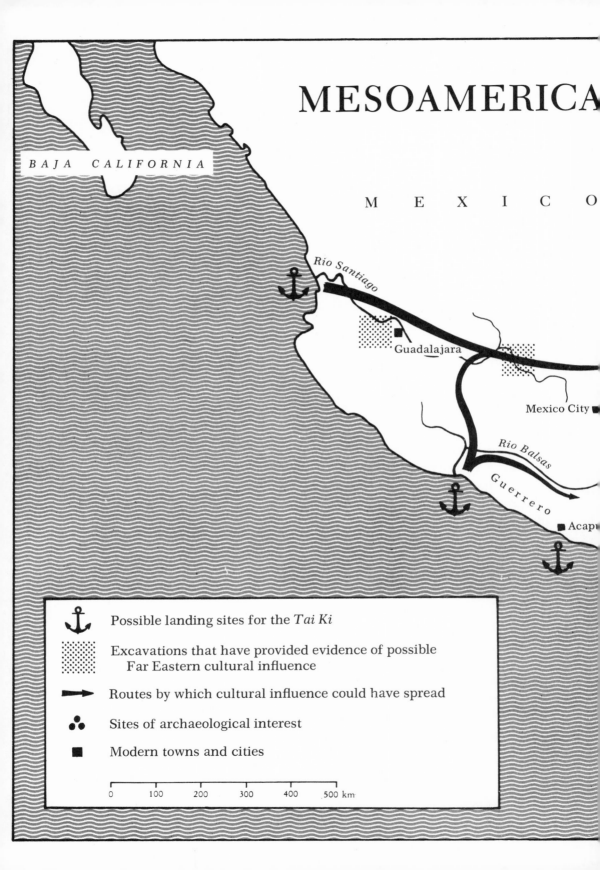

MESOAMERICA

BAJA CALIFORNIA

M E X I C O

Rio Santiago

Guadalajara

Mexico City ■

Rio Balsas

G u e r r e r o

■ Acapu

⚓   Possible landing sites for the *Tai Ki*

        Excavations that have provided evidence of possible
          Far Eastern cultural influence

➤   Routes by which cultural influence could have spread

∴   Sites of archaeological interest

■   Modern towns and cities

0   100   200   300   400   500 km

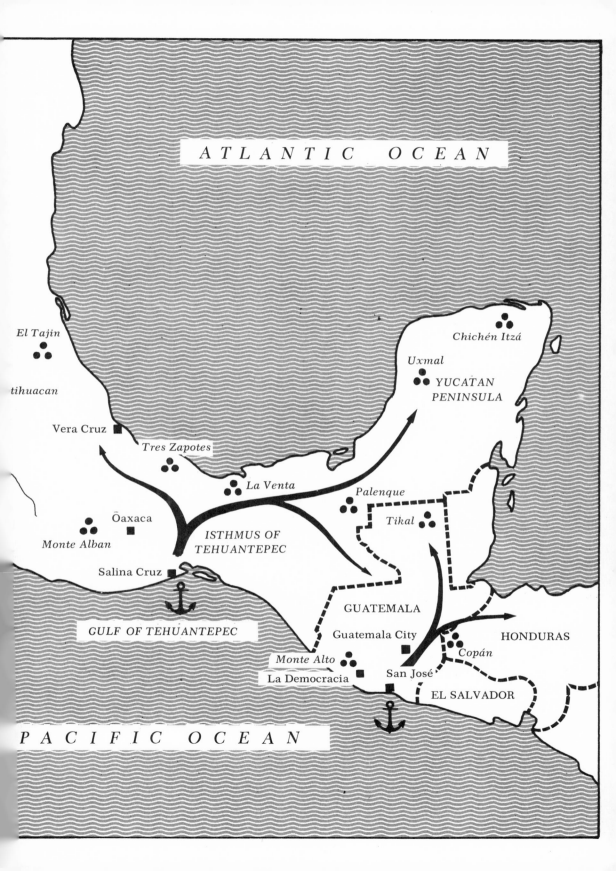

intended to incorporate all available literature on shipbuilding in the Han period into their plans. The article indicated that they were having only one difficulty, and that was money. So far, they had a hundred thousand dollars at their disposal. George Belcher, the man behind the expedition, was thirty-two years old and hoped to set out in 1974. He had already made one voyage of this kind. In 1969, he had sailed from Norway to Newfoundland in a reconstructed Viking ship.

There we were, faced with the possibility of a race from Hong Kong to Mexico. "Quite something," I wrote to Arno, "a Grand Prix across the Pacific."

I contacted Belcher and received a prompt answer from him. "Yes, Dr. Meggers is right when she says that I've been planning this expedition for a long time now. . . . I've invested two years and my own savings in it. . . . I was surprised last year when I heard of your plans for a similar voyage."

Together with three friends, Belcher had incorporated the Transpacific Society in Honolulu, had completed all his plans, and was now preparing to set out on the expedition. Things could well take an amusing turn for us.

Arno and I had also taken a look at our "definite" landing site in the Tehuantepec isthmus. We reported to Carl what we had observed. His response was something less than enthusiastic. "Salina Cruz is a rotten port. Its lighthouse functions only intermittently, and the harbor is frequently struck by heavy storms. The approach to the harbor is four hundred feet wide rather than two hundred, as you estimated, but that doesn't make any difference to us one way or another. All we need is twenty-five feet. Salina is hard to enter because there are often heavy seas right at the mouth of the harbor." Carl went on to quote from a guide to seaports: "Landing in Salina Cruz can be difficult to dangerous. Stiff breezes occur frequently, and the harbor entrance is plagued by dangerous currents." Carl's comment was: "Cheerful prospects, but the other harbors in the area aren't any better. We'll just have to take what we can get."

The deck of our junk had been finished on Ap Lei Chau. The shipbuilders were at work on the footing for the mast. Carl was kept busy, as he put it, being "designer, supervisor, historian, and buyer of equipment."

"Everything is going along just fine," our captain reported. "But I could use a thirty-two-hour day. Twenty-four just aren't enough. But you know all about that."

True enough. We, too, were racing against time. We had finished our research in Central America in March and had returned to Europe. Now Arno was busy planning the provisions for the journey and deciding what equipment we needed. Together we continued our search for the remaining crew members. I collated the material we had gathered in America and worried about our competitors.

In the middle of March, Carl arrived for our last talks in Europe. He looked thin and tanned in his faded jeans as he came toward us at the airport. "Hello," he said cheerfully. "Everything is O.K." Good. We wanted to go over all the details once more together, and we still had final decisions to make about the rest of the crew. A young doctor from Vienna had expressed an interest in joining our expedition. Five hours after Carl's arrival we were talking with him. Arno and I had already interviewed him, but since he claimed to have extensive sailing experience, we wanted Carl to have a chance to talk to him, too.

It turned out to be a rather unpleasant meeting. The doctor, who later proved most helpful in assembling our ship's medical supplies, was skeptical.

"The ship is a lemon," he said after no more than a preliminary description of it.

"A junk," Arno replied.

"What are you going to do if she swings broadside to the waves?"

"Ride it out," Carl said.

"How close can you sail to the wind?"

"Seventy degrees."

"That's not close enough."

"It'll do," Carl said.

That was that. The doctor declined to come along. He had no confidence in the ship. Carl and Arno remained unperturbed, just as they had when I told them about George Belcher.

"We'll be the first," Carl said calmly. "But I think we'll have to move up our departure date. Changes in the climate seem to be making the monsoons start somewhat earlier. Europe isn't the only place where weather patterns have gone nuts."

On May 10 we would have a public showing of the ship. We had to have the entire crew assembled in Hong Kong by the beginning of May at the latest. It was March 10. Only six weeks to go. Our countdown had begun.

Then Carl returned to the shipyard. A bit later he showed the junk to the Austrian foreign minister, who was visiting in the People's Republic at the time. I was still in Austria, nervously, impatiently, frantically making final preparations; but when I saw our junk in a TV news report, I felt for the first time that our project finally had official sanction.

Shortly before his departure for Hong Kong, Arno came to see me, accompanied by a young German who had already spoken with Carl about the expedition and wanted to join it. He was from Hamburg, twenty-six years old, a tall, gangly, shy student of theology and history by the name of Wolf Werner Rausch. He had attended the German Merchant Marine Academy and had a few years' experience on merchant ships behind him. It was up to me to decide if he should come with us. I said yes, and the young man beamed with pleasure. He was to arrive in Hong Kong on May 1, a day ahead of me. Our crew now numbered five.

I also received a letter from George Belcher. He explained that lack of funds would prevent him from making his own expedition and he would like to join ours. I felt that Carl and Arno should have a say in that decision. We would talk about it in Hong Kong. But I was relieved that there would be no race across the Pacific now.

I took my leaves, made one hurried phone call after another. Then I was off, made a layover in Canada, where I met our film producer, Phil Hobel, and Bill Martin, who would be our cameraman on board the *Tai Ki*.

"Hi," Bill said, shaking my hand. "I'm Bill."

Bill Martin from Santa Barbara, from Pennsylvania, and from New York, a tall, blond American who enjoyed his port wine, who could laugh and grin and swear in a league by himself, who loved his cameras and his women, who honed the *Tai Ki*'s harpoons to a fine edge and dove overboard in search of prey with them, who loved making films, drinking, working, living to the full. Bill Martin, thirty-three, a head taller than the rest of the crew, a Jack London figure.

We took off on the last leg of our journey, the flight to Hong Kong. The wide reaches of Canada spread out beneath us. Phil plied me with questions. I answered absentmindedly, my thoughts elsewhere. The phrase "shared costs" struck my ear, then "BBC, NBC, ORF, maybe ARD and CBS, too." I burst out laughing.

"What's the matter?" Phil asked.

"I feel as though I were still in my office in Vienna. The talk's just the same."

"You can't ever get away from it," Phil answered, then went on with questions about film locations in Mexico, production costs, production partners.

We left the West Coast behind us, flew over cloud banks south of the Aleutians. The rippling water below us mirrored the rays of the sun. The surface looked calm, motionless. It seemed inconceivable to me that this water could ever be dangerous.

Our chic stewardess was displaying an interest in us that went beyond the requirements of professional charm. Bill ordered dessert and some port. I lost a game of chess to him, just as I would lose many more later, thirty-six thousand feet below on the surface of the Pacific. This transoceanic flight gave us the last few hours of peace and physical comfort we would experience for

71

a long time. It almost seemed like a betrayal of my friends who were already slaving and sweating in Hong Kong while I gave myself up to the pleasures of the jet age.

Landing in Tokyo, and the making of a first film clip. We stepped out onto the gangway and waved like returning heroes. Then we were supposed to go down the steps and walk toward the cameras, laughing and smiling all the way. Bill, in his exuberance, kissed a girl who was standing next to the cameras. She turned red, then pale, struggled furiously, then acquiesced to the tall blond's embrace. Bill let her go and threw his arms up into the air. "We're here," he said with a laugh and then embraced me, too.

Hong Kong, more precisely Kowloon, May 2, 1974, 9:30 P.M. local time. Arno's face is pale under his black, disheveled hair. His deliberately relaxed motions and slow speech are meant to inspire a sense of tranquility he obviously does not feel. He has been waiting a long time to unburden himself.

"We're having trouble." Then, after a pause, he adds, "Carl is very nervous."

That was all. There was no need to say more. We would see all we needed to see ourselves.

A few hours later. Carl's room in the Cathay Hotel, Tung Lo Wan Road, Causeway Bay. The floor is covered with charts, other papers, sample provisions, navigational instruments, lengths of rope, fishhooks. A chronometer, protected by a wooden framework, is sitting on a bamboo stool.

Our shipbuilder seems the same as ever. Gaunt, calm, taciturn. His slaps on the back convey little warmth, seem more an empty gesture of masculine camaraderie. He has a can of beer next to him.

"What's new?"

"Nothing much," Carl replies. "Everything's going well."

Nothing much? There is no mention of trouble, but a lot of talk about details. We discuss provisions, when the water tanks will be delivered, where we can get what canned goods and when.

Wolf Werner Rausch bursts into the room. He wipes his sweaty hands dry on his blue T-shirt. His face is dirty. All of him is dirty. He has just come from working at the shipyard. He laughs, seems in good spirits, lighthearted. There are no signs of problems to be seen in his face. He has been here for two days, his first time in Asia.

Arno jumps up, says, "Let's go see Allan."

We're six stories higher in the hotel, seem to have stumbled onto another film set: a bed covered with books and charts, barely space enough left to let a man squeeze through, desks to either side piled high with electronic equipment — dials, gauges, knobs, switches, lights, an antenna sticking out the window. A man is sitting in front of the equipment, bending forward, listening intently, huge earphones on his blond head, his fingers working delicately at the knobs. He starts as though roused from a dream or from deep concentration. Almost frightened. A sign of recognition plays across his face. He snatches his earphones off, shakes my hand. Friendly but reserved.

"My name's Kartin."

I would learn later that he was not a man of many words. He would speak if there were good reason for speech but not merely for the sake of conversation. He was a typical Scandinavian in appearance: blond, blue-eyed, broad-shouldered. He was small but surprisingly strong. He seemed awkward at this meeting, as one often is at long-expected meetings that are supposed to be of great import but that in fact are dominated by petty details. And what did we really have to discuss after all? Everything of significance had been settled long ago.

Allan turned back with unnecessary haste to some papers, strewn in front of his radio equipment: tables, lists, codes, all the secret scripts of the initiated. He shut down his set. We would go out to eat together.

A half-hour later we were seated around a table for what would be the first of many meals together in Hong Kong: Arno Dennig, Carl Grage, Allan Kartin, Bill Martin, Wolf Werner Rausch, and I, six of a crew that would soon number eight.

"We've got a doctor," Arno said, "but he couldn't make it tonight."

"Englishman," Carl added.

"His name is Bob Kendrick," Arno said. "Tonight is his last night on duty in the hospital."

"I'm hungry," Wolf interjected. We would be hearing this announcement often in the weeks to come.

This first meeting of the *Tai Ki*'s almost complete crew turned out to be a strange one. Too much was held back; a peculiar silence reigned in the group. Carl tried to fill the silence with talk, drank port with Bill, told stories about the Chinese, how odd they were both in their manner and in their work. He told about the Royal Hong Kong Yacht Club, of which he was a member; told of the races he had sailed in it, the trophies he had won for it. He was the center of attention, spoke of junks and storms, but finally said very little. All of us behaved similarly. Wolf, I felt, was the only one who seemed impervious to the loud silence that hung over our table. He assumed the pose of a colonial officer, ordered a bigger and better meal than the rest of us, displayed his critical judgment, laughed at others and himself. The role he would play in our crew was beginning to take shape already. He was the young, exuberant sailor, an adventurer from North Germany who, with a twinkle in his eye, let us all know how much he liked everybody and everything, the crew, Hong Kong, the shipyard, the *Tai Ki*, only to do a turnabout the next minute and start complaining about how stale the bread was. He was given to sententious statements delivered with self-indulgent pathos, and he had a touch of irony that suggested objectivity but may have had another intent altogether.

Arno held himself aloof. He did not react to Carl's stories, and whenever he did have anything to say or a question to ask, he restricted himself to concrete details. Sometimes he would burst out in brief, loud laughter. His eyes remained inexpressive. Allan tended silently to his meal.

I was ready to be cheerful, but that was no easy task. The silence, everything that went unsaid, dominated the atmosphere at our long table in a dark restaurant that advertised "the best steaks in town" and belonged to a U.S. Marine who had fought "for freedom" in Vietnam.

Bill seemed subdued, too. Although I had known him only a few hours, I could see the change that had taken place in him. The tall American who had been so outgoing in Tokyo was holding himself back now. He spoke only if a question was directed to him personally. Otherwise he just hacked away at his tough steak Diane, sipped at his wine, rarely looked up from his plate, and tried to listen to what was going on around him. He must have felt the importance of this first meeting, too. This young American cameraman hoped our voyage would be a turning point in his career. He was out to make a major film, and he was ready to take any kind of chance for this opportunity. He wanted to join that exclusive company of filmmakers who dealt in the extraordinary. Now he had fallen silent.

The next morning we set out for the shipyard on Ap Lei Chau. I was going to see the *Tai Ki* for the first time. At 9 A.M. Bill was sitting in front of the hotel at the wheel of a rental car. We drove across Victoria Island toward Aberdeen on the south shore of the island, swooped down around the switchbacks to Deep Water Bay and Aberdeen. Junks lay moored to our left, one after another; then we ran alongside a narrow waterway where junks and sampans moved back and forth with diesel motors chugging loudly. In earlier times, the boats that anchored here moved under silent sails, but most of them then served the same purpose as their modern descendants: they were floating houses. Sampans, small boats built along the same lines as junks, used to be propelled

75

with oars. Now they are almost all motorized and carry all kinds
of cargo: wood and grain, tourists and fruit. Floating restaurants
lay on the far side of the canal. The film set had worn thin here,
the grandeur gone shabby. Across from the restaurants was a
sampan station, next to it a ferry slip and a dock for the tourists
who take colorful boats across the water to the restaurants.

Unfamiliar faces, unfamiliar smells. Arno led the way. A
young Chinese girl came up to him, beaming. *"Lei-ko sampan,"*
she said and pointed to herself. Arno grumbled, "Why not?" and
went down the algae-smeared steps to the water. The motor clat-
tered into action. We headed for the floating restaurants, then
swung off to the left. More new smells: salt water, seaweed, oil,
and garbage. Very different smells, at any rate, from those on
Causeway Bay. Every region and every city has its own smells.
London smells of fish and chips, Marseilles of pizza, Munich of
plastic, Mexico City of dust. The characteristic odor of the Far
East that I'd found in Saigon, Phnom Penh, and Singapore was
missing in Hong Kong, but I came on it again in Aberdeen: the
stink of overripe oranges.

We rattled across the water. Children were swimming in the
filthy brew. Junks surrounded us on all sides. Then I saw her.
Some three hundred yards past the Tai Pac and Sea Palace restaurants lay the *Tai Ki*. Even a first impression showed her as distinct from all the other boats moving in and around Hong Kong.
She was much simpler than the others, and perhaps for that very
reason she was more beautiful, more elegant. That is how I perceived her, anyhow, for we are always ready to view with an
uncritical eye things we have long been looking forward to
seeing. Things are often beautiful or impressive or awe-inspiring
simply because we have decided in advance that they should be.
Just as with opinions we have unconsciously taken over from
others, here too we make judgments we consciously have to step
away from to revise.

Even though I had seen photos of the *Tai Ki*, I was still expecting something more primitive. There was nothing crude about

her. She was, as Carl suggested, a "nonmissing link" that represented the transitional stage between Chinese ships of the distant past and those of today.

A sheathing of blond wood partially covered the dark hull and formed a graceful line that seemed, even in this setting, ready to cope with the waves of the Pacific. Carl was unable to explain why the hull followed this particular line, which also determined the shape of the ship's interior. "That's the way the model was," Carl said, "so that's the way we built the ship."

The superstructures of woven rattan rose from the deck in soft, rough-textured arches. The mushroom-shaped roof of the large room that would serve as our quarters stood amidships. Toward the stern was the gable-roofed helmsman's cabin; behind it the massive rudder housing, then the rudder itself, shaped from an immense tree that no storm would ever be able to break. The mast, not yet rigged with its sail, rose naked from the dark planking of the tabernacle.

Carl took me on a tour of the ship, explaining important points as we went along. Movie cameras whirred behind us, for even this first meeting with the *Tai Ki* was to be recorded on film.

"The *Tai Ki*," Carl intoned like a tourist guide, "is built of Chinese pine and makes use of the carvel principle in its construction. The hull is made up of seven separate watertight compartments; and some three thousand wooden pins and a thousand wooden bolts have been used to hold it together. No metal — neither bronze nor iron — has been used in the ship. Other crucial joints have been sewed together with bamboo fiber, and bamboo fiber has also been used in the mast stays.

"The hardwood rudder is shaped like a huge oar and is mounted on the stern. This is an important point, because the vertical, stern-mounted rudder first replaced the side-mounted steering oar in Chinese shipbuilding precisely in the period from which our model dates: that is, sometime around the birth of Christ.

"The sail is made of woven rattan reinforced by horizontal

bamboo spars, and each spar is controlled by its own sheet. The sail weighs about five hundred and fifty pounds. Halyards, sheets, and all other running lines are of sisal and jute. The structural elements of the cabins are of wood; rattan matting has been used for the covering material."

"And how large is the ship?" I asked, assuming my role of interviewer in the film.

Carl was grateful for this bit of prompting. He pulled a piece of paper from his breast pocket and read off the dimensions of the *Tai Ki*.

Overall length	64 ft.
Length above-deck	58 ft.
Length at waterline	42 ft.
Draft	3 ft.
Freeboard	4 ft.
Beam above-deck	18 ft.
Beam overall	20 ft.
Beam at waterline	16 ft.
Height of mast above-deck	52 ft.
Sail area	1,188 sq. ft.
Water displacement	31 tons

Later we all sat down together on any available boards, boxes, and coils of rope that were lying around on the forward deck and got down to business. When would we be able to set out? In ten days? Two weeks? When would the ship be finished down to the last detail? What still had to be done? The answers to all these questions were vague, and the entire discussion ended with Carl's statement that we would have to wait for the right winds. Wolf was eagerly dragging tools around the deck. Arno had disappeared. He had had to drive back to town to see to our provisions. Bill was stalking around on board, looking for photogenic motifs. Allan had gone back to the hotel to make some further

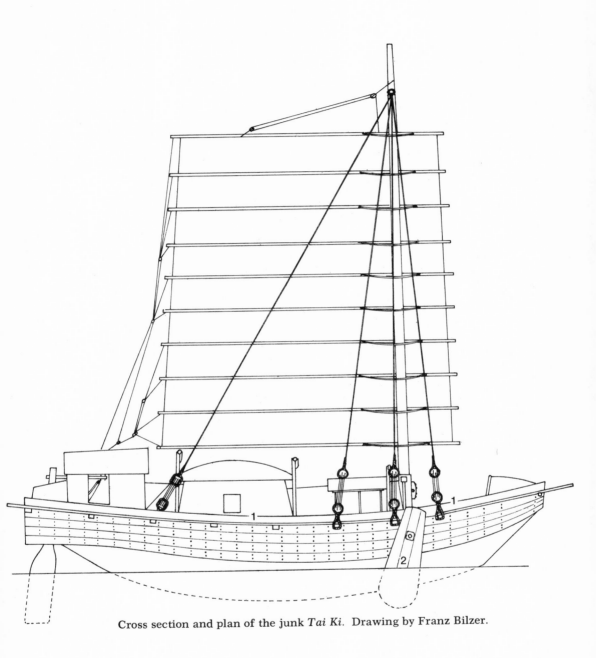

Cross section and plan of the junk *Tai Ki*. Drawing by Franz Bilzer.

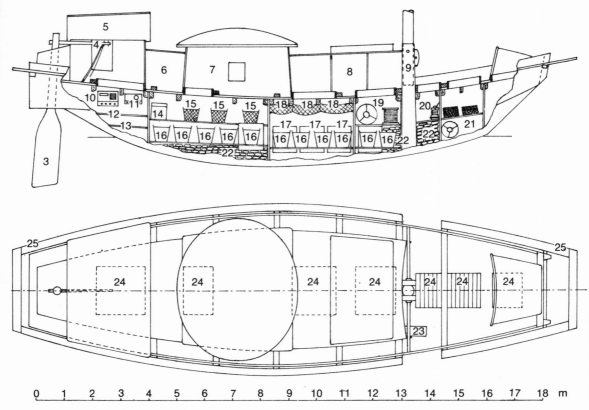

1 Bulwarks	14 Camera gear
2 Leeboard	15 Baskets
3 Rudder	16 Barrels of canned goods
4 Tiller and tackle	17 Water tanks (capacity 172 gals. ea.)
5 Helmsman's cabin	18 Baggage nets
6 Covered passageway	19 Ropes
7 Crew's galley and living quarters	20 Spare lanterns
8 Crew's sleeping quarters	21 Storage for ropes, firewood, coal, kerosene
9 Tabernacle	22 Ballast stones
10 Ship's radio	23 Spare mast
11 Ham radio set	24 Hatchways
12 Chart table	25 Catwalk
13 Bench	

adjustments on his equipment. A toothless Chinese joined us on the forward deck. He was smoking a heavy bamboo pipe, and he responded with a grin to any glances we cast his way. Inclined to pulp-magazine romanticism as I am, I was convinced he was smoking opium. In fact, he was smoking a local rough-cut tobacco.

The ship's interior: we had to stoop everywhere but under the rattan roofs of the cabins. The floor was made of heavy planking, and compartment hatches cropped up here and there. They provided access to the storage and ballast areas below. Some stone ballast was already in place. Tanks containing 840 gallons of fresh water — enough for nine months, according to Arno's calculations — would provide additional ballast. Food containers with a total capacity of well over two tons would be lined up on either side of the tanks.

Seated amid scattered tools and equipment, two Chinese were placidly weaving rattan mats that would serve as doors. "They're so slow it's enough to make you puke," Carl grumbled as I stopped to watch the two men work. We stumbled on over ropes and sacks, heading for an open hatch near the rudder. A canvas chair marked "Capt'n" stood near the hatchway. On a film set, it would have read "Director."

The hatchway led to the captain's cabin, which lay on one side of the ship. Directly across from the captain's quarters was the area reserved for the radio shack. Not even a start had been made on the racks for Allan's radio equipment. A table for charts would eventually stand where a pile of rags, ropes, and scraps of wood now lay. The helmsman's bench would be installed farther astern and slightly above the cabin area.

At first glance, a great deal seemed already done. The ship seemed almost finished. But a more exacting inventory showed just how much remained to be done. Would we be able to meet our deadline of May 15? I experienced my first doubts.

"So we put it up to May 25," Carl answered gruffly. "That was the date we'd first planned on, anyhow."

Arno had been right. Carl was nervous. The fact that time was running out on us had put him on edge. And our questions put him on edge, too. How could I have any idea of what he'd had to put up with from the very beginning of this job, or how could Arno know either, even if he had been in Hong Kong for a few weeks now? There was no point in rehashing the past. We all simply had to do whatever was demanded of us and whatever we demanded of ourselves day by day. Tensions began to develop. Carl felt responsible for everything himself, felt all decisions should be left to him. But we felt responsible, too, and felt our demands should be heard. We were a team now, and we had to coordinate our efforts. It was a difficult situation for those of us who were new to it and to Hong Kong, and it was equally difficult for Carl, who was accustomed to working and making decisions alone.

A day of unsettling talks had done nothing to dispel the doubts our first few hours in Hong Kong had evoked.

That evening Arno came to tell me that Bob Kendrick was upstairs. We found our ship's doctor bent over our medical supplies in a room next to Allan's. He sorted, arranged, made notes, mumbled a brief greeting, continued writing with strong, nervous hands. He wanted to join us. This thirty-five-year-old Englishman had been in the Far East for six months now and had planned to return home in any case. "Interesting, very interesting," he mumbled in response to my brief words of explanation about the purpose of our voyage. And he kept writing out his list of medications. He had shoulder-length hair, a small mouth, small eyes. With hardly a word, he slapped out of the room in his rubber sandals. So that was our seventh crew member.

A few days later another candidate presented himself in my room. I'd talked briefly with him on the phone before he came up. Curly hair, a full beard, light-colored T-shirt, rimless glasses.

"Hal Price," he said, introducing himself. "I couldn't get hold of Carl. I hear you need another man."

I would have to confer with Carl and Arno before a decision could be made, and I answered him in vague terms.

Bob Kendrick had told Hal's wife, Mary, that the *Tai Ki* needed another experienced sailor.

"I called Hal immediately," Mary told me later. She was a young woman with a soft voice. "I knew how important this would be to him, so I let him know right away."

"Aren't you afraid when he goes off on a voyage like this?"

"Yes, but that's an issue quite apart from what Hal wants."

Hal was born in Dublin, had gone to Canada, had studied in Vancouver, and had been teaching the children of wealthy Chinese families in Hong Kong for the past two years. He was a sailing buff par excellence. Just a few weeks before we met, he had taken part in the South China Sea Race from Hong Kong to Manila and back, and now he wanted to go to sea again. "The sea is my second element," he said. "I can't get along without it." Two days later Carl, Arno, and I agreed that he should join us. Our crew was complete, but the date when the ship would be finished was as uncertain as ever. We kept telling ourselves it would be May 15, even though we knew better, and kept reassuring each other that we might just make it by then after all.

On May 11, the entire crew gathered for a press conference. Journalists from all over the world were there; some of them had come to Hong Kong especially to cover our departure. Cameras, flashbulbs, questions, interviews. Yes, we would be leaving soon. When exactly? That depended on the winds. Yes, on May 15 probably, maybe a little later, but before the typhoon season began, of course.

More questions, more pictures. Smiles. Answers. Kobi, a cameraman of Phil Hobel's from Japan, shot one roll of film after another. Of course we would be leaving in a few days. We were on top of the world. Carl shone like a star, sparkled with wit. Arno laughed. I ran into two fellow journalists I'd last seen in Vietnam two years ago. No, it wouldn't be long at all now.

And then the sail wasn't delivered on time. And we found we didn't have enough wooden containers for our provisions. And the wet suits we had ordered for every crew member hadn't arrived yet. And that by no means completes the list of what we didn't have and of what hadn't been done. But nothing bothered us much. We accepted invitations, attended dinners, hobnobbed with the consul general, the ambassador, and other interested dignitaries.

Wednesday, May 15. Instead of setting out on our voyage, we made a trial run.

My journal reads:

A big day, sort of a big day. The *Tai Ki* was towed out to the typhoon shelter and then continued on alone in a light wind. The crew doesn't feel at home on the ship, but Carl creates the impression of being in control. A leeboard to port broke loose. The sail is too heavy. Carl says the mast nearly broke. We all work with a will, but to little effect. Carl and Arno move about the ship with Oscar — the brother of our legendary Rocky So, who has fled to Canada in the meantime — and check out mast, rudder, and rigging. Hal knows what to do and is a great help. If it hadn't been clear to us before that we had a long way to go before we became a crew, it certainly is clear to us now. Wolf coils and stows lines meticulously. Is that the result of his training in the merchant marine or a manifestation of German thoroughness?

It was clear after this trial run that a number of adjustments and changes had to be made. The mast had to be shortened. The mountings for the leeboards had to be improved. The sail had to be set lower on the mast. The rudder wasn't functioning as smoothly as it should. There wasn't a chance that we could leave by May 25.

A week passes, and little has been accomplished. Wolf is painting the Tai Ki symbol on the sail. The work that has to be done seems to be going forward in a haphazard manner. We aren't able to do much ourselves, and the tempo of the Chinese workers doesn't mesh with ours. We stand around at the shipyard, looking at our ship and knowing exactly what needs to be done, yet we can do nothing but gawk into the smiling faces of calmly diligent Chinese workers who weave and hammer and saw away, completely oblivious to the impatience of these European adventurers who want everything done faster, faster, and still faster yet. There's no point in getting worked up.

Carl feels himself in greater isolation than ever. The crew is growing increasingly restless. Work on the ship proceeds at a snail's pace; time races by. We slave away like coolies loading our stores and provisions on board. Every last tin can has to be handled six times; every item moves from the store where it is purchased out onto the street, from the street into the car, from the car onto the sampan dock, from the dock into the sampan, from the sampan onto the deck of the *Tai Ki*, from the deck into the hold below. We move eighteen tons in two days. Then we have our first blowup.

A dog is responsible, a little mutt we'd fished out of the water and who had made himself at home on board the *Tai Ki* and on the ship moored next to her. One faction argued that he should be our mascot.

"He came to us out of the blue," Carl said. "He's clearly a good-luck charm."

"What good is he to us?" Wolf asked.

"It's out of the question," Arno said. He spoke as a farmer accustomed to dealing with animals. "We don't know where the dog comes from or what diseases he could be carrying. He's a potential threat to the whole expedition."

And as so often happens, feelings that had gone unexpressed before burst out now over this ridiculous issue. This trivial incident released pent-up aggressions that had nothing to do with the matter at hand, and we suddenly found ourselves divided into pro- and anti-dog camps. The opponents emerged victorious. Or, to be more accurate, there were no victors at all, because Jenny Croppers, who was doing a film story on us for the BBC, resolved the strife by turning up with another mascot for us. This dog was a mutt, too, but a veterinarian had given it both a clean bill of health and a set of standard inoculations. We christened this small, perky beast "Lap Sac," which, freely translated from the Chinese, means something like "shit heap." Some of the crew called him "Hong Kong." Bob Kendrick settled for the appellation "Dog."

But a residue of anxiety and antagonism remains. We schedule another trial run and then postpone it. May 25, the latest departure date we had set for ourselves, comes and goes without departure being anywhere in sight. The monsoons set in. The weather turns muggy. We get wind and rain on schedule. The meteorologists can rejoice in the accuracy of their predictions. Two days later the Austrian consul general in Hong Kong, Dr. Peterlik, holds his official send-off for the *Tai Ki*. The Austrian flag is raised, then the flags of the other nations represented: Denmark, the Federal Republic of Germany, Great Britain, Ireland, the U.S.A. Once again the ship and gangplank are overflowing with reporters and cameramen.

And two days after that the *Tai Ki* moves out to sea, not, however, on her voyage across the Pacific but on another trial run. We're all hoping it will be the last. The weather in the morning was fine, but the afternoon brings thunderstorms. We slop around off Aberdeen in pouring rain. Our experienced sailors — Carl, Hal, Wolf, and Arno — are hard at work. Allan has no immediate responsibilities. Bill is seasick, and I'm feeling queasy myself. Bob pitches in awkwardly but energetically. The mariners are satisfied with the results of this test run, and Carl says we can set out as soon as we get the west winds we need.

The required west winds arrived, but they were too far out to sea off Aberdeen to bring the *Tai Ki* away from the dock.

Arno and I sit down to consider our schedule again and go through our checklist for these last few days in Hong Kong. We simply have to get underway. Carl is aware of this, too, but he still

This is where the *Tai Ki* was built. In the foreground is Aberdeen, a port and suburb of Hong Kong. On the far side of the channel lies the island Ap Lei Chau. Its shore is lined with shipyards, all of them family businesses. (D)

Upper left: So Hawk Sum, "the All-Knowing One." He agreed to build the *Tai Ki* and did so at an unhurried Oriental pace that put our Western expectations to a severe test. (D)

Upper right: Carl Frederik, designer of the *Tai Ki,* at work in one of the storage compartments. Carl's official job was to supervise the building, but more often than not he worked along with the crew. (D).

Below: The hull is finished. But our troubles and our race against time were just beginning. (G)

We hoisted the Japanese cameraman Kobi up the mast on this specially constructed seat so that he could film our activities from above. Kobi ended up not sailing with us, but we took the "elevator seat" along. Mounted at the stern, it served an all-important daily function. (D)

The *Tai Ki*'s sail. The rattan mats are sewn together on a playing field (*upper left*). (D) In the shipyard the spars are fastened to the sail (*upper right*). (D) Then the sail is raised for the first time (*right*). (D)

Final jobs before setting sail: the ballast stones lying on the forward deck still have to be stowed in their compartments; the rattan matting for the cabin walls has still not been completed; the leeboards are still not properly mounted. There seems to be no end to these last-minute chores. (D).

Two weeks before sailing. The spare mast and the wooden barrels for provisions are still waiting to be brought on board. (D).
Facing Page: We are finally ready, but we do not leave port under our own sail. On June 16, 1974, the *Tai Ki* is towed out of the harbor. Hong Kong is behind us. We are heading for the open sea. (P)

First disaster: the rudder is damaged. After three days, towing in rough seas we have to head for the harbor of Kaohsiung in Taiwan for repairs. The wood of the rudder we had thought indestructible has splintered. *Left:* Arno is trying to draw the ropes of the rudder mounting taut. (KK)

Right: With the help of ropes and pulleys the rudder is lifted up to be remounted in the *Tai Ki*. The rudder has been reduced in size, and the rhomboid holes cut in the blade are designed to lessen the force of the water pressure. (KK)

Above: Carl and Arno replace the torn ropes of the sail. (BM)
Below: The helmsman's cabin. Bill and Kuno are at the tiller. Both are wearing life jackets because of heavy winds and rough seas. Behind Kuno on the left is the log; on the right, the barograph, which, unfortunately, ceased to function after a few weeks. (D)

Above: The seams in the rattan matting of the sail keep coming apart and have to be resewn again and again. Here Arno is busy mending. (BM)

Right, above: The mushroom-shaped roof of the cabin and one of our two "windmills" used for generating electricity. Also visible here are the kitchen door and "sink." (D)

Below: The radar reflector. (K)

Right: Arno takes our position with a pocket sextant. (KK)
Below: Kuno at his "desk" on the forward deck. (D)

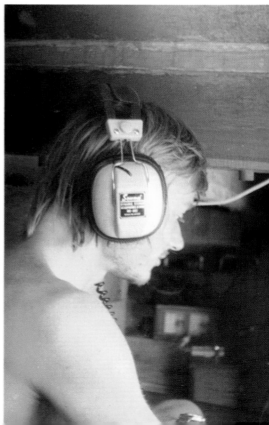

Right: Allan in his radio shack. (KK)

Overleaf: Bird's-eye view of the *Tai Ki.* The first sunny day after a spell of wind, rain, and fog. Towels, air mattresses, and sleeping bags get a thorough airing. (D)

Left: Our ship's doctor is not exempt from KP duty. Here he is patiently scrubbing a pot. (K)

Below: Mens sana in corpore sano. Hal keeps his mind in trim by reading as he pedals his daily quota on the generator bike. (D)

Another storm behind us. Allan and Carl raise the sail to full height again. (к)

keeps finding additional work to be done on the ship. We need some ropes here, some planking there. Allan is totally absorbed in his radio gear and won't take a minute for anything else. Arno finally informs him in no uncertain terms that we're trying to get an expedition underway, not launch a radio ship. Allan snorts and disappears inside his radio shack again.

Carl had wanted to see the *Tai Ki* leave Hong Kong under her own sails. Arno and I had agreed with him, but now it seemed more important to us to get out to sea, even if we had to be towed out to get there. We were considering a tow of a hundred or two hundred miles, hoping to make up for some of our lost time. It was June 2 now. The next day we had a talk with Carl. He agreed that we should take a tow as far as the southern tip of Taiwan. That would be the equivalent of at least a week's sailing and would bring us halfway back into line with our schedule. Carl started looking for a boat that could tow us and soon found one, an old steel-hulled yacht that had been converted to engine power. Her owner was an American who forced us to view some ancient photos taken in the "good old days" of the opium trade. "My boat is in good shape," he declared with the grand gesture of an old-timer who wasn't prepared to take a bunch of frivolous adventurers very seriously. He clearly saw himself as a high priest of the mariners' caste, willing enough, if hard pressed, to grace novices like us with a nod of condescending approval.

"My boat is in good shape. But I'll need a little money in advance. Have to make a few little repairs." He taps reflectively at his chin with his fingertips, flicks a nonexistent thread off his blue jacket. Really, he assures us, just some minor details that need attention.

One of these minor details was a new compass. The one he had on his "completely renovated ship" didn't work. And then he had a little bill to pay to the shipyard that happened to be overhauling the boat at the moment. Otherwise, his boat was in tiptop shape.

Carl laughed and cursed. Our new departure date was June

9, and we intended to leave that day at twelve noon no matter what. If our American couldn't tow us with his tiptop ship, then we'd have to find someone else who would. We had several more uneasy days ahead of us. The crew grew more impatient still, split up into camps. We talked about what measures we might have to take to overcome imagined obstacles. What would we do if some act of God made our departure impossible? What would we do if the typhoons caught us still in port? What would we do if the British port authorities forbid our departure? In discussions that lasted into the night we considered innumerable remote eventualities and innumerable wild schemes to cope with them. We simply had to set out, no matter what the consequences. And what if the weather prevented us from continuing? Then we would have to head for the closest available land, even if it happened to be in Red China.

"You know that's impossible," Wolf said in an attempt at humor. "We don't have any visas."

We experienced periods of incredible depression. Maybe we should put the whole thing off for a year. But that was out of the question, and we all knew it. Besides, we all wanted to set out. Carl was even prepared to go in August if we had to. The prospect of winter weather on the North Pacific and along the American coast didn't seem to faze him.

Negative reports began appearing in Hong Kong newspapers. Nobody could understand why we hadn't set out. Phil Hobel had left us, and he too had worked himself into a case of nerves before he flew back to the States. He had been as nervous as we were, and we were on the verge of losing our self-confidence — the worst thing that can happen to men preparing to embark on a great adventure.

Journal entry of June 7:

Our situation grows worse by the minute. Received calls from the BBC and the English Navy: storm warnings for the area south of Formosa.

This news reached us at 2:30 P.M. in the midst of a heated discussion. At five in the afternoon the storm warnings went up on Ap Lei Chau. The weather station reports a low-pressure system about 160 miles southwest of Hong Kong. The storm is moving toward Hainan, but we are still planning to sail on Sunday, June 9.

I drove straight to the Royal Observatory in Kowloon. A narrow lane turns off from Nathan Road, leads to a high iron fence; beyond that a graveled driveway winds through the dank heat and dark, opulent vegetation of a tropical garden. A long path with palms to either side of it leads to a clearing on the top of a small rise and to a white villa in colonial style. The visitor passes between columns, into a hallway, then through office doors. Our need for current and complete weather information had sent us on this pilgrimage often. What I learned on this particular visit was not encouraging. The low-pressure system would affect Hong Kong. Seas were heavy, and we would have to postpone our sailing.

Even more disturbing than this news was a further report that was just coming in on the ticker tape at the Royal Observatory. Still another low was developing southeast of the Philippines. "That could turn into a typhoon," a young meteorologist told me. "But it's impossible to say for sure now whether it will or not."

I returned to the shipyard. Carl was in a rage. Someone had stolen five thousand Hong Kong dollars, the equivalent of one thousand dollars in U.S. currency, from his wallet. And we had other money troubles to boot. The shipbuilders had presented us with a much higher bill than we had expected. We haggled and bargained endlessly. The next day we received a revised bill for twice as much as the first.

We were ready to sail, but the weather seemed to be against us in earnest now. The cautious forecasts the weathermen of Nathan Road had made proved correct. The first low-pressure system had already turned toward the mainland and was no longer a threat at sea, but the low off the Philippines had developed into an STS, a "severe tropical storm," and had been christened with the name of Dinah. The storm was about 350 miles across and was producing wind velocities of 60 miles per hour at its center. The observatory predicted this storm would hit the Hong Kong area and make our sailing impossible before June 13 at the earliest.

Sunday, June 9. Bob has been sleeping on board already, and Allan has joined him so he could have more time to work on making further radio contacts. The crew is irritable, the weather humid and cloudy. We're sitting on deck wrapping lemons in old newspapers. This occupational therapy helps ease tensions. We do some more bargaining with Oscar. The contract provides for a penalty if the ship isn't completed by the date agreed on. Since the boat was not done in time and Oscar has to forfeit a percentage of the set price, he wants to make up for that loss with the padded bill he's been trying to foist off on us. The negotiations are fast and furious, but Carl doesn't give an inch and finally persuades Oscar to accept our terms.

By Monday, tropical storm Dinah has worked herself up into a full-fledged typhoon. And she still seems intent on visiting Hong Kong. Carl and I take another walk down the graveled path to the Royal Observatory and call on Dr. Chu, one of the directors there.

"You might as well forget about sailing on the thirteenth," he says. "The fifteenth sounds more like it to me."

"And I'd thought the thirteenth would be our lucky day," Carl says.

So we had to wait some more. Arno would sleep on the boat tonight. The ship had to be under constant guard now. All our equipment as well as all our personal gear was on board. We didn't want to risk finding the *Tai Ki* cleaned out some fine morning, and Lap Sac, descendant of a long and venerable line of stray Chinese mutts, was not dog enough to defend the ship.

We waited and then waited some more. Only a calm at sea, day after day without wind, would prove more wearing and debilitating than this seemingly endless waiting. All essential work on the ship had been completed. We were ready to go.

We partially filled this empty time by conferring with Mr. Wei, an elderly Chinese scholar at the University of Hong Kong, who had done considerable work on diffusion theory and who paid us an unexpected visit at the shipyard one day. Cyrus Gordon, another noted scholar in the field, happened to be in Hong Kong at the time to present a lecture in City Hall. In the course of his talk, he said: "The significance of the *Tai Ki* expedition can hardly be overestimated. If this ship manages to reach Central America, then the possibility that ancient ships made this same crossing will be beyond dispute." Before his lecture, Gordon had visited the *Tai Ki* and wished us bon voyage. It is hard to say how much that word of encouragement meant to us during those otherwise bleak and barren days.

We would sail on Saturday, June 15, weather permitting. One Chinese fisherman who had agreed to tow us had backed out at the last minute, and even a thousand Hong Kong dollars couldn't convince him to change his mind. The whole enterprise struck him as too dangerous. Another fisherman said he would think about it. A third said he would do it, but he wanted more money than we could afford.

Dinah struck Hainan on June 13, and the impact of the storm made itself felt in Hong Kong. Ferry service in the harbor was discontinued as the winds climbed to forty knots and the rain streamed down. But we could at least rejoice in the fact that a storm that was hitting us was also a storm going past us. We visited the Royal Observatory again, only to be greeted with still further glad tidings. Another low-pressure system was forming to the southeast of the Philippines, where most typhoons seem to rise. On June 14, this low was moving toward Luzon at a speed of twelve knots. But at this point there was no clear sign that it would develop into a typhoon, and our sailing date remained firm.

Corvette Captain Redmond of the British Harbor Patrol tried to dissuade us from sailing.

"It's too late," the lean naval officer told us. He spread out some charts he had brought with him. "Here," he said, pointing to an area east of the Philippines. "The water temperature here is between eighty and eighty-four degrees. That means one typhoon after another."

His final words were brief and to the point: "Postpone the whole show. You have no other choice."

My journal for Saturday, June 15, 1974:

We build up our hopes only to have them scattered by one storm after another. Dinah has gone on by, but Emma is on her way. Another typhoon or STS is developing east of Luzon. The barometer reads 29.3 and is falling. The computers at the U.S. Weather Station in Guam have come up with three possibilities:

1) Emma will head for the southern tip of Taiwan.
2) Emma will move up the east coast of Taiwan.
3) Emma will head for Okinawa.

Winds have been clocked at 54 mph, and the storm itself is moving at 20 mph.

Arno and I insist on sailing Monday if it is humanly possible. We will simply have to take our chances on rough seas off Taiwan. Carl and Hal have their doubts. The others remain silent.

In any case, we cancel the towboat we had lined up for Sunday. The crew is depressed. Strain is taking its toll. And we are no longer certain of having a naval escort for the first 100 miles. This escort boat was supposed to take the BBC camera crew off the *Tai Ki*, and Jenny is frantic.

Bob, who has spent the night on board, reports that there are rats on the ship. We choose to see their presence as a sign that our ship is not a sinking one. We are running desperately low on money. I've never had as little in my pocket during the previous fifteen years as I have now. Allan is just as badly off.

Emma turned out to be more amiable than Dinah. She contented herself with turning into a mere tropical storm rather than into a typhoon, but her kindness in this respect did us little good in practical terms. Seas between Hong Kong and Taiwan were rough, with waves running between twelve and fifteen feet. Carl was doubtful about a towing operation in such heavy seas, but he might just as well have spared himself his doubts, because our tow ship failed to appear. There didn't seem to be a skipper in Hong Kong who cared to venture out in this weather with the *Tai Ki* in tow. Carl took the brunt of the troubles that plagued us during these last days. Nothing was working out, everyone was nervous, and directly or indirectly the captain was made to feel responsible for everything that was going wrong, even though it was ridiculous to hold him accountable for storms, difficulties with the towboats, and the drastic warnings that rained in on us from all sides.

"I'll pray for you," an American newspaperman said to me on the phone. And when Wolf and I went to Captain Conway of British Naval Headquarters to have our sailing permit approved, he said to us: "You're a bunch of bloody idiots." But Conway, who looked something like a younger brother of Orson Welles, wasn't through with us by any means. "I ran weapons up and down the Yangtze during the war," he bellowed at us. "I've sailed the Yellow Sea, and I know the Formosa Strait like the palm of my hand. I've even sailed it," he added, breathless with anger, "in a junk. I know this corner of the world backwards and forwards. Now just take a look at this." He threw a thick book across his desk at us. "You'll find the weather statistics for the last fifty years in there, and I can tell you right now that the chances are ten to one you'll run into a typhoon." Then he burst out laughing and wiped the sweat from his forehead. "A junk!" he hooted. "A sixty-foot junk!"

He picked up a weather map for June 1974 that showed all the computer forecasts for winds and currents. "That's where they come from," he said, pointing at the Philippines, "and that's where they go. If one of them happens to hit you on the way, you've had it." His thick hands crumpled the map up into a ball and tossed it into my lap. We added this map to the ones Carl had on board, and in the "kitchen" of the *Tai Ki* we hung up a calendar that Conway gave us as a souvenir. But despite these well-meaning gifts, he had hardly made a significant contribution to our peace of mind.

Oscar So finally located another fisherman who was prepared to tow us as far as Taiwan. But because the weather conditions were extraordinary, he would have to ask an extraordinary price for his services. This little fisherman was obviously out for a fat catch. When he quoted his price, we just laughed in his face. Another boat we'd had in mind was out of service with a broken-down engine. Oscar So had run out of possibilities.

After so many months of preparation, all these last-minute difficulties drove us frantic. We simply had to sail. Any further delay would force us to cancel the whole expedition. Carl insisted we could still sail in August, but our actual situation made that possibility purely academic. Quite apart from the fact that we had nearly demolished our last financial reserves already, we could not ask the crew to endure several more weeks of suspended animation. We had to make a decision one way or another.

Wolf and I ran into town in search of another and cheaper tugboat while the rest of the crew stayed on board the *Tai Ki* to make final preparations for sailing. Rain was streaming down, and we were drenched in a matter of seconds. Neither the Aberdeen Harbor Authority nor the Hong Kong Marine Department nor the Kowloon Marine Department was able to help us. We found a few fishermen who were willing to tow us out at a reasonable price, but they all had to think about it for a while. We would have to wait a day or two. The professional tugboat skippers were all booked solid. If we had only come a little earlier . . .

I was boiling with that helpless rage that overcomes us when we feel defenseless yet guilty at the same time. What had we done wrong? Who was to blame? We had been running around in Hong Kong all morning. It was noon now, and we were standing on Connaught Road in front of the Hotel Mandarin. We had planned on going into the Clipper Lounge for a farewell drink to civilization, but we were soaking wet, and Wolf's yachting shoes had dissolved into a muddy paste. Our attire was hardly suitable for the setting. That was a matter of indifference to us, but we wanted to spare ourselves the humiliation of having the doorman kick us out.

In the meantime, a patrol boat from the Harbor Authority had come up alongside the *Tai Ki*. An officer who obviously had several years' service behind him came on board to speak with our captain. Were we in for more trouble? The officer explained to Carl that we couldn't take a tow from a fishing boat.

"Why not?" Carl asked calmly, struggling to conceal his dismay.

"Fishing boats aren't licensed for towing."

Another monkey wrench in the works. Would we never get out of Hong Kong? Arno wrote in his journal later: "A frantic few hours. Nothing panned out as it should have. Kuno and Wolf have reported back that Hong Kong is supposedly full of tugs at a fair price, but they can't seem to get their hands on a single one. China is China. It would be a relief to us all to get underway."

Time is running out on us. Perhaps we will be able to turn up a boat yet. Carl and Arno negotiate with the English harbor officer. The crew, in turmoil but outwardly calm, is standing around on deck. After long and earnest talk, Carl and Arno win their case. The Harbor Authority agrees to look the other way.

"You realize that I'm acting contrary to every regulation in the book," the officer says.

"Yes."

There was nothing more to say, and no one in the crew offered to say more.

"All right then. Good luck." The officer turns around, steps onto the catwalk, and jumps onto his launch. A last wave of the hand and he is gone.

A bit later, Wolf and I returned to the boat, drenched, filthy, still in a rage. There were no reasonably priced towboats to be had unless we were ready to wait a few more days. If we were going to leave today, we would have to pay that little pirate his price.

The entire crew and Oscar So's family were assembled on the forward deck. We had stumbled unaware into a farewell party for the *Tai Ki*. No one had told us about it beforehand. Everyone from the So Brothers Shipyard was there. Mary, Hal's wife, stood leaning against one of the leeboards. She would ride out with us a way, then return in a sampan. Jenny was there, too, carrying Lap Sac in her arms. She and her cameraman, Eric, would stay with us and film our first twenty-four hours at sea. Then a British naval ship would pick them up. "I hope," Jenny said, resigned to her fate.

Bill busied himself taking pictures, worked quietly yet nervously with his cameras. Allan had disappeared into the radio shack to make a few final checks and adjustments. He seemed to be the calmest of us all. Bob gobbled up fish and rice, grumbled to himself. Hal stood with Mary. Carl was exceptionally calm, but that kind of tranquility is often a sign of inner agitation.

Our high-priced, snub-nosed fishing boat soon pulled up alongside the *Tai Ki*. Streaks of rust showed through dirty white paint. Her forward deck was built high as protection against the waves. This boat that would tow us was not much larger than the *Tai Ki*. The crew from the towboat joined the party, cracked jokes, laughed with the shipyard workers. We understood nothing. Cloudy skies. Wind. Light rain.

We had pictured our sailing differently. We felt little excitement, hardly any pleasure. All that mattered was finally leaving, finally clearing this harbor, finally putting an end to this interminable waiting. We were indifferent to what faced us at sea. It could not be worse than this forced immobility that was exhausting us all.

I go ashore with Arno to confer for the last time with Oscar So in his little house on Ho King Street on Ap Lei Chau. Arno and I are on edge. Arno is making an obvious effort to be calm. He lets me do the talking, listens, than stands up abruptly. It's time we were off. Neither of us bothers to consider as we return to the *Tai Ki* that this is the last time we will have solid ground under our feet for many months. We aren't in the mood for nostalgic reflection.

The farewell party is over. A few reporters interview us briefly; others are waiting in sampans moored nearby to accompany us out of the harbor. We see only a few familiar faces. Hectic activity sets in. We gather on deck, cast off. We are lashed side by side to a harbor tug that will take us through the narrow channel out to the typhoon shelter. There is a lot of shouting. Carl issues orders.

At 5:10 P.M. the *Tai Ki* and her tug begin to move away from the dock. The So family and the shipyard workers are standing on shore and waving. Faces peer at us from junks moored in the harbor. The crew has nothing to do at this point. The transfer to our towboat won't take place for another hour or two. We sit quietly together. Carl is standing on the roof of the helmsman's cabin with the rudder lines in his hands. He is taking his leave of this harbor where he has worked for a year and a half. He waves, but hardly anyone waves back. We leave him alone, and he seems to prefer it this way.

We pass row upon row of junks, and the gray stone walls of the typhoon shelter rise up in front of us. The harbor for sailing boats lies to our left. At 5:30 we clear the last stone wall and move out to sea on a southeasterly course. Lamma Island is off our starboard bow. A few sampans are still with us, but they soon turn back. The seas are noticeably rougher once we have passed out of the harbor zone. Someone calls over to us that we should pose for the cameramen. None of us wants to move. We feel nothing but exhaustion.

We glide out into the misty evening. Our voyage across the Pacific has begun.

CHAPTER FOUR

Sharks, Jade, and a Day on Board

THE TAI KI WAS UNDERWAY, FINALLY UNDERWAY. HER shallow hull skimmed across the water. Waves slapped against her sides, threw spray on deck. The mast groaned in its tabernacle. The rigging creaked. The *Tai Ki* was underway. Hong Kong lay behind us; the land disappeared. Soon we saw nothing but the sea under a hazy light.

Finally underway. Carl is still at the rudder. The rest of the crew members are sitting on the forward deck with the guests, who will be leaving us soon: Jenny and Eric from the BBC and Mary, Hal's wife.

Cigarettes are offered. Allan refuses. "I've decided not to smoke anymore," he says. And he stuck by his resolution. We drink beer, crack jokes. We're underway. The long, enervating wait is over. We were in the clear. The *Tai Ki* had begun her journey. She leaped, glided, danced across the waves. Only a few hours ago it had seemed we might never leave the dock on Ap Lei Chau. Now we could breathe easy. We slap each other on the back, grin, fall suddenly pensive, burst out laughing again. A great load has been taken from our shoulders.

Bill is filming these first hours on board. He is smiling now, too, even though it was he who had announced just a few hours ago on the rain-soaked dock on Ap Lei Chau, "I'm not gonna hang around here letting moss grow on me. If we don't sail today, you can count me out. I'm gonna head for Paris, and you can sell my ticket to somebody else."

We were underway, and not one of us would have seriously believed the day before or even a few hours ago that we would in fact be underway today.

Jenny is sitting on a white life raft, holding our mascot Lap Sac, whose presence we owe to her. She'll accompany us on the junk for one day; then she'll have to take her leave. Mary will have to go, too. She is standing next to the mast now with Hal. The time for farewells is approaching.

As the day turns to evening and then to night, laughter becomes more subdued. There is little time left for talk. Carl is issuing the first commands of the journey. The *Tai Ki* bounces and staggers along behind the rusty white fishing boat, crashing into approaching waves. The weatherman at the observatory in Kowloon had warned us a few hours ago that the seas would grow rougher, and he was right. The exuberance of our departure is gone.

Carl organizes the watches. He splits us up into four two-man teams. Every six hours each of us will stand a two-hour watch, one hour at the rudder and one at the lookout. We'll have to adjust our sleeping habits to this cycle as best we can.

Then we split up and go about our chores. Bob and Hal are stationed on the forward deck to keep an eye on the towlines. Arno, Wolf, Allan, Bill, and I set eagerly to work, but our enthusiasm soon wanes. The sea has taken hold of the *Tai Ki*, but not the way we had pictured it. We had had visions of our sails billowing in the wind and of our bow skimming elegantly over foam-topped waves. Reality has nothing in common with these romantic fantasies. A rusty cable connecting our junk to the stern of the boat ahead of us is all we can see. We can barely make out the towboat dancing over the waves, rolling from one side to the other but always righting itself. Just watching its motions sets our stomachs fluttering. What kind of contortions must the *Tai Ki* be going through? We can't see them, but our bodies will soon be responding to them.

Being towed through rough waters isn't much of a treat under the best of circumstances. But it is worse if your boat happens to be a junk: that is, a box without a keel. A junk is built to slide over the surface of the water, not to cut through it. It cannot function in tow the way it is designed to; it can't pitch freely and ride with the waves as it normally would. The towboat drags it through the water like a lump of wood. The impact of the waves is magnified, and the boat responds unnaturally and unpredictably. The towline yanks and slings it about. Whenever the ship tries to glide off to port or starboard, it is jerked back; whenever the bow tries to rise on an approaching wave, the line hauls it down into the water. The whole crew was soon feeling the effects of this rough treatment.

The waves were running nine to twelve feet. That is not an abnormally rough sea, but for a towing maneuver, especially as long a one as we had undertaken, the conditions were far from ideal for either ship or crew. We had pictured the beginning of our voyage differently.

Eric, the BBC cameraman, and I are the first victims of seasickness. Apathy sets in with nearly everyone. The tensions of the last few days give way to new ones, to outright fear for some of us.

The *Tai Ki* leaps about like a cork behind the fishing boat. This damnable heaving and tossing of the deck. I give myself up to sleep, to dozing, to forgetting, to wanting to forget. If only it would stop and stop soon. Standing, walking, any simple action is impossible. In a few weeks this will all be routine; our bodies will have made the adjustment. But they haven't yet.

I emerge from my fogged sleep, sink into lethargy again. At 0200 Carl wakes Arno and Hal with the first bad news of the voyage: the rudder has been damaged. The towing that has prevented the *Tai Ki* from reacting naturally to the waves has also exposed the rudder to unexpected pressures, twisting, wrenching, and battering it in its mounting until it cracked. It's hard to imagine what a terrible beating is necessary to harm that rudder. The rudder shaft is made of iron-hard billian a little over a foot through. Ten men at So's shipyard had worked several hours to mount it; and once mounted, it could be moved in the water only with the aid of pulleys. The rudder was the last thing any of us would have expected to be damaged.

Allan contacts the towboat by radio and tells the skipper to slow down. We're going to try to raise the rudder so that less of its blade will be exposed to the pressure of the waves. Arno, Carl, Hal, and Wolf crawl into the rudder housing. They have cut a hole in the cabin roof so that the rudder can be moved up and forward once it is lifted out of its mountings. Arno is dangling overboard in the night. Hal or Wolf holds the light for him. With the help of a block and tackle, the rudder is slowly raised. It isn't broken, but there are long cracks in it. Arno is hanging upside down over the water, someone or something holding onto his heels. Carl is working alongside him. The heavy seas grow rougher still. Both men go on working stubbornly, cursing and groaning. The motion of the ship finally conquers Carl; he hangs over the rail, and Hal is soon with him. Arno and Wolf are the only members of the crew whose sea legs prove reliable.

A dismal beginning. How could so much go so wrong in so few hours? Our first dawn at sea breaks gray over the *Tai Ki*. Our meal schedule has to be organized, but we haven't even worked out a KP roster yet, or any other duty roster, for that matter. Carl had hoped to arrange our work plan while we were in tow, but he has other things on his mind now.

Arno and Wolf prepare our first breakfast. No one else helps them or shows the slightest interest in food. Everyone is wrung out after this sleepless night. Arno is enraged. The crew has to eat!

The first two days on board pass by me as though in a fog. I'm simply absent, somewhere else altogether. This isn't just seasick-ness. I'm not nauseated, don't have to vomit. But something is draining my strength. I lie motionless, unconscious. Every once in a while I wake up and try to do something, only to collapse again. My sense of balance isn't functioning. It's not that I'm dizzy. I'm just totally disoriented.

Arno's journal for June 19:

o6oo. Stood watch with Bill. I'm worried about the rudder. Wolf, Hal, and I have to bear the brunt of the work. I don't like it, and I hope this state of affairs will pass when the others are feeling better. Kuno seems to be suffering from more than seasickness. He's trying desperately to get hold of himself, but his inner ear won't cooperate, and he keeps falling over.

Irritability is turning up in the crew, aggravated by sickness. No one had reckoned with two thirds of us being out of commis-sion. The damaged rudder has been a bitter pill for Carl to swal-low. His rudder, the rudder he designed, has proved inadequate already. He's depressed, and the rest of us are depressed with him.

Even after these few hours at sea we begin to consider a question that will crop up again and again: will we have to give up? Can we go on? Will the boat hold together? We start at the sound of wood groaning, sometimes cracking. We sit in silence, helpless. Hours pass. Arno is the only one of us who is fully able to do KP. Bill feels rotten, but he sticks by his camera work anyhow. Seas grow heavier and the contortions of our ship more violent. Should we cut loose from the towboat? How can we, with a rud-der we can't depend on? Will we be able to continue our voyage with this rudder at all?

Jenny and Eric have left the *Tai Ki*. A British gunboat came alongside, and two sailors took our guests off in a motorized life-boat. The heavy seas threw the lifeboat against our hull, forced the sailors to pull back. For a while it looked as though our two visitors would have to stay with us. Then we tossed Jenny into the lifeboat as if she were a sack of potatoes, and Eric finally managed to tumble in during a brief lull between waves. No time for good-byes.

After 420 nautical miles, the *Morning Cloud* — M 66192 YU with the *Tai Ki* in tow finally sighted the southern point of Taiwan. We had originally planned to take leave of our towboat here, but Carl seems undecided now as to what course he will take. Or if he has come to a decision, he certainly hasn't communicated it to the crew. It seems as though he wants to take a chance on going on. The rest of us are on edge. Everyone else thinks we should make use of the opportunity to repair the rudder. The rudder is still functional, but its mountings seem inadequately designed, and the surface area of the blade should be reduced to cut down its water resistance. Arno argues for a repair layover on Taiwan. Carl is still undecided. His main argument against Arno's plan is that there is no port on the east coast of Taiwan equipped to do the work we need.

More indecision. The southern tip of Taiwan is nearly astern of us. This is where we are scheduled to cut loose from our tow. Everything depends on our captain, for we had all agreed in advance that he would have the last word in all nautical matters. Then he passes on his instructions to the towboat by radio: reverse course and head for Kao-hsiung.

The *Tai Ki* turns around, and we go back toward the west against increasingly heavy waves, stronger winds, and an ebb tide. This was the worst stretch of our entire journey in tow behind the *Morning Cloud*. We had been warned in Hong Kong about sea and weather conditions off Taiwan. The forecasts had been correct, but reality was worse than what they had led us to expect.

After seven more hours, we are outside the harbor. Carl is in his cabin, studying charts and relaying orders to the *Morning Cloud* for our approach. We see other ships, a seawall, ships at anchor, a dock. We put into port and tie up. We're immediately surrounded by troops and police. Astonishment and suspicion reign. We see rifles and machine guns, hear questions we can't understand. Then a patrol boat appears. It seems we have stumbled into the military harbor of Kao-hsiung. That might have meant trouble for us, but the Taiwanese show considerable understanding. The patrol boat escorts us into the commercial harbor. Despite this kind gesture, it soon became clear to us that we were still held under suspicion. The *Tai Ki* was placed under close guard for the duration of her stay in Kao-hsiung. Armed guards stationed on the pier kept both boat and crew under constant surveillance. Sensing that something might happen on the short stretch from Hong Kong to Taiwan, I had procured visas for Taiwan before our departure. But our visas proved to be insufficient documentation here. We each received a special pass and a tag as well. If we wanted to leave the ship to wash or go to the bathroom, we had to show our passports, our special passes, and our tags, which we would have done well to wear around our necks like dog tags.

Port authorities. Customs. Police. Immigration authorities. Police and customs again. All our visitors seem to want gifts that we aren't prepared to give them, and before long we, who are subject to customs authorities, are playing customs officers ourselves. Every official or policeman who comes on board is accompanied by at least two crew members. We would have been vexed to see a camera, a sea bag, or some other item suddenly disappear on us. But the bureaucracy managed to have its sport with us anyhow. We were requested to prepare a list of every item on board, right down to the last can of beans. In consideration of a slight fee, of course, this requirement could be waived. . . .

But we haven't any money to spare, and who knows what they'll demand next if we give in on this point. So we talk at great length with the officials concerned, ask if we can't take their pictures — they refuse — shake their hands warmly, a gesture they look on with some suspicion. I fetch my journal and ask for their autographs. We are full of humility and reverence; we obviously admire their resplendent uniforms. They are kind enough to sign: Mr. Hsu Jen Kuei, Mr. Ten Kuo Hsu, and Mr. Lee Chung Lin. We proffer groveling thanks and escort them off the ship. The guards remain. A bottle of whiskey softens them up a little, but we are still subject to passport checks every time we want to go to the bathroom a few yards in back of where the guards are stationed.

Carl starts organizing the duty rosters. He thinks we should assign a steady cook. The rest of us think we should all take turns at that job, although we all agree that Arno, who was in charge of laying in our stores, should retain final authority over their use. We finally decide that the crew will be divided up into kitchen teams of two. One man cooks, the other washes up. At the next meal, the jobs are reversed. At first, we changed teams every three days, later every two.

The morale of the crew is wretched during our layover in Kao-hsiung. Everyone is depressed, and no wonder. We seem to be moored in a sewer, plagued by filth, flies, rats, cockroaches. Armed police stand guard over us. We are faced with the work on the rudder, important organizational tasks, and — remote as it may seem at this point — the mission we hope to accomplish. But here, surrounded by concrete piers, filth, stench, and noise, the ocean's broad sweep seems distant indeed.

Everyone's spirits are low, and each crew member deals with his depression in his own way. Arno tries to dispel it with a burst of activity. Carl retires into himself, works, says nothing. He seems to want to avoid us. Are his responsibilities weighing on him? If so, which ones? Bob mumbles under his breath. The police, fearing we might transmit military information, have forbidden Allan to use his radio, and he is trying to make up in Kao-hsiung for some of the pleasures he missed in Hong Kong. We are all concerned how his radio contacts will react to the *Tai Ki*'s sudden silence. We send a telegram from a hotel, hoping it will go through and not be censored or held back as a coded espionage report.

Wolf, Arno, and I discuss the mood of the crew and the need

to bring everyone together as a team. We all express and repress complaints about Carl, who is proving to be competent as a nautical technician but not, it seems, as a team leader. Bill is isolating himself in his work as filmmaker and photographer. Hal is pitching in, yet finding that he remains an outsider despite his willingness to work.

The rudder is removed from the ship. It has two cracks about four feet long in it and looks as though a splinter had broken out of it. The decision to come into port had been the correct one. We find some workmen, and with their help, Carl and Arno are able to dismount the rudder. Heated debates on what should be done to the rudder follow. Simply reinforcing it with iron bands around the splintered area doesn't seem to be enough. The rudder is too large and therefore too easily damaged by heavy seas. It is agreed to shorten it, to make it narrower, and — after much discussion — to cut rhomboidal holes in the blade to reduce water pressure on it.

More sweaty, dirty work. Anger, irritability. Talks late into the night. Or long, painful silences. More sweat and stench. Long faces.

Bill and I escape into town. We want a bath, a shave, and a haircut. In a little shack we discover what is probably the best barbershop either of us has ever come upon in his life. The place was unusual not just because it stood out in such sharp contrast to the filth of its surroundings, but also because it had real class. A small room. Two chairs, two mirrors, two girls — who were sisters — and the necessary implements. Clean, everything clean. Who would have expected it in this street lined with bordellos?

BILL: "These two are good enough to earn fifty dollars a haircut in New York."

KUNO: "Seventy."

BILL: "A hundred! I'm gonna hire them."

Kuno: "We'll open a shop in New York with the one and a shop in Paris with the other."

Bill: "Right! A hundred dollars a cut. The most renowned barbershops in the world. Just look at these two. Here in this street full of whores."

Kuno: "Incredible, absolutely incredible."

After two hours we're polished within an inch of our lives. The bill amounts to nothing, a mere pittance. Smiles and farewells are exchanged. Then one of the pair says, "Come back this evening. Cheap, very cheap."

We're taken aback, then we burst out laughing and head outside, trimmed, shaved, and perfumed, into a teeming tropical rainstorm.

Back to the filth of the harbor. More work on the rudder, trial runs, mountings, dismountings, arguments. Bob disappears. Wolf pokes around in the secondhand bookstores of Taiwan. Then the rudder is mounted again for the last time. We can sail again. Arno and I are determined to discuss the problem of leadership with Carl before we set out. We have to clear the air, speak openly about our individual failings. If we can't be frank with each other, we won't be able to complete the expedition together.

We start with me. We'll have to find out whether my physical difficulties were just a result of the towing. Arno is next. He can't demand as much from the others as he does from himself. Then Carl is up. He has to be more communicative, has to take over the role of leader. If Arno or I took over this role, that would lessen his authority as captain. Each crew member has to know what his duties are. We may well have made a mistake in preferring a crew picked randomly to a half-trained one. But in any case, the crew members have to know where they stand. That is our only hope. Tomorrow we'll be setting out again, and nothing will be able to stop us, we think, if the crew works together, if everyone is prepared to make sacrifices for the others, if every crew member knows precisely what his tasks and duties are. All this lies in the hands of the captain.

Carl listened quietly, then expressed his thanks. He would do his part, but he wasn't given to many words. Good enough.

We're back on board, ready to sail. The police have become friendlier and more polite. Maybe they're expecting some farewell gifts. They'll be disappointed. We have a last-minute crisis with Bill. He is a crew member like everybody else. His work on board has to assume top priority. Once that's taken care of he can pursue his camera work. . . .

He sits silent and draws circles in the red sawdust with his toe. I'm sitting on a chunk of wood to his left. Arno is leaning on the dirty wall of a shed.

"We need a full-time crew of eight men," I say.

Silence.

"The ship comes first. For everybody and at all times," Arno adds.

"And if we run into a storm or something else happens? I'm here to take pictures!" Bill objects.

"Agreed," I reply. "But we've had the impression so far that you haven't wanted to do anything else but make films. And that won't do."

The rest of the crew is calling to us from the ship. The tug is waiting. We're supposed to sail any minute now.

"Just a second," I call back. "Think it over. Fast."

Arno is impatient.

"If I can't take pictures, then I'm staying here. You can make do without me." Bill is raging now.

"O.K.," Arno says.

"Wait. Just try to understand what we're saying," I break in again. "The expedition comes first. We've got to make it across. That's the main thing."

"If we don't make it, then the best films in the world won't do you any good," Arno adds.

Silence. More waiting. Bill stares at the ground. More yelling from the boat. Everyone is impatient and on edge.

Bill jumps up and walks to the edge of the pier. The *Tai Ki* lies before him. He has some camera gear with him; the rest is on board. He presses his hands together, looks down, throws his head back, turns, walks a few steps away from us, turns back; he is still furious.

"O.K.," he says. That's all. He jumps on board without looking at Arno or me again.

Bill would later prove to be a devoted crew member. If anyone earned the title of loyal comrade, it was certainly he.

Shouting, scurrying about. Ropes are loosened, tossed, caught, coiled. The ship moves away from the pier. Ten or fifteen spectators gather to watch the *Tai Ki* move out of the harbor under escort by the harbor patrol. Dock workers on shore wave. By 1230 we have cleared the harbor zone. Twenty minutes later a naval ship crosses our bow, comes in close; sunlight glances off field glasses. We respond by ignoring our observers. The *Tai Ki* sets a course of 210°. The barometer reads 29.7. The sun is shining; it's warm; light clouds fleck the sky. We have set only half our sail but are still making four to five knots across gentle swells.

The mood of the crew changes instantly. We're moving under our own sail. The wind is picking up. We measure a velocity of 6 on the Beaufort scale, and our speed increases correspondingly. At this rate we could make a hundred nautical miles today. A hundred nautical miles! Everyone radiates good spirits. Was everything we went through in the last ten days — or in the last three weeks — really not as bad as we perceived it to be, or were we simply not used to dealing with difficult situations? Wolf, our theologian, is singing a Bach motet.

Taiwan is behind us. Relieved, we see it disappear over the horizon. We start making calculations, playing the "if" game we will play hundreds of times over: "If we make x knots per day, then we'll reach the other side in y weeks." Depending on our rate of speed for any given day, this game evokes laughter, high hopes, vexation, impatience.

We make our boat shipshape, and each of us arranges his own sleeping place, stows his own gear. On Taiwan we hadn't had any time to take care of personal needs. Now we hang nets to take our duffels and personal effects. We haggle over the best sleeping places, pack ropes away, untangle them, tangle them again only to untangle them once more. Arno acts as foreman and divides up the work among us.

Our days pass in swimming, chores, chess. Bill is the undefeated chess champion. Arno and I are in about the same league. Wolf, our novice, to whom I had given some basic lessons back in Hong Kong, begins to come into his own. He's taking lessons with Bill, the Grand Master. Bob plays only occasionally. When he does, he stages long battles with Bill and usually loses. He can wipe up the board with the rest of us. We have free time for reading and talking, for settling in and getting used to each other, for adjusting to a situation that will remain constant for weeks and months. Time passes slowly hour by hour, but the days fly by.

Allan makes radio contact with the Norwegian coal ship *Thorunn* and receives a message that shakes us considerably: typhoon warning. The center of the storm is two hundred nautical miles northeast of our present position. After four peaceful days, the seas turn rough, with waves rising fifteen to eighteen feet. Carl heads south to avoid the brunt of the storm. A head-on collision with it is unlikely, but we see all we want to of it even on its fringes. The seas grow heavier still, and the crew has to step lively to lash down or stow away the movable gear. The helmsman is often hard pressed to hold the rudder steady against the force of the waves.

I'm the cook today; cooking aboard the *Tai Ki* is not pure joy. Our kitchen is located under the domed roof of the central cabin. A wooden box contains coffee, sugar, salt, and condiments. Tin cans are kept in a basket. Arno has mounted our two-burner kerosene stove in another sturdy wooden box. Next to the stove are two plastic water containers. Knives, forks, and spoons hang on the wall in tin cans. For plates, Wolf has devised an ingenious gadget that looks like a stool turned upside down. Still another box holds pots, pans, and a pressure cooker.

My menu calls for soup. The first step is to fetch any necessary tin cans from the storage containers below deck. In heavy seas, this basically simple act can become complicated. With a pencil flashlight clamped between his teeth, the cook opens the hatch, descends, jams himself into an angle of the ship's timbers, paws through cases, loses his footing and is tossed into a corner, cracks head and back on the planking, rejoices if he can emerge again with only a few bruises. Then he primes the stove, pumps up pressure in the tank, turns the burner on. He puts on water to boil. A wave slops the water out of the pot; the flame goes out; the stove is drenched. Clean up and start over again, once, twice, three times, over and over again until you can do it in your sleep.

The water is finally warm, the soup half-done. The cook stands in front of the stove, his hands on the pot and pot cover, playing gyroscope for his soup. He succumbs to another massive wave, dumps the whole brew out again. Cook and pot sail through the kitchen. Hot soup — or coffee or stew or rice — splatters on the deck. Innocent bystanders suffer scalded hands or feet. Lap Sac, unsteady on his legs, tries to lick up the accident but retreats before a dishrag tossed his way.

The decision to restrict ourselves to cold meals during storms by no means solved the cook's problems. More often than not he was sent flying with a potful of cold oatmeal in his hands and was unable to prevent dumping it on himself, the deck, or another crew member.

If seas are only moderately rough, with waves between fifteen and twenty feet, cooking aboard the *Tai Ki* is still possible; but if the waves are higher than that, mealtimes become a dubious pleasure for cook and crew alike. Under extreme conditions, even the experienced shipboard cook is relatively helpless. There are, of course, certain tricks of the trade that make the job easier, and some crew members show more talent for rough-weather cooking than others. Arno is a magnificent storm cook, and Wolf — who said at the beginning of the voyage, "I don't know anything about cooking. I'll just do the dishes" — turns out to be a natural. His enthusiastic descriptions of marinades and spicy sauces and the exotic names he gives his dishes inevitably set our mouths watering, and even if the product doesn't fulfill the claims of his advertising, we have still worked up hearty appetites for the meal. Public relations make the difference, even in the small world of the *Tai Ki*.

Bob is a first-rate salad maker. Using tuna fish, corned beef, rolled oats, and green beans, using ingredients both complementary to and incompatible with each other, he comes up with truly remarkable creations. Bill prefers hot Mexican dishes that often scorch the palate. Arno is our expert on calories, and as chef he sticks to solid home cooking.

"The important thing isn't how much you eat," he intones, "but how many calories you take in."

"I want enough to eat," Allan grumbles.

At almost every meal during our first few weeks at sea there was disagreement between the eternally hungry radioman and our frugal quartermaster. Months later, after the voyage was over, Allan admitted that Arno's rigor in distributing rations had been essential.

"Meals are the high points of the day," Bill notes, and it is a fact that much of the crew's interest focuses on food. Aside from matters relating to the ship itself and to our work on board, no other subject is discussed as often. Arno has no difficulty in restricting his intake of food. That kind of self-discipline is routine for him. But others are constantly plagued by hunger that is only aggravated by the additional exertion the ship's movements demand of the crew. The body is seldom truly at rest, even in sleep, for only an exceptionally calm sea permits deep slumber. And during waking hours, even if one is sitting or lying down, the ship's motions force thousands of muscles into play that are rarely used on shore.

"Sailing always demands a lot of energy," Carl opines.

Arno maintains that the crew would do well to shrink their stomachs down to healthy proportions. Allan registers violent protest. Our ship's physician concurs with Arno. Hal, who is always ready to accept the will of the majority, remains silent. Neither Wolf nor I have anything to offer at this point either. Although Arno successfully defends his rationing plan, the question of food remains a problem throughout the entire journey. We come to discuss it less and less, but that is far from a sign that we have reached a consensus.

Fish provide us with some variety in our diet. Shark is an acquired taste, and even then, it requires a knowledgeable cook to make it palatable. We are lacking such a cook aboard the *Tai Ki*. Dorados, on the other hand, are delicious no matter how inept the chef.

I have KP. I'm sweating away, scratching burned Hungarian goulash out of a pot that had been left on the stove too long. Looking out onto the water, I see something stir under the surface. I'm unable to tell what it is until two sharp fins emerge about ten yards to port and then disappear again.

"Shark!" I yell.

The whole crew is assembled in seconds. The hunt is still a novelty. Bob is the first on the catwalk, his knife in his hand. Arno and Bill follow with harpoons.

"Where is he?"

"Out there somewhere," I answer, pointing in the general direction.

The water is calm; then we see it stir again. Bob lowers himself gently into the water, Arno and Bill after him. There's more splashing in the water, much closer to the ship this time, and we can see now that I was mistaken. It's a sea turtle, not a shark, but

A page from the ship's log

Time	Course	Log	Knots	Wind direction	Wind velocity	Baro-meter	Temper-ature
16	340	97	0	180	1,5	759	30
18	310	01	0,5	160	2,5	759	29
20	330	03	2	160	3	759	28
22	330	06	1	200	3	758	28
24	330	08	1	150	3	759	27
02	330	08	0	140	1	759	26
04	270	08	0	0	0	758	26
06	330	08	0	30	1	758	25
08	330	09	0,5	50	3,5	758	28
10	330	12	1,5	50	7	758	28
12	330	16	2	50	6	758	28
14	350	22,5	3	60	10	759	28
16	350	27,5	3	60	9	759	28
18	350	34	3,25	60	9	758	28
20	350	38	2	80	8	759	28
22	340	44	3	70	5	760	27
24	340	46	1	70	3	760	27

Every watch made these log entries on the blackboard in the helmsman's cabin, and the data gathered in this way made it possible to calculate the position and progress of the ship.

no one can stop the hunters now. Carl and Wolf pull on their diving masks and go overboard, too.

Arno moves in on the turtle quietly. It seems to be flying in the water, moving its broad flippers as if in slow motion. Arno takes aim, fires. The shining steel harpoon shoots past the turtle. Frightened now, the turtle turns quickly and tries to dive. But Bill has moved in to within ten feet of it. It turns and swims straight at him. He swims aside, hesitates for a second, his finger ready on the trigger, then he fires. The harpoon stabs through the turtle's neck. With a sudden turn and violently thrashing flippers, the turtle dives. Bill lets it take some line, then tries to snub it, but the turtle is more than Bill can manage alone. Arno and Bob take hold of the line with him. Together, they halt the turtle's run, and badly wounded as it is, the turtle loses strength quickly.

Wolf and Carl join the other three, and all five haul the wounded turtle toward the stern of the *Tai Ki*. Hal and I are waiting to pull it on board. It is still alive, its wide flippers still thrashing.

Bob's training in anatomy stands him in good stead. He adroitly dissects the turtle on the forward deck. Bill will get the shell as a trophy for his study at home, and Lap Sac can look forward to a rare treat. Crew and dog will be eating turtle stew for the next two days. The tough, gray meat has to be chewed forever — Bill calls it "indestructible chewing gum" — but the taste is excellent.

Then Arno starts baking bread, and after some preliminary difficulties, bread making becomes a high art on board. Special breads like onion bread, sweet bread, and cinnamon bread are produced; special names for special breads are invented. Allan was the first to follow Arno's lead as baker, but he did so without much success. Since Arno had taken a dim view of Allan's consumption of meat and canned goods, Allan resolved to round out a frugal meal with some bread. Arno recorded the incident in his journal: "Our gourmet Allan seems rather subdued. He's making bread. That is to say, he's trying to make bread. He mixes and kneads his dough, puts it on the fire the way I've shown him. The results are dismal, and Allan is particularly downcast. He had forgotten to put in the yeast, and when he was done, he had nothing but scorched, stone-hard lumps of dough that bore no resemblance to bread at all. We ate them anyhow."

Breakfast, the first meeting of the day. Although the limited space aboard the *Tai Ki* would seem to make sociability inevitable, this was not the case with us. An individual can always isolate himself, no matter how small the area he shares with others, can always withdraw from his neighbor who is sitting only inches away from him. He can read, refuse to speak, muse to himself. The only activities that are communal are those that are declared communal. For this reason, mealtimes were focal points in the order of our day.

Breakfast is usually served about 0800. We have oatmeal; occasionally someone attempts pancakes. We drink instant coffee, tea, or lemonade, all of which taste of chlorine. We talk about the past night, about messages Allan has received over the radio. We organize — or try to organize — the day's work. Discussions become heated, develop into arguments, are followed by silence. Carl withdraws into himself, hardly speaks with anyone. When he does speak, it is always with individuals, never with the whole crew.

Mountains are made of molehills. Butter, for example, was the spark that ignited the first major explosion in the crew. We run out of butter at breakfast, and Bob heads for the storage compartment to fetch some more. Arno reminds him that we are allowing ourselves only one container of butter per week. Bob ignores him and starts to lift the hatchway. Arno roars at him. Bob yells back, something about "miserable organization," then adds, "I've had enough of this crap." Arno is seething; Bob's hands shake as he continues working at the hatchway. Carl remains silent. Then Hal speaks up.

"You're behaving like children," he snaps. "We're a team with a common goal. If we have disagreements, we should settle them by a vote." He doesn't wait for anyone's reaction but simply goes on talking. "Who thinks we should stick by Arno's rule of one container of butter per week? And who thinks Bob is right?"

Everyone votes for Arno. Bob abstains and grumblingly accepts the majority's ruling.

We fought over trivia, of course. But the important thing was that our aggressions could find release in these arguments. We could get our feelings out into the open rather than repressing them in silence. We pushed ourselves and each other to the limits of our patience during those first weeks at sea. That was part of getting to know each other and of coming together as a crew.

Like all the typhoons we encountered during the initial phase of our voyage, the first one to strike us on the open sea also moved on toward Taiwan, but before it did it left its mark on the *Tai Ki*. The rudder, which was our major worry, suffered no damage in the thirty-foot waves and gale-force winds. But the lowest spar on the sail shattered, and the rattan bindings that held the sail to the mast tore. Some of them would have to be replaced entirely.

We had come very near the center of this typhoon. According to Allan, we were within 150 miles of it. Since the storm had measured some 500 miles across, we had clearly been in one of its vortices. We could appreciate in retrospect how sound Carl's judgment had been when he headed south. If we had held to our north-northeasterly course, we would probably have moved directly into the eye of the storm. This would not be our last experience of this kind, and no wonder, because we were on the Pacific during the typhoon season.

An entry from my journal:

This typhoon was something of a fluke in terms of usual weather patterns. Early in July, the storms tend to head for Hainan or Taiwan. This

117

one passed over Okinawa. The barometer is rising now, and Bill is trying to tape some interviews with the crew about the storm we've just experienced. Everyone is tired. The last few hours have been demanding. Arno and Wolf held up best of us all, working like madmen the whole time, but their ambition did not seem to be contagious. As cook, I may have provided a great deal of amusement for others as I juggled pots, plates, and soup, but from my own point of view, this stretch of KP was pure hell. In the evening we received a distinctly unroutine bit of news from Sweden: The Federal Republic of Germany will play Holland in the soccer world championship. Wolf is confident of victory.

The *Tai Ki* performed well in the storm, far better than the crew, which is still far from broken in. Arno is doing his best with what he has to work with. Carl is assuming that the crew will gradually teach itself what it has to know. Either the tail end of the storm or a fresh wind — the crew of the *Tai Ki* could care less which — is moving us along at a stiff pace of about 90 nautical miles a day, sometimes a little more, sometimes a little less. In any case, we're making good time.

We hear a radio report about the typhoon we've come through relatively unscathed. Japan has counted 27 dead, 80 missing, at least 10,000 homeless. Korea reports 8 dead and 40 missing. Seventeen ships have gone down. The BBC considered the typhoon important enough news to warrant special news flashes. Massive property damage has been reported in all areas struck by the storm. We had come away lightly from what had been a major catastrophe for others.

Despite the radio contact we maintain and the news we receive, our isolation at sea weighs on us. I have spoken with Wolf, Arno, Hal, and Bob about this. A thousand links tie us to the world we have left behind, and we find it hard to break these links. We realize this only when we consciously come to grips with our isolation.

Wolf is speaking of "temerity" and the "need to prove oneself worthy of good fortune." The crew seems to have turned philosophical now that the storm has given way to calm. Bob is sketching faces and objects. Arno is hard at work. He comes into the cabin after hours of labor outside, stretches out on his back and breathes deeply like a miler after a race, jumps to his feet and sets to work again. Allan is sleeping. Hal has rigged a hammock that hangs out over the water at the bow. Allan is taking his repose there. Bob and Hal are also frequent visitors to this bird's nest. Lap Sac is snuffling around on deck. Wolf is seated on the rudder housing, a pipe in his mouth, a Mao cap on his head. The cap is decorated with a red star he cut out of a can of Japanese "Saporro" beer. He sits like a stagecoach driver, his legs spread, the steering lines like reins in his hands. Carl is poring over his charts in his cabin.

We have brought along two big sea bags full of books, literature to suit any taste. Wolf is deep into Musil's *Man without Qualities*. Bob and Bill are learning German. In the net over my air mattress, I have a volume of Needham's *Science and Civilization in China,* a history of the Incas, a few short monographs on diffusion theory, and a couple of mystery stories. After a day's work of whatever sort on board or after a dip in the ocean, I find myself usually preferring the light reading.

My journal of July 18, 1974:

Light breeze. The night is somewhat cooler than we are used to. Our more northerly position is making itself felt in the temperatures. We're at 142° east longitude, 30° 40′ north latitude, just about on a level with Rome, Tashkent, and New York. Wind velocity: 5 mph. Barometer: 30.1. Course: 20 to 40°, though our direction is determined more by the current than by our manipulations of sail and rudder.

Our morning is full of activity. Arno and Wolf are pumping out the bilge. Hal is the cook. Allan and Bill are at work on the safety lines. Bob and I are resealing the cabin roof. Carl is occupied with his charts and has KP duty.

Sealing the roof is a miserable job. We mix up a pasty liquid of tung oil and sawdust, then carry it over to the roof in big tin cans that used to have dehydrated potatoes in them. We smear the stuff on with heavy brushes, one square foot after another. The roof is in dire need of this treatment. Rain and spray have washed the original sealer off, and water is starting to leak into the cabin. This is particularly irksome when the drops come down on your head during the night.

We paint hour after hour. The job is more unpleasant than ever along toward noon because the oil, heated by the sun, can give the feet a nasty burn. But then the work is so monotonous that one's thoughts can wander as they please.

I'm somewhat concerned about Wolf. He is very young. He has shown me a page of his journal, and I quote it here only to show how his mood is totally determined by external circumstances. This passage in Wolf's journal was written on July 22 in the thick of the storm. Today, in the glory of this weather, what we experienced then seems so remote as to be unreal.

Day breaks on our misery. Everything is dank and clammy. Rain is setting in, and our cabin roof leaks like a sieve. Sleeping figures stretched out everywhere; musty smell; wet, rusted kitchen utensils and eating gear scattered about. Cold. Our situation borders on the intolerable. Not a square inch one can call his own, not a square inch that's dry, no trace of human warmth, no sense of security. . . .

I wonder what he will put down in his journal about today.

Books. We read, think, speculate. I regret that we don't have a more extensive selection of books on board. I dip into Needham late in the afternoon and leaf through what he has to say about jade. I have already made some notes on the subject:

Jade has always been regarded as a precious stone in the Far East, where the most valuable varieties were given the names of birds. Some of these varieties were valued more highly than gold, and jade was shaped into ceremonial implements such as symbolic axes. The extreme hardness of jade demands a high degree of skill from the artist who works with it, and in the Far East the jade carver was granted special privileges in society.

Jade was the first material to be traded in overseas commerce, and professional jade collectors jealously guarded their knowledge of how and where to find this precious stone.

Jade staffs, like scepters in other cultures, were used as symbols of rank, and jade discs colored with cinnabar were placed in the mouths of the dead. Jade was also used as an ornamentation for teeth. Holes were bored in the incisors, then filled with jade. Death masks of eminent personages were fashioned of jade, too, a strange use for this highly valued material.

It is surely not a matter of mere coincidence that similar jade objects appear both in China of the Shang period (ca. 1200 B.C.) and, only a short time later, in the Olmec culture of Mesoamerica. The Far East and Mesoamerica are the only places on earth where the idolization of this beautiful and relatively scarce material occurs. And in the Olmec culture this use of jade crops up without any apparent preparatory phases. Olmec artifacts of jade seem to have materialized out of thin air. But the artisans who fashioned the figures uncovered in the Olmec graves of Cerro de la Mesas obviously had a thorough knowledge of their medium and of the methods for shaping it.

If we consider, too, that in Olmec jade figures a facial type that has nothing in common with that of the American Indian appears seemingly out of the blue, then we can come to only one conclusion: transpacific contact must have taken place.

I hear Wolf shouting. Bill comes rushing into the cabin and snatches up his camera gear. I automatically grab my camera bag off a bamboo nail over my head and follow Bill outside. The crew is gathered on the forward deck. Allan points at what first seems to be a thoroughly unremarkable stretch of open water. Then we see a dark back rise above the surface, then another, then two more. A fountain shoots up and is soon followed by a second. A pod of whales is passing us about three hundred yards away. They pay no attention to us. They rise to the surface, disappear, rise and disappear again with unhurried, elegant motions. They swim calmly along, following some path invisible to us, moving toward an unknown goal. Our meeting is like that of two gliders sailing quietly toward each other through the air, passing each other, and fading from each other's view. We watch the whales as they move away from us. They are the only living thing rising from the sea, these arrogant brutes that show not the slightest interest in our magnificent ship. Bob stays on deck longer than the rest of us and stares after the whales, even when they are no longer to be seen.

These days at sea stood under the sign of storms. Typhoons or severe tropical storms — Gilda, Ivy, Jean, and Kim — were a constant threat during the journey from Hong Kong to Japan. According to the weather reports, Kim was scheduled to reach us during the last days of July. But she was kind to us, passing us by and sending only slightly heavy seas and winds our way.

0200. Somebody is shaking me awake. I start up out of a deep sleep. Where was I? Where am I now? Awareness of my surroundings comes suddenly, almost frighteningly. We sleep fully dressed, if shorts and a T-shirt can be called fully dressed. It's my watch at the helm. My partner feels his way to the lookout post on the forward deck. I glance at the log: how fast are we traveling? What's the course? Then I am alone for an hour, the steering lines in my hands. At 0300 the posts are changed. I pass through the cabin and out on deck, sit down, lean back on the low, rounded roof, have a smoke, look at stars, moon, clouds, the phosphorescent glow of the sea, the sail looming threateningly overhead, listen to the slap of waves against the bow.

0400. Changing of the watch. I wake my relief, then collapse on my air mattress. Four hours' sleep. The summons to breakfast. We eat without washing, we talk, hear the latest news. Arno has asked Carl to teach him how to use a sextant, and Carl is happy to oblige. Arno has been studying the theory and working with the device for the last few evenings. Jack London said the sextant lends the seaman who knows how to use it the mysterious aura of the alchemist. It is hard to picture Arno as an adept of the black maritime arts. Jack London was probably exaggerating a bit. Arno begins his studies with an English pocket sextant from Carl's "Maritime Museum."

Morning. The KP detail has cleaned up after breakfast. Two men are working the bilge pumps. This is still a simple job that takes only two hours every other day. Very little water is coming in. Compartment four is the only one that seems to be taking on more water than expected. Scraps of wood the shipbuilders left behind are a constant nuisance, blocking the pump valves time and again. This causes problems for those of us lacking in technical skills. Arno often has to come to my rescue, freeing the jammed valves with a sovereignty that strikes me as downright arrogant, probably because I am forced to recognize each time how little dexterity is actually called for.

Some spars are in need of repair and reinforcement. Hal's efforts to do this work with original materials fail. He and Wolf finally decide to use nylon rope to bind sail and spars together. They bore holes in the heavy bamboo spars and file the edges of the holes smooth to prevent them from cutting into the ropes. Wolf runs up the mast and out on the spars like a squirrel. He works with panache, Hal with precision.

Carl is sitting next to Bill on the helmsman's bench and sewing at some as yet unidentifiable object made of canvas. When Bill asks him what he's making, he replies, "A washbowl." He would later use the same material to sew a hammock and an apron for special tools.

A narrow strip of filth and garbage drifts past us to starboard. The nearest land is hundreds of miles away. Bob jumps into the water, submerges, surfaces with a black lump in his hand. He passes it up to us, a glob of what may have been heating oil a little larger than my fist. I lay the black, stinking lump on the catwalk and take a picture to document this instance of pollution on the open sea. Bill says he wants a shot of it too, and I leave it lying where it is. We both forget it, and by the next day it has dissolved into black, sticky rivulets that trail onto the deck and over the side. Carl and Arno start cursing. I get a broad chisel and try to scrape the tacky mess up but only manage to drop the chisel overboard. Arno is far from pleased. I replace the chisel with a tin can squashed flat, and after long and arduous labor, I have the deck clean again. Wolf christens me "The Polluter." Despite my successful efforts at purification, the onus remains with me.

At lunch we have still another discussion about food rationing. This is almost a daily ritual now. Allan is pressing for snacks between meals. Arno objects that "nibbling," as he calls it, will only make self-discipline in rationing all the more difficult. These debates are wearing on all of us, and they are also having the side effect that some of the crew members who have previously had no trouble controlling their appetites are now clamoring for more food. We agree once again, as we had several days earlier, that Bob and Arno make an inventory of our provisions and that we work out a new rationing system on the basis of this inventory and of Carl's estimates of our projected time at sea.

Afternoon. Rattan matting emerges from compartment three. Some of it has been water damaged. Carl and Hal set about repairing it. After half an hour of work, the forward deck is littered with minute fragments of sail matting. Wolf complains that the place looks like a pigsty and begins an overzealous clean-up campaign that sends many a useful item flying overboard: a small bucket, several tin cans we had meant to use as containers for odds and ends. Cleanliness may be next to godliness, but it can be carried too far.

Bill harpooned a small dorado during the morning, and this success has increased his bloodlust. He sets out to try his luck again in the afternoon, but at the cry of "Shark! Shark!" he comes leaping up and over our four-foot freeboard as though he were a trained dolphin. His performance is particularly impressive considering that he's weighted down with harpoon, knife, and swim fins. Hal had jumped in with him just for a little dip, and he too climbs back on deck. The element of sudden terror is lacking for him, though, and he takes a little longer than Bill did.

Bill had been swimming close by the hull the whole time. "Then all of a sudden this ten- or twelve-foot monster turns up in front of my nose. I was really startled. Goddam! I was almost afraid. Imagine that!" Our cameraman laughs and runs his hands through his thick blond hair. He doesn't look very frightened, not now, at any rate.

The shark turned up next to the ship again a little later, swimming six feet or so from the hull and surrounded by a horde of pilot fish. He cut an imposing figure. Even though several of us had sworn we'd never go after shark again because we might find our prey served up to us at mealtime, we put our resolution aside in this case and began to organize the hunt. Arno will take snapshots; I'll be in charge of the movie camera. Bob and Bill will be the harpoonists. Our plans complete, we discover that the shark is nowhere in sight. He reappears off the stern a little later, tantalizes us awhile, then disappears. Lap Sac accompanies his departure with a lot of barking.

The focus of the hunt changes. This time our prey is a rat. Bill claims to have seen it, but we're still not sure whether rats or cockroaches are getting into our provisions. We prefer to think it's rats, probably because we think we'll have better luck dealing with them. But as it turned out, even our rat hunt proved a failure. If we suspected rats of nesting in some of the bamboo spars we had stored below deck, we would drag the bamboo behind us in the water to drown the invaders. We dragged bamboo behind the ship for two days in a row but never saw a sign of a rat. And marauders still kept nibbling away at our bread, our chocolate, and our sugar.

1900. We set our night-lights. Wolf is an expert lamplighter. He usually needs only four matches to light the position lights, the helmsman's lamp, and two lamps in the cabin. His record is two. I use up almost a whole pack of our supposedly waterproof matches to the same end.

Supper. This meal passes without debate about calories. We laugh about Bill's confrontation with the shark. Hal tells us about his wealthy Chinese pupils. I talk about jade. We discuss a reorganization of the duty rosters. Carl will draft new ones, and so will Arno and I. The conference we had on this subject the next day turned out to be an unhappy one for all concerned.

Evening. Allan climbs on his bicycle-generator and sets off on his daily tour. Others take turns on the bike, too. Anyone who wants to send a message home is obliged to produce his share of the electricity consumed. We decide to organize a two-mile bicycle race, the "Tour de *Tai Ki.*" Allan covers the stretch in good time. I'm next. Arno follows and matches my time. Bill pours on the steam, pedals faster and faster, betters Arno's and my time by five seconds. Hal can't match that. Then Wolf swings onto the bike with a grand gesture. "I'll show you how it's done," he says. "I used to ride a bike to school every day."

"On your mark, get set, go!"

Wolf's boast wasn't empty. He tops us all. We plan a daily race. Whoever makes the best average time during the voyage will be Champion of the Pacific. But because of lack of time or interest, that first race was the last, and Wolf's championship went unchallenged.

Bob and Allan sit down on a hatchway on the forward deck. Lap Sac, greeted by a curse from Wolf, runs to Bob. He is the only one of us the dog takes to. A month has gone by, and the dog still hasn't let me near him. When Arno tried to pet him, he bit his hand.

Familiar sounds emerge from the radio shack: ditdadadit-ditda. "Here I am trying to learn German," Bill groans, "and they're practicing their Morse code back there again." He tosses his vocabulary notes into the corner. Carl relieves me at the rudder, and I head for my post on the forward deck. In the cabin Arno is stretched out on his air mattress, playing chess with Wolf, who squats across the board from him. Bill watches the match. It is 2100. Night has fallen. Stars shine overhead. A light haze hangs on the horizon. Beneath it is the sea.

Quiet settles over the ship. Bob pumps up his air mattress. Hal has put aside his journal. Allan has disappeared behind the spare mast and is already asleep. He possesses the enviable talent of being able to fall asleep from one minute to the next. Wolf has turned in. Arno takes over the helm from Carl. Bill relieves me on deck. 2200. I wash under the stars, then roll up in my sleeping bag.

Thoughts about the day pass through my head. We could have used more wind. What's on the agenda for tomorrow? Arno and Wolf ought to get together for a talk. Carl needs more support from the rest of us. He is isolated from the crew and becoming more so. He finds it difficult to talk. He started to tell me about his son last night. That's the first time he has opened up, and we've stood a lot of watches together by now.

The water slaps softly against the hull. The mast, creaking gently in its tabernacle, is an accurate indicator of the wind's force. The breeze is light now. Yes, we really could have used more wind today. We made only 45 nautical miles. That's a bit under the average we'd like to make. We need more wind. Maybe we'll get it tomorrow. My next watch begins in five hours.

CHAPTER FIVE

Typhoon Warning Number Six

OUR COURSE WAS 60° NORTHEAST AT FIRST; LATER IT WAS 90° east. To the east lay our destination; to the east lay America. Our junk traveled at an average speed of three knots. Long, heavy swells picked her up, let her fall. The wooden hull creaked and groaned, maintained a steady dialogue with the crew, even during a calm.

My journal for July 20: "This is my mother's birthday. Cloudy skies. Wind out of the northwest. The sea is turning rougher, the barometer falling. At 0800 it read 29.9; two hours later it had dropped to 29.8. Temperature: 84°. Wind velocity: 7 knots and increasing."

Our position was 142° east longitude and 30° north latitude. We were about 600 miles east of Okinawa and not far from Iwo Jima, the largest of the Volcano Islands off Japan. The mood was tense that morning as the crew gathered for breakfast. There was something in the air, quite literally. Allan passed along the weather reports he had picked up just before midnight. Bob and Carl, who had been standing their watches then, already knew what was coming.

Our main radio contact, located in Nynäshamn, south of Stockholm, had received a report from San Francisco that three low-pressure systems were threatening the *Tai Ki*. The typhoon

Ivy and the STS Jean both lay southwest of our course, and a third low was forming barely a hundred miles due west of us. All three systems were moving at about 20 mph. Ivy and Jean would probably blow themselves out to the northwest of the *Tai Ki*, but it was obvious that Low Number Three, which, in defiance of all tradition, I called "Frederick," would catch up with us. Frederick was moving from west to east, heading directly for us at a speed of 15 knots. The only thing that was uncertain was whether Frederick would choose to become an STS or a typhoon.

The routes that tropical storms will take are never completely predictable, of course. Dr. Chin, one of the meteorologists at the Royal Observatory in Kowloon, had passed this comforting information on to us several weeks ago. But within the short distance of a hundred miles, give or take a few, the most capricious storm was unlikely to alter its course significantly.

Allan predicted that Ivy would probably head for Hong Kong and Jean for Taiwan. He was right in both cases. Frederick would strike the *Tai Ki*. This gloomy forecast had a depressing effect on our breakfast conversation.

My journal contains this entry:

Our talk this morning differed greatly from the usual breakfast chatter, even from that on mornings when we had been threatened by other typhoons. Allan spoke, with appropriate Nordic reserve, about life after death. Hal concerned himself with nautical questions and preparations. Bob rumbled into his sprouting beard. Wolf cracked jokes and abounded in forced gaiety. Arno, who placed very little faith in weather forecasts, said he had the impression that every thunderstorm that came along in these latitudes was advertised as a typhoon. Our nerves were a bit ragged from the actual storms we'd experienced and the flood of storm warnings we'd received during the last few weeks.

Broad swells were the first signs we felt from the storm behind us. Then the waves started growing heavier, rising to between five and ten feet but no higher. Carl Frederik gave the order to secure the ship, and we spent the morning hours working frantically. There was no time for reflection. We had to shorten and set the stays, lash down the light superstructures, and take everything below deck that wasn't fastened to the ship: ropes, baskets, boxes, Allan's generator bike. Four men were detailed to pump out the bilge. Hal and Allan worked together on one pump, Bob and I on another.

During our brief breaks, we discussed what might be in store for us. The low-pressure system could well develop into an STS and then into a typhoon. "That's probably what'll happen," Hal observed tersely. His opinion carried some weight. He'd been living in the Far East for two years now and had some experience with the storms of these latitudes. "The storm will hit us about 2100 tonight," Allan had told us at breakfast. Maximum winds of 60 to 75 mph were expected. Our chances for avoiding the storm were as good as nil.

It seemed as though the Pacific, which owes its misnomer to the fact that it happened to be calm when Magellan saw it for the first time, wanted to test us just once more now that we stood before its gates. Perhaps it would deny us entrance altogether. We had passed 140° east longitude and reached the outer limits of the typhoon belt. By all rights we should have been left in peace.

In Chinese, typhoon means "great wind." Thousands of ships and hundreds of thousands of people have fallen victim to these tropical storms in the course of history. In 1974, they seemed to be acting up in erratic ways that puzzled the most experienced meteorologists. A cyclone struck Central America, killing thousands and making thousands more homeless; a typhoon destroyed a city in Australia; and the "normal," predictable typhoons were far more violent than usual.

Typhoons take their rise near the equator, but the physical processes involved have still not been fully understood. One condition essential to the formation of a typhoon is a high water temperature. The heat the water releases forms the eye of the typhoon, and the atmospheric pressure in the eye drops below that of the area surrounding it. The result is a low-pressure system that is centered in the eye of the typhoon and that spreads in an ever-increasing circle. The first sign of a typhoon is a rapid drop in barometer readings.

Damp, warm air extending over a large area will breed a typhoon. During our journey from Taiwan to Japan, the average water temperature we measured was 84°. Somewhat farther south, at about 10° north latitude and 130° east longitude, it must have been around 86°. The rotation of the earth sets the circular winds of the typhoon in motion, and in the northern hemisphere they necessarily move counterclockwise. Typhoons cannot form directly on the equator because the vertical component needed for their rotation is lacking.

The eye of a typhoon is usually anywhere from thirty to fifty miles across, but the diameter of an entire typhoon system can often reach massive proportions. Storms six hundred to seven hundred and fifty miles in diameter are not unusual. If such a storm were centered at Pittsburgh, its outer edges would easily reach as far as Chicago and New York. Peak wind velocities can go over 150 mph, and at sea the waves reach proportionate heights.

In the Far East, typhoons rise to the east or southeast of the Philippines and usually follow regular paths. They can occur in any month of the year, but late May has come to be regarded as the beginning of the real typhoon season. More than half the storms during the initial phase of the season move to the northwest and end in the Gulf of Tonkin or over the island of Hainan. Some touch the coast of southern China; relatively few reach Japan.

Almost five times as many typhoons and tropical storms occur in the South China Sea as in the same latitudes of the Atlantic off the coast of North America. In contrast to the American hurricanes and tornadoes that move over land masses and cause untold damage there, the Asiatic typhoons are predominantly sea storms. As soon as they touch land or come in contact with the cooler, drier air of a high-pressure system, they rapidly lose force. As a result, these Asiatic storms are a threat only to islands and coastal areas.

The number of typhoons rises throughout June, and July and August are the peak period of the season. During these months, the pattern of storm movement changes, shifting more toward the east. Tonkin and Hainan are no longer in danger as the typhoons begin to press north and east, hitting Taiwan first, then the Ryukyu Islands, and eventually the major islands of Japan. But the statistics that reflect the general pattern of typhoon movements, like any other statistics, have their failings, and the year 1974 went drastically against the norms of the past. In the first typhoon months of May, June, and July, only two out of eight storms followed the rules and moved west to Tonkin and Hainan. The other six struck Taiwan, Okinawa, or Japan.

The meteorologists of the Royal Observatory in Kowloon and the weather experts of the British Navy in Hong Kong had emphatically warned us not to sail any later than the end of May. The danger of typhoons was too great; worse yet, the *Tai Ki* was simply not capable of dodging storms at sea even if she were informed of them in advance and remained in constant contact with weather bureaus.

We were aware of this danger, and this is why we grew increasingly nervous as our departure kept being delayed week after week past our planned sailing date of May 15. We were all quite familiar with photographs that showed what typhoons had done in the past: scenes of devastated streets in Hong Kong, of oceangoing ships capsized or tossed up on land, of houses demolished. One picture in the Royal Observatory had particularly captured our attention. It showed the remains of a junk that had been smashed against the cliffs of Lantau Island west of Hong Kong in 1962. Nothing was left but a pile of boards. "The crew must have been swept overboard hours before the wreck," a young British meteorologist commented drily. "No survivors were reported."

This photograph reminded me of a Japanese woodcut I had once seen: several junks surrounded by foaming waves. Sailors huddled together on the boats, hung on by their fingernails, clung to every available handhold. They were bent under the lash of the storm, seemed almost in an attitude of prayer on the decks of ships that had long since lost both mast and rudder. Would we too find ourselves helpless before a storm someday soon? Would we too be whirled about in the raging waves, stripped of mast and rudder, until we gave up hope and prayed for the end?

The *Tai Ki* had encountered five typhoons on her trip so far, quite apart from a number of tropical low-pressure systems, and she had come away from them all relatively unharmed. "We're running a typhoon slalom here," Arno had remarked. Would we have to face another one now that we were just about in the clear? Whether typhoon or STS was all one to the crew of the *Tai Ki*. The difference between the two may interest meteorologists working over their maps, but for us it was meaningless. Wind velocities in a typhoon are 75 mph and above. In a severe tropical storm, they reach a "mere" 70 mph. Five miles per hour less doesn't make the waves any lower, the gusts any weaker, the duration of the storm any shorter. No, as far as we were concerned, the difference was purely academic. There was no harbor where we could seek shelter, only the open sea for hundreds of miles around us.

Every five days or so during the first leg of our voyage we received a storm warning, and the crew registered each warning with a deep sigh. We all knew that the first few weeks of our expedition would be the most dangerous and that the possibility of being struck full force by a typhoon was great. But so far the gods of the sea had been kind to us.

Once free of the typhoon belt, we might conceivably have to cope with storms in the open Pacific. Cyclonelike storms occur

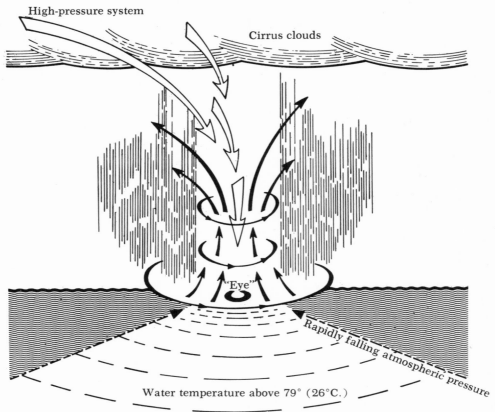

High-pressure system

Cirrus clouds

"Eye"

Rapidly falling atmospheric pressure

Water temperature above 79° (26°C.)

How a typhoon takes shape

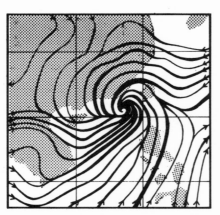

Wind velocity and direction during a typhoon southwest of Taiwan. The increasing thickness of the lines represents increasing wind velocity.

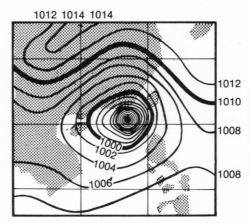

1012 1014 1014

1012
1010
1008

1000
1002
1004
1006
1008

Atmospheric pressures during a typhoon southwest of Taiwan. Each line represents a difference of 2 millibars. Atmospheric pressure at the eye of the typhoon is 980 millibars.

near the international date line, too, storms that meteorologists have only recently become aware of and that are still not recorded on U.S. Navy pilot charts. But the odds of our crossing the mid-Pacific without ever encountering one of these storms were good. We weren't likely to run into any serious trouble again until we neared the American coast. If we found ourselves off Mexico toward the end of November, then we would have to reckon with the possibility of hurricanes, another hazard that could have been avoided if we had sailed from Hong Kong according to our original schedule. But November seemed so remote that we gave it little thought. It was July now. The stretch of time that lay between July and November appeared to us on board the *Tai Ki* like a near eternity. We thought in terms of minutes, possibly hours; even a single day seemed too long a unit of time to comprehend. Plans that stretched weeks and months ahead of us were meaningless. What counted was the job at hand, the here and now. In our tiny universe of some 350 square feet, there was no room for plans and schedules conceived of on a normal time scale. Just as men in prison cannot think in large spans of time, cannot permit themselves to think in such terms because doing so would make it impossible to endure the long wait ahead of them, so the crew of the *Tai Ki* developed a new sense of time. Today was as far ahead as any of us could look.

The ground swells and the waves grew heavier. The ship rose and fell. We waited. We were not particularly preoccupied with the coming danger. There is little point in expending mental energy on events that lie completely beyond our control. We didn't permit our thoughts to race ahead into the future; we concentrated instead on what had to be done right now. For many of us whose normal line of work involved planning far ahead, the adjustment to this kind of immediacy was not easy. We had only simple tasks to perform but didn't find them all that simple. We felt ourselves removed to the mental world of generations long past and began to understand how they, confronting time and the natural world with little more than their primitive beliefs, their native intelligence, and the skills of their hands, could come upon ideas that may strike us in a more rationalistic age as absurd.

Our adventure had two dimensions: one had to do with putting our theory to the test and proving our case. The other had to do with proving ourselves. The crew of the *Tai Ki* consisted of eight men who had deliberately submitted themselves to this test, who had gone out in search of that moment when they would be forced to live to the full. Eight men made up of flesh, blood, and nerves. Eight men in constant danger. Eight frail, vulnerable beings. Shove one of them into the water, leave him under for three or four minutes, and his life is over. Let a spar come crashing down in a storm because someone didn't tie a knot properly a few days ago and his skull is smashed, his brain spattered all over the deck along with all the thoughts, desires, and dreams that had filled it. Nothing is left of him but a few friends' recollections.

We had thought about these things and discussed them in arid hotel rooms in Hong Kong, at the shipyard on Ap Lei Chau, and during leisure hours on board. Now, early in the morning with the storm nearly upon us, the crew members are not occupied with their thoughts but are coping with the stress of the moment in their characteristic ways. Arno works with silent determination. Bill is preparing his camera gear with the calmness of the professional. He keeps out only a bare minimum of equipment and stows the rest below deck. Bob is sitting on his air mattress, studying German. Allan was up all night working at his radio and is stretched out on his back fast asleep now. Hal is checking knots, splices, sheets with agile hands. Wolf tramps around noisily. He is trying to control his nervousness by ceaseless activity. He seems to think that if he hasn't checked the stays four times — no more, no less — they won't stand up to the storm. Maybe he thinks that if he checks three times to see that the life rafts are lashed down securely, that if he does a great many things over and over again in a certain order now, then the storm will be less likely to defeat us later.

I'm sitting on a bamboo stool, trying to put down my impressions and feelings on paper. I'm tempted to write something about courage and heroism, but that would strike a false note. We are simply eight men in a boat on the Pacific, waiting for whatever this storm will bring us. If I wrote about courage, that would be an oversimplification of a complex reality. If I wrote about fear, that would be equally far from the mark. No one is afraid. Everyone is simply braced for what is coming.

Sunday, July 21, 1974. The effects of the tropical low-pressure system are making themselves felt. Wind 25 to 35 mph out of the north. The low must be somewhat to the northeast of us. Wind velocity is increasing and will later rise to gale force, 9 on the Beaufort scale. Heavy seas, low cloud cover. During the night the barometer dropped only a few points. By 2200 it had fallen to 29.3 and is steady there. Temperature: 80°. Waves: 20 feet, sometimes higher. Course: 90°, but we are drifting rapidly off course to the south. Ship's speed: 2.5 to 3 knots per hour. At 0400 the low was centered at 32° north latitude, 145° east longitude. Heavy seas throughout the night. Sleep was well-nigh impossible. We were tossed from our beds repeatedly. I was thrown on top of Arno, then onto Wolf, nicked my head pretty badly. It's a wonder that we got any sleep at all. Toward morning I decided to tie myself down. I pawed around in the dark but couldn't find any rope. Result: I was thrown again and smashed my back against the mast.

In the morning I was a bit seasick. Bob tried to help me recover my sense of balance with acupuncture treatment on my right ear. I haven't noticed any improvement.

The ship is tossing so much that it's almost impossible to write. My journal has been "washed out" by two waves. One of them smashed into our dog, too, and sent him hightailing below deck. In the morning we set our watches ahead two hours. Now we have our own special ship's time. We did this to make the evening longer and save kerosene that readers and chess players would otherwise consume.

Afternoon. Whole gale, 10 Beaufort. Very heavy seas. Average size of waves: 25 feet, peaks up to 30 feet. Our course is still 90°. Wind still out of the north. We've experienced some crosswinds. The *Tai Ki* is heeling heavily, and we continue to be driven off course to the south. This drifting has clearly cost us a number of miles headway. Hal, Wolf, and I have asked Carl Frederik to change the course to at least 120°, but he has refused.

Seen through the narrow doors of the helmsman's cabin the sea looks more threatening than it is in reality. When the ship heels over to a forty-five-degree angle, it seems to take an eternity to right itself again. The horizon disappears. The sea becomes a self-contained landscape comparable to a desert with its dunes and swells of sand or to the snow-covered peaks the alpinist sees lying motionless all around him once he has reached his goal.

But the sea moves. Its waves are peaks in motion, and it is precisely this motion that throws the force of the sea into relief, makes the power of this element so vividly clear. The phrase "waves as high as a house" comes to mind, but the comparison is a poor one, the image inadequate. True, many buildings may stand much higher than any wave that ever rose out of the sea. But buildings are motionless. They convey nothing of the unpredictable force of the sea, nothing of the life contained in these waves that angle toward our ship, heave it up into the air, plunge it into a valley, smash against its planking, explode into thousands of foaming torrents, pour over the deck, rise and subside again, driven by a force that we can only begin to comprehend when we consider how easily, how playfully it tosses this thirty-ton ship about time after time, all day long. What kinds of mechanical aid and what kind of energy would men have to develop to duplicate just once what nature does here repeatedly — in play and with her left hand?

Bob jumps up from his air mattress to go after some canned goods below deck and fill up the water container. He takes hold of the hatchway with his broad, laborer's hands, then hollers for the water pump. Wolf is lying on deck and reading. He hears Bob call and yells back, "You can kiss my . . ." But he gets up and helps Bob nonetheless.

Cursing the whole time, Bob drags the freshly filled water container back up on deck. On August 6, the ship's doctor of the *Tai Ki* will celebrate his thirty-fourth birthday with a bottle of whiskey. He is a stocky, muscular Englishman who had come to Hong Kong to study acupuncture. He joined the expedition because he "felt like going to America again." He'd traveled there once before as ship's doctor on a passenger boat that had sailed from England to the east coast of South America.

Bob had a penchant for drastic language and jokes. As a rule, he took things as they came and rarely lost his temper. He could be angry, but his anger usually found release in bouts of intense work, unless one of our debates about food had roused his ire.

At night he studied the stars, together with Bill, Allan, and Arno; sat on the railing, playing Spanish and South American songs on his guitar; spoke Spanish; learned German on board and made incredible progress in it in a matter of a few weeks; studied Morse code with Allan. This last project was so important to him that it sometimes interfered with work that had to be done.

Nothing seemed to touch him directly, and an ironic, almost cynical, attitude, which sometimes expressed itself in a biting humor more appropriate to a sixty-year-old than to a man of Bob's age, helped him maintain a certain distance from people and events. With hands that seemed totally unsuited to holding a pen, much less to guiding a scalpel or syringe, he made delicate sketches of fish and seashells. He groomed his beard carefully and gave as much attention to his short shipboard haircut as he had to the long locks he had cut off early in the voyage. Beautiful women were an important part of his life. His American girl friend, whom he had brought on board the *Tai Ki* in Hong Kong, could easily have decorated the cover of a magazine, and many a *Playboy* reader would have envied him the pictures he had made of her, not to mention the model herself.

It was easy to imagine Bob as a Kitchener or Livingston, sent by Queen Victoria to find an oasis somewhere in the Sudan and establish a trading station there. He would quietly set about his business, overcome all hardships in his matter-of-fact way, set up the post, sing songs to a Nubian maid in his free time, draw her face, her body, would return to England and submit his laconic report: "Mission accomplished." Then he would set out for the nearest pub and order himself a beer, just as if he'd returned from a day's outing on the Thames.

Every crew member is dependent on the others, and just how he reacts to that dependence is crucial not only for his personal psychic balance but also for his effectiveness as a member of the crew. Later, in Seattle, we would be able to determine who had played what role and how. The extreme conditions of the expedition stripped away much more of our shells than any "laboratory experiment" could have, not, surprisingly enough, because it forced us to show what we were and what we were feeling, but because it prompted us to show what we thought would heighten our personal prestige in the group and so heighten the pleasure we took in being part of the crew.

It was unimportant whether one crew member expressed admiration or ridicule for another. Indeed, ridicule was a much more direct way of relating to others than admiration, and it is possible that the sum of impressions of and admiration for another crew member amounted to a far less positive social result than the sum of impressions plus ridicule plus the distance from the other that the ridicule provided. The opportunity to smirk at someone else or make fun of something he did created in the person making the judgment a sensation of pleasure that helped him befriend the person he was ridiculing. But anyone who stifled his reactions, be they positive or negative, and closed himself off to the others, anyone who refused to let anyone else have any share in his actions, feelings, and desires, constituted a danger not only for the crew but for himself as well, himself most of all, for he committed the most mortal of sins that can be committed in a tightly knit group of this kind: he isolated himself and at the same time offended the others. He continued to take from them, but he returned only very little or nothing at all. This was the man who sinned most against our small shipboard society.

The typhoons we experienced subjected every one of us to what might be called a series of experiments in group behavior. Differences in national character began to appear in a variety of subtle manifestations: Bill Martin displayed American sociability and affability; Wolf, a German penchant for order; Hal, the openness of the Irish; Arno and Kuno, the rough and bumptious ways of the Austrians; Carl and Allan, the quiet reserve of the Scandinavians. These are obviously clichés, but during our first days together there was evidence enough that these clichés had some basis in fact. Only after weeks and months together were we able to penetrate these patterns of behavior and really see the man next to us; only then could we recognize all the ramifications and subtleties of his mind, assuming he was willing to share them with us.

It was interesting to see, for example, how Hal Price, an experienced sailor who had taken part in the South China Sea Race only a few months ago, did not try to impress us with his nautical knowledge but kept himself in the background and was hardly noticeable except for the fact that he went about his work with the confidence and competence of the expert. Yet despite his near invisibility, he was fully integrated into the group and an essential part of it. His journal entries for this period focus on his wife, Mary, whom he had left behind in Hong Kong and with whom he shared a close bond that still left him his freedom.

Allan was the image of Nordic stoicism and calm. He went about his work with the precision of a machine and remained unruffled no matter what the circumstances. Conversations with him were always brief; he never said a word too many; perhaps he said too few sometimes. He never voluntarily extended conversations, and he usually concluded them with a brusque nod, a gruff "Yes" or "O.K." Anyone who wanted more than a minimum of communication with Allan would have to carry the conversational ball most of the time himself.

From the very beginning of the voyage, he held to a rigorous training schedule worthy of a professional athlete. He pedaled three miles a day on his generator bike, then worked up to six miles, finally to ten. He was the only crew member who really held to his resolution to stop smoking. At breakfast he heaped malt extract, dextrose, and cocoa on his cereal to help him "build up strength," as he put it. Allan did neither more nor less than what he conceived to be his share. He could lie still for hours at a time, waiting for who knows what, and if one of us asked him what he was doing, he would answer, "The sea has taught me the art of waiting."

None of us could help noticing that Arno liked to speak sarcastically about other people's fear. He certainly wasn't doing so to hide his own, because he, with all he had experienced and accomplished, was probably the last of us who would ever feel any. But it was clear nonetheless that he was searching for some way to deal with this new situation. And since he was unable to articulate exactly what it was he was feeling, he initiated dialogue by means of provocation. He did so by passing judgments on others without being willing to consider whether his judgments were correct or not. He challenged, attacked, and exposed himself to both challenge and attack. The reactions he elicited in this way were dialogue enough for him in the first phase of the journey.

"You have to be ready to open up," he said. "It's the same on any kind of expedition. You've got to be open to everyone else."

He made his first close contacts on board with Wolf and Kuno, but that had less to do with personal preference than it did with the fact that they shared his native language. Arno worked hard to form a community and to keep it alive.

Carl Frederik tried to avoid it, or he at least created the impression that he was trying to avoid it. Perhaps he just had a totally different conception of it than we did. He and Allan were something of a pair in their willfulness and in their insistence on their rights. Grage wasn't prepared to give an inch, neither to storms nor to the crew. He seemed to be engaged in a special personal struggle, not only with the sea but with something else as well.

And then there was Bill Martin, big, blond, broad-shouldered, energetic; big Bill, who loved to talk about sangría and port wine and who could revel like a French gourmet in the glories of foods, spices, specialties, and restaurants. He kept inviting us all — "as soon as we're ashore again" — to join him in this restaurant near Washington or in that one in Boston or in still another in Santa Monica. And he had as hearty an appetite for women as he did for food and drink, this tall American with a Latin temperament.

As the storm grew more intense around us, he fell silent, disappeared for a few minutes, then turned up again with his life jacket on. He didn't act from fear but from caution. He had acted more rationally than any of us, had simply made use of the means available to him to improve his chances against sea and storm. Old tars might have considered him over-cautious, but there wasn't one of us who could claim to be an experienced sailor on this kind of ship, not in those first weeks, at any rate. There is no one around who can teach the handling of ships designed at the time of Christ's birth. And if anyone thinks these ships function like any other sailing ship, then he is suffering under more illusions than we harbored when we first conceived of our expedition. Bamboo spars are made of different stuff and react differently from spars made of oak, pine, or other woods. A sail of rattan matting doesn't bear the faintest resemblance to one of canvas. It behaves differently both in light and heavy winds, fills differently, does not belly out but simply yields a little to the pressure of the wind.

The kinds and combinations of woods used for hulls of different types and even in individual ships of the same type can vary a great deal. A junk is no more a North Sea cutter than it is a Malayan prau. I have never seen boats maneuver as effortlessly as the junks in Aberdeen harbor, nor have I ever seen such apparently clumsy vessels as the fishing junks off the Chinese coast wheel and turn with such grace. Then, too, planks that are held together with wooden pins behave differently from ones that are nailed or bound together with metal strapping. A rudder controlled by ropes requires a different touch from one controlled by a lever or wheel. During the first run we ever made in a junk, we were particularly impressed by the helmsman, by the way he stood in the stern, controlling the rudder lines with the delicacy of a puppeteer and steering his boat with a precision that the most modern steering mechanism would be hard pressed to match.

Every ship, and a wooden one especially, has its own life, follows laws that not even the builder can predict and that he can come to understand only after long acquaintance with the finished ship. No, anyone who claims we were experts in our field is far from the truth, and anyone who assumes we could have been or should have been experts has no idea of what our ship and our undertaking involved.

It could not be said that the *Tai Ki* was an easy ship to sail. Her construction was too complex to allow for that kind of simplicity, but, on the other hand, she wasn't so complicated that only a highly experienced crew could handle her. She was a cross between a raft, a cutter, and a yacht, and in reality she was every bit as unusual as this description of her makes her sound. The lines of her hull distinguished her from all other junks in the Far East, and she differed from them in just about every aspect of handling, too. And any comparison with European vessels of comparable size seems so farfetched as to be impossible. She was, to put it succinctly, unique. She reacted to every wave and every breath of wind as only she could react.

No, we were far from being experts. Whenever Carl, Arno, and I sat proudly on the forward deck and traded glances of satisfaction, we were not indicating by them that we thought we had accomplished anything grandiose with our ship. We were conveying to each other not so much a sense of pride in our expertise as a simple delight in having accomplished what we had set out to accomplish. How often in his life does a man experience that kind of delight? It had taken us eight years to do everything that needed to be done. In that time we had found someone who had faith enough in us to put up the necessary money; we had built a ship, organized an expedition, found a crew. We had done all that in spite of everyone who had tried to discourage us and written us off as fools. Many people had laughed at us, especially while we were still in the planning stage and still living our normal, everyday lives. We had met with ridicule and amazement. This ridicule had piqued us, of course, but not wounded us deeply. We even had to admit that those people who called us arrogant might be right. But isn't there an element of arrogance in any venture that breaks out of the routine?

Perhaps we were arrogant, but if we were, our arrogance took a naive form. Indeed, naiveté often appears to be arrogance, particularly when it is a naiveté consciously assumed. We had deliberately chosen to be naive. We couldn't begin to pretend that we were acting on reason. We had kicked over the traces, had left careers temporarily behind to follow a will-o'-the-wisp. We didn't pretend to be acting rationally.

The crew of the *Tai Ki* was braced for the worst. The ship staggered under the heavy seas, pitched from crest to trough, climbed, pitched down again. The ship's clock read 1500. The wind was gusty and probably reached top speeds of 60 mph. I gave up my place at the rudder to Carl Frederik, stumbled forward to my sleeping place, put on my life jacket and blue safety belt. I moved toward the bow, thrown against the cabin walls at every step, and finally reached the forward deck. Normal movements were impossible in such heavy seas. The crew members either kept to their air mattresses or grumblingly performed essential tasks. Our ship's dog peered wretchedly out from under the deck boards he had chosen as his retreat. I had never seen a seasick dog before, but Lap Sac was seasick. There was no doubt about it. Bob remarked that Lap Sac looked appreciably paler than usual. Nothing could move this otherwise eternally hungry mutt to approach his dish. And for a seafaring dog of his appetite that's saying a lot. His ears hung over his eyes; the furrows on his brow were deeper than ever; and every unusually violent motion of the ship elicited groans from the poor beast. He had come on board as a puppy; the ship was the only world he knew. And now, in this storm, it was a world gone mad. No wonder he sank into utter despair. He couldn't take a step without being tossed one way or another, either onto Wolf, who cursed him for a goddam miserable mutt and shoved him away, or onto Bill, who reached out to pet him. But before Lap Sac could receive this gesture of kindness, he was thrown into still another corner. Even his retreat under the deck planking offered little peace or security, for the ship often pitched so steeply that Lap Sac suddenly disappeared, slid forward under the deck, and smashed up against a timber, only to come crawling and whining into view again a few minutes later. Lap Sac's world was definitely out of kilter. It had been out of kilter at 0700; it was no better at 1200; and in the course of the afternoon, as the seas grew heavier still, it became a perfect hell.

The blurred pages of my journal, drenched by the storm, read:

A bit after 1500. Carl Frederik has just relieved me at the rudder. Now I have the watch on the forward deck. Bent over, I step out from under the sheltering roof and stand face to face with what we usually, and inadequately, describe as an "elemental force." Now, six hours later as I write this, the only expression I can find that conveys what I saw is: mountains rising up and rolling toward me.

I tied my safety line around the mast and clipped the snaphook into the ring on my blue nylon belt. It was impossible to stand up, so I squeezed myself between the mast and cabin. The sea boiled and seethed around me. The *Tai Ki* soared out of the water, then plunged into depths from which it seemed the ship could not possibly emerge again. At the same time, massive waves rolled into her from the side, picked her up, sent her diving down again. The heavy cross waves made themselves all too clearly seen and felt, waves rushing in from different directions, smashing into each other with incredible force, tossing up mountains of foam, breeding new waves, thundering against the hull and setting the whole ship trembling.

We had reefed most of our rattan sail, leaving only two spars and the one span of matting between them set. That much sail was essential for steerageway. Still, we could almost feel the drift, could almost see our ship being driven to starboard and to the south, but there was nothing we could do to prevent it. Our rudder had been a source of woe to us from the outset of the expedition. Now it creaked and groaned in its mountings. Its complaints could be heard anywhere on the ship, even on the forward deck, where the roar of the storm was deafening.

Suddenly there seemed to be some kind of change taking place in this raging seascape. I didn't notice it at first but perceived it only a bit later, just as one perceives the silence that follows a loud noise only a few seconds after the noise has ceased. I didn't want to notice the change. But I felt it despite myself. In the distance, beyond all the waves that surrounded us, one wave rose up and towered above the others. It was coming toward us from the north. The fact that it was higher, larger, more powerful than all the others around it did not come home to me immediately. My consciousness simply couldn't absorb what my eyes were seeing. Only after a minute or two did I understand.

The *Tai Ki* rose up on a wave about thirty feet high, and right behind that wave, perhaps a hundred or two hundred yards to port, stood a wall of water that seemed to reach into infinity. Our ship slid down into the trough, and then I saw nothing but this living wall, this green-gray, foaming, hissing organism, moving toward me. Waves formed within the wave, small breakers racing down this precipice of water and wind. But despite them, the wall — some three hundred, perhaps five hundred yards wide — remained relatively smooth. The sea spread itself out before my eyes like an abstract mural framed in foam. Streaks of color stabbed across the dark, muted tones of the background. What I saw had the force of a huge sacred painting in the cathedral of the Pacific, a masterpiece born of the sea to her own greater glory.

I could only guess where the peak of the wave might be. I was unable to see it or even to estimate how high it was, just as I was unable, in these first moments, to think in any dimensions adequate to the reality before me. All comparison failed. And, of course, I had failed. As a lookout I had failed completely and totally. I hadn't given any signal at all, hadn't given the slightest warning. I deserved the worst punishment anyone could have devised, for I had forgotten everything around me and had surrendered to the fascination of a spectacle that seemed to be enacting itself in slow motion but that in fact moved to its conclusion with incredible speed. What I saw had cast a spell over me, and nothing could have pried me loose from my post.

Six hours later I wrote in my journal:

A wall of water rose up before me. Our boat struggled to climb it. It was difficult to estimate the size of the wave. I thought at first that it must have exceeded the height of our mast by quite a bit. The mast is forty-eight feet high. Mounted in the boat it stands some fifty-five feet above the water. The mountain that rolled down on us must have been a good sixty feet high, but I wouldn't be at all surprised if it had been several feet higher still. I can't say for sure. My first association was a film I'd seen in New York, *The Poseidon Adventure*. The film showed a passenger ship capsizing in a 120-foot tidal wave. Then I thought, "I've got to get my camera. We've got to have pictures of this." My next thought: "I should get Bill to take the pictures." Only then did I finally think, "I ought to warn the crew."

This could be the end. Maybe it is! Yet there's something almost beautiful about it. The *Tai Ki* hangs on. I'd like to be watching from another ship. How long can we keep on going up? How much longer? We've almost reached the top. We can almost look down into the next trough. Only fifteen or twenty feet to go. Then the wave breaks over us with an ear-shattering roar. The water pins me down between cabin and mast. I cling to whatever will offer me a hold. Air, I've got to have air! There seems to be no end to the water pouring down on us. I feel the ship twist about under me. Have we gone over? A moment of terror and panic. I'm going to drown! Then the boat breaks free, glides into the trough, releasing me from the grip of the water that had held me down. I'm lying on the deck, gasping for breath. My hands fumble for the snap-hook and open it. I crawl into the cabin. Disaster reigns there. Everything that wasn't tied down — and even what was — is tumbling about inside. Water is still streaming in through the roof. Bill is the first to speak. "I thought we'd had it." What are Hal and Allan feeling? I'm struck by the fact that Arno is very calm. Wolf says, "That ought to be against the rules. That kind of stuff ought to be against the rules."

Bob has been thrown up against the bamboo wall. All our kitchen utensils, all the things that are usually hanging on the opposite wall, are lying around him. He has his arms full of pots and pans, cooking spoons, plastic bowls, tin cans, cooking oil. A ridiculous picture. He snorts and curses. The dog is with him, soaked to the skin. In his first panic, Lap Sac ran to his master, Bob Kendrick. Now, dripping wet like everything around him, he is searching frantically for a place to hole up again.

Hal's journal:

I was sitting in the cabin, talking to Bob, who was getting something out of the medicine chest for me, when the wave hit us full amidships. The

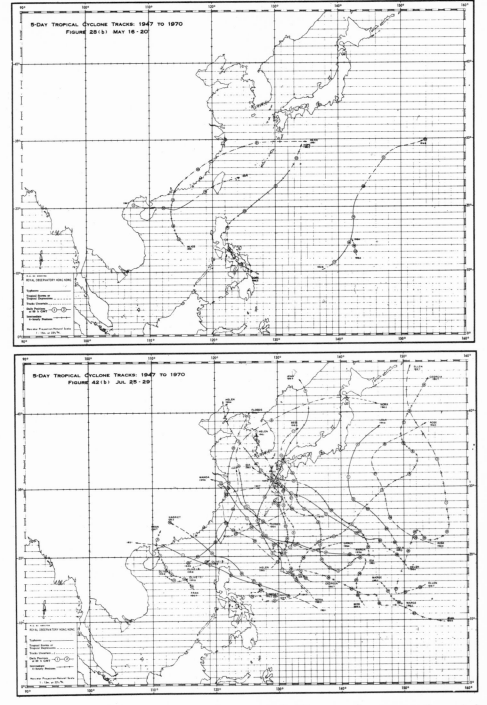

Frequency of typhoons in the years 1947 to 1970. The map above covers the period from May 16 to May 20; that below, from July 25 to July 29. (Maps published by the Royal Observatory in Hong Kong, 1972)

Left and previous page: Nobody kept track of the number of storm warnings that we received or of the number of typhoons we encountered. Again and again waves rose up before us, broke and spilled over deck, poured through the ship. That may sound romantic, but for the men on board, the romance soon wore thin. We could not photograph or film the worst — or most dramatic — storms because at those times everybody was much too busy to man a camera. (Both к)

The junk struggles against waves that sweep over the forward deck. The sail seems to be dipping into the sea, and every last square inch of the ship is drenched. (K)

Above right: The worse the storm becomes, the more essential it is to check the stays and keep them taut. (D)
Lower right: Arno at the helm. Even though the tiller was controlled by an elaborate system of pulleys, heavy seas could still make a watch at the helm a Herculean task. (K)

Between storms the Pacific Ocean occasionally lived up to its name. At such times Lap Sac sought human contact and refused to let Bob and Allan's intentions to practice Morse code stand in his way . . . (BM)

Right: The metamorphosis of Robert Kendrick. Our long-haired doctor suddenly reached for the scissors and began trimming his abundant foliage. When he was done, he looked like a galley slave. "Quite an appropriate guise under the circumstances," Hal observed. (BM)(D)(D)

. . . or Bob would pick up his guitar, settle himself on the forward deck, and pick out Spanish melodies. "I've got to practice," he said with a grin, "so that I'll be able to make a good impression when we get to Mexico." After a long day's work moments of quiet contemplation in the rays of the setting sun . . . (BM)

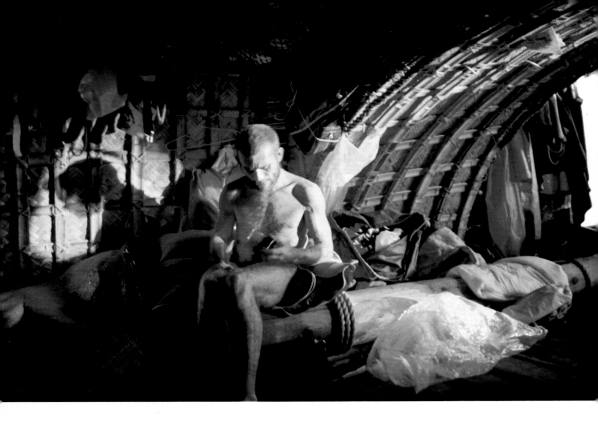

Above: Bob in his private quarters. Here, in this corner behind the spare mast, he lived, slept, studied German and Spanish, smoked his pipe, lounged, and meditated. It was his monastic cell on board our tiny ship. (D)

Above right: After a three months' hunt, Carl triumphed over the rat. All its cleverness finally proved of no avail. Here, locked up in its cage, the rat is confronted with evidence of its maraudings: a canvas bag and Allan's plastic sack, both with holes gnawed in them. (P)

Lower right: Lap Sac sniffs curiously at his new shipmate. Now that the rat has become an "official" crew member, it receives a name: "Pericles of the Pacific." (K)

Above: A sea turtle that had been foolish enough to come too close to the junk was the most unusual prey captured during the voyage. After we hauled the turtle on board, Bob put his surgical skills to good use and prepared the turtle for the kitchen. For the next two days, we had the opportunity to develop a strong aversion to turtle stew. (D)
Left: Dorados circled the ship in great numbers and were our favorite table fish. Arno harpooned this one. (D)

Guests on board the *Tai Ki*.
One of many flying fish that landed on deck. Bob had meant to take this prize specimen home as a souvenir, but the next morning there was nothing left of it but a few bones. The rat, still at liberty at the time, had struck again. . . . (BM)

A small bird makes itself at home on one of our charts. Although the *Tai Ki* was hundreds of miles away from the nearest land, we suspected that this visitor was a land bird, not a sea bird. But then none of us were knowledgeable enough about birds to be sure. (G)

A remora we found attached to our captured sea turtle. (D)

This elegant, white-vested sailor was our first visitor. He spent two days relaxing with us. Here he is taking his ease next to Allan on top of the helmsman's cabin. Since there were no ornithologists among us who could tell us what his proper name was, we called him "John." (BM)

Encounters on the high seas. *Above:* A Chinese warship crosses our bow and continues on its course without taking any apparent notice of our nutshell. (ʙᴍ)

Right: A Japanese fishing boat comes up alongside the *Tai Ki*. Four of our crew leap into the rubber dinghy and row over to the visitor, fired by hopes of a few bottles of beer. All they got for their pains was spaghetti and soda pop. The Japanese fishermen called over to us, "Hong Kong — America?" We gleefully replied in the affirmative, delighted that our reputation had already spread so far on the seven seas. (ᴅ)

Overleaf: Sunset in the Pacific. (ʙᴍ)

roar was deafening, and the ship trembled violently. Somebody was pouring water over me, one bucketful after another; there seemed to be no end to it. . . . The floor was flooded, and water streamed in endlessly through the roof. We'd taken a direct hit. . . . Kuno was outside when the wave struck. He was lucky it didn't sweep him off the deck. . . . As soon as we'd recovered a bit, Carl asked me to check everything below deck. He and Arno would check topside. . . . There was no obvious damage anywhere above the waterline. No doubt about it: we were plug lucky. It's clear that we shouldn't sail the *Tai Ki* parallel to such heavy seas. We'll have to watch out for that in the future. The next big wave may not be so kind to us. . . .

Bill wrote:

It happened in the early afternoon, something like 1530. I should mention that we were warm, dry, and contented and feeling secure. That was at 1529. A minute later we were groaning and moaning in terror. The wave must have been at least forty feet high . . . seawater poured through our roof of rattan matting and flooded everything in a matter of seconds. Inside the cabin, it looked as though a gigantic hand had picked up the *Tai Ki* and shaken her. I looked at Bob Kendrick's face, and hard as it may be to believe, I could see in it that he thought we were finished. I know I thought so myself. We were incredibly lucky that only one wave like that hit us.

We were sailing a course that I can only describe as insane. Most of the day we were running parallel to the waves in a very heavy sea. I would have given a lot to get some pictures, but I didn't have a chance to take any. The overall length of the *Tai Ki* is about sixty feet, and she's heavy; I don't know exactly how many tons. But she was still tossed around like a cork. And what we've been through is by no means the heaviest sea we'll run into. How will she take the next one?

Bob's journal:

The watch had just been changed when it happened. Kuno had just gone outside, and he saw this damn monstrous wave that was probably fifty feet high, maybe more. The bloody thing took us right amidships. I was sitting inside on the spare mast and pawing through my medicine kit when it struck. Torrents of water poured through the woven mats and sent the kitchen gear, along with everything else in sight, flying in all directions. Most of the stuff seemed to land on me. The dog howled and looked like a drowned rat. The whole place was flooded. We spent the next few hours getting the ship — and ourselves — back to normal.

Kuno's journal:

Arno is hanging overboard on ropes, looking for damage. Practically nothing seems to be broken. But everything, absolutely everything, is wallowing in the flood. Our clothes are drenched, our cooking gear, our sleeping bags. Carl has retired to his cabin. He has decided to change the course; we're sailing 120° to 150° now. It's the general opinion at supper that if we run into two or three more waves like that, one after another, the voyage of the *Tai Ki* will be over. Carl thinks we must have been hit by a tidal wave, because a single wave of that size in such a heavy sea is extremely unusual. It is obvious that our winds are coming from two directions with the north wind dominant. The circular air currents of the low-pressure system to the north-northeast of us are sending the north wind our way. That we were experiencing two separate winds was also clear from the fact that we felt two distinct temperatures.

The crew members recovered quickly, even though they still had to cope with continuingly heavy seas. The typhoons Ivy and Jean reached Taiwan the next day, just as the weather reports predicted they would. Tropical storm Frederick hadn't struck us with its full force, but the *Tai Ki* was very close to the storm center nevertheless, probably no more than fifty miles away from it. The seas continued heavy, with waves ranging from fifteen to twenty or twenty-five feet. Storm conditions held through the afternoon and night. The winds abated only gradually. At 1600 the next day, we measured a wind velocity of 30 mph, still quite a fresh little breeze.

According to our most recent weather reports, our low-pressure system has moved ashore over Japan. Allan received these reports on his special radio equipment. The crew of the *Tai Ki* will have to do without its weather reports from the cabin radio for the time being. The set was ruined in yesterday's flood.

It would be something of a distortion to call the crew's mood good at this point. Everyone is nervous, still tense, still over-wrought. There are arguments. Mistakes are made. Bill, who has KP, loses his footing as he goes to wash out the bread pans. He almost goes overboard. Carl and I are able to catch him by the ankles at literally the last moment. We leapt for him like two tigers on their prey. If he had gone over in this weather, his chances would have been close to nil. In a matter of minutes, certainly before we could have done anything concrete to save him, he would have been swept away in the boiling waves. And all because he miscalculated the force of an oncoming wave, or didn't even notice it, or possible had his weight shifted onto the wrong foot, or happened to turn his body at just the wrong mo-ment — silly mistakes that can be deadly on shipboard — and also because he, Bill, our most careful crew member, had forgot-ten to wear his safety belt.

After that incident, we were more cautious. For the next two nights after the storm, Wolf and I kept our life jackets handy next to our sleeping bags. As I recall, Bill and Bob did the same. And Wolf went out onto the forward deck every hour, day and night, to check on the life rafts.

CHAPTER SIX

The Silence of the Sea

THE CREW MEMBERS WERE BEGINNING TO KNOW EACH OTHER, beginning to know the sea, her storms, her swells, her stillness, beginning to know their ship, her sounds and her reactions.

We had had a chance to prove ourselves in action during the storms we had been through but hardly a chance to come to terms with ourselves and each other. Arno made attempts in this direction by trying to systematize our work on board. Carl made no attempts to mold us into a crew because he assumed what he could not legitimately assume either for himself or for the rest of us: namely, a thorough understanding of what had to be done in any situation. He declined to talk about the crew as a team and how it could be made into a team. Communications from him were limited to orders, the organization of duty rosters, and announcements of course and position. Slim pickings.

External circumstances kept tension high. We would barely have come clear of one storm before Allan received word that the next one was on its way. During the first leg of our voyage, he was the most important individual in the crew, for it was he who kept us in touch with the rest of the world.

Back in Hong Kong Allan had set about developing a radio network for the *Tai Ki*. He hoped to stay in constant touch with radio hams all over the world for as long as possible. His main contacts were Danny, an American working in the United States Consulate in Hong Kong, and a team of hams in Sweden.

The radio club in the little Swedish city of Nynäshamn had set up a *Tai Ki* radio service and, by means of a special postcard, had notified other amateur radio men throughout the world that it would maintain radio contact with OZ-6 QK/MM for the duration of the expedition. Behind that mysterious designation lurked none other than Allan Kartin.

We soon became familiar with all the names of our Swedish friends: Arne Andersson, Erik Rothstein, Alf Svensson, Kjell Andersson the "Wednesday Man," Axel Westgard, Lennart Durèn. And they would show themselves to be real friends in need later on.

Allan's decision to concentrate his energies on a network of ham radio stations proved to be a sound one. The radio shack on the *Tai Ki* contained sets designed for contacting coast guard stations and other ships, but the range of this equipment was limited. Depending on conditions in the ionosphere, we could communicate over distances of 600 to 1,000 nautical miles. On land, those distances may seem considerable, but in the vast reaches of the Pacific they shrink to insignificance. Contact with ham radio stations is at least theoretically possible over any distance.

Allan had three means of supplying his radio shack with electricity. The first was his generator bike, which provided about 50 percent of the required electricity. Windmills mounted on the helmsman's cabin provided another 30 percent but had, of course, their serious limitations. In a calm they were worthless. Allan's third source was solar energy. The collectors he used were excellent, but they too were dependent on the weather.

The coast guard stations and other official transmitters could offer us only terse routine messages, but our amateur contacts gave us much more extensive service. Quite apart from the detailed reports we each received from our homes, we also had the

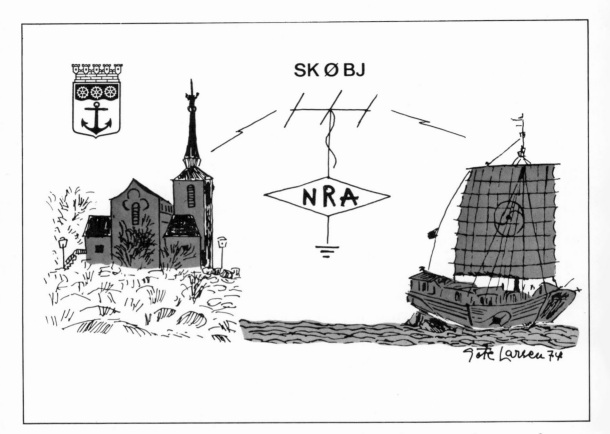

It is customary among amateur radiomen to confirm radio messages by means of a so-called QLS card. Because the ham radio club in Nynäshamn, Sweden, planned to maintain constant contact with the *Tai Ki,* it had this special QLS card printed.

peculiar experience of first learning about developing low-pressure systems in our area not from the Japanese or Taiwanese coast guard but via Hong Kong and Sweden. Danny would send the message over a distance of seven thousand miles to Nynäshamn, and from there it would be sent another eight thousand miles to us on the *Tai Ki*.

After a while at sea and with the help of his Swedish contacts, Allan was able to expand his network even farther to in-

To Radio   **Confirming QSO:**

DATE	GMT	MHz	2 way	RST

LAEN B FOR WASM   B 11 for SCA

Rig: .... W

Ant.: ....

Rmx.: ....

....

PSE **QSL** via SSA, S-122 48 Enskede,
TNX   Sweden or direct

Operator SM...

TNX FER QSO ES VY 73!   ....

Amateur Radio Station SK Ø BJ
Box 71, S-149 01 NYNESHAMN Sweden

To Radio ....

....

....

....

The Nyneshamn Amateur Radio Club will during June-October 1974 have radio contact with OZ 6 QK/MM (Allan Kartin from Denmark) on board TAI KI.
TAI KI is an expedition, with 8 persons, using an old Chinese junk sailing over the Pacific. The purpose of the expedition is to prove that the Chinese could have discovered America about fifteen hundred years before Columbus.

Printed in co-operation with Lion:s Club, Nyneshamn.

clude a station in the Philippines, one in Ceylon, and one in Austria. Arno and I were quite touched one night to hear the unmistakable accent of our Austrian contact come through to us as he said in English, "This is Leo speaking. . . ." Leo was located near Wels, a small town about 120 miles west of Vienna. He was seldom able to make direct contact with us. "But," he told us later, "my radio contact with Nynäshamn was as good as anybody could want it." Leo kept our families and friends regularly informed of the *Tai Ki*'s position and related to them how both crew and ship were faring.

Although our expedition roused little interest in Austria, it held considerable appeal for Scandinavians, perhaps because two Danes were involved. At any rate, a bookstore in Stockholm displayed a map of the Pacific in its show window and marked the *Tai Ki*'s progress on it as reports of our positions came in.

Allan was envied for the invisible link he had with the outside world. News flowed to and from our ship via his radio shack, and he went about his work conscientiously and untiringly. The watches were so organized that no crew member ever got more than six hours' sleep, but Allan came away with even less than that. He was in his radio shack every night at midnight — the agreed-on time for receiving and sending messages — and he usually put in at least an hour's work there each night. He was always at his post, regardless of whether he had just come off a watch or had one coming up in two hours. The rest of the crew took over night watches for him frequently, but his burden still remained greater than anyone else's.

I wrote of Allan in my journal:

He tends to his radio duties with a care and earnestness that I find remarkable; perhaps equally admirable are his systematic approach to his work and his rigorous adherence, even here on board the *Tai Ki,* to the laws his radio operator's license imposes on him.

And there is something downright conspiratorial about him when he turns up at breakfast with tiny letters in his hand and passes them over to one crew member or another. They rarely say more than "Everything's fine here at home" or "We're all well," but even these communications, reduced to a bare minimum by distance and circumstances, seem to him much too private to be revealed to anyone but the person to whom they are addressed. Messages of this kind don't reach us often, and much as we may talk about that faraway world beyond the horizon, these signals we receive from it arouse little interest. The crew is too preoccupied with life on the ship to react to Allan's carefully folded notes with anything more than astonishment over the fact that we are still in contact with the world we have left behind.

Only later, when Allan's radio equipment failed and all contact with the outside world was cut off, did the crew understand how much this tie had meant to us.

Toward the end of July the *Tai Ki* lay becalmed about four hundred miles southeast of Japan. The water dropped off below us to a depth of thirty thousand feet; we were over the Ramapo Deep of the Japan Trench. The Pacific was living up to its name.

We enjoyed an ideal day for swimming. But then it was followed by another equally ideal day. And another and another. Wolf wrote in his journal: "Nothing is more nerve-racking than a calm at sea. A calm is far more dangerous for the morale of the crew than any storm or typhoon. Two weeks of calm, four weeks of calm interrupted only by occasional puffs of air are more debilitating than a voyage through endless storms." Wolf was quoting from the journal of Captain Cook, the great English explorer who sailed around the world three times and discovered almost all the islands of the Pacific from Hawaii and Tahiti to New Zealand.

In the past weeks, the steady stream of storm warnings had caused the crew many a sleepless night, but at the same time storms had their encouraging aspect, too, because they meant we would have wind, lots of wind. And that meant we would move rapidly ahead and make up for lost time.

But now we lay becalmed. Not a breath of wind for days on end. At first we enjoyed the rest the calm afforded us after the strain of the storm. A holiday mood prevailed on board. But then there seemed to be no end to the heat. The air temperature hovered around 90°, the water around 85°. There was no way we could cool off, no cold shower, no iced drink. Things were no better at night. We ran around naked; even the lightest piece of clothing soon hung dripping wet on the body. The heat began to take possession of us. Our movements were languid; the slightest activity drew torrents of sweat. We crawled into the shadows, but there was no breeze to clear the cabin of damp, sticky air. The sun poured down unmercifully on the open deck, day in, day out. We soon had enough of doing nothing, of killing time. And we started to worry: how many miles have we lost today? How far behind on our schedule are we now? Our days are lost, empty. We almost wish for a storm.

Carl had fallen ill with fever and nausea a few days ago. "I feel like the whole ocean is weighing on me," he said. He had to force himself to eat, and when he did, he soon jumped up to run for the railing.

Then Hal became sick, too. He had a fever of 102° and lay immobile on his air mattress for a whole day. He was pale and dripping sweat. Then Allan succumbed, complaining of headaches and fever. And I had another symptom to add to my collection: I had suddenly collapsed in the cabin, then wakened in a different place. I couldn't guess how many seconds or minutes had passed. My pulse was racing, and I was drenched in perspiration. I was losing control of my body, and I began to feel shame, to search for an explanation, tried to hide my weakness but only felt it more and more. . . . Bill was not feeling in top form either. He didn't have any fever, but he too was sick to his stomach. So was everyone else, and it was clear that we couldn't blame this nausea on seasickness.

Some strange disease had taken hold of the crew. Arno spoke about it with Bob. Bob thought there were two possible explanations. Either an infection — "Nothing very serious," he grumbled — had broken out among us after an incubation period of several weeks, or the drinking water in our wooden tanks was bad. Bob had noticed that the symptoms seemed to be worse after the crew had had something to drink and particularly after breakfast.

Arno wrote in his journal:

We're considering whether we shouldn't stop in Yokohama for a fresh water supply. I'm against this plan, but if this sickness doesn't pass, we may have no choice. The virus still seems to be spreading. But it's also worth noting that these varied symptoms could well be of psychological origin and indeed probably are.

Allan is complaining that the water is giving him headaches and some undefinable pains in his calves and feet. Allan's ills inspire more laughter than concern, but Kuno is a different story. He's lying around like a dead man. Bob thinks he may have suffered a heart attack. Carl's condition is hardly salutary either. He looks like a walking skeleton and spends most of his time asleep. When he gets up, all he can do is stagger around. And he's been this way for several days now. . . .

Back during the storms, our youngest crew member, Wolf, had celebrated his twenty-sixth birthday. It was our first party at sea. Arno gave him a bottle of whiskey. Bill wrapped two rolls of film in aluminum foil and handed them to Wolf with a grand gesture. I gave him a pipe I hadn't had time to make use of. Wolf reciprocated by presenting the crew with some beautifully rigged sea anchors. He and Hal had folded the canvas sea anchors and coiled their ropes neatly just before the birthday party. "That's my gift to you," he said, "a contribution to your safety." In the course of their work, Wolf and Hal had prepared a second gift that wasn't particularly well received by Arno. They had knocked a sack full of books into the forward compartment. That in itself wasn't so tragic; but, unfortunately, the compartment had taken on some water. Cursing to himself, Arno had fished the sack out of the water and spread the books out on the forward deck to dry. So it was that Wolf's birthday party took place amid soggy volumes of St.-Exupéry, Engelmann, Dostoevsky, Handke, Lorenz, and Wells, amid nautical textbooks and histories of China and America. The decor for the party was festive, the mood hardly one of untrammeled gaiety. Neither Bob's performance on the guitar nor Wolf's jokes did much to improve spirits.

The *Tai Ki* lay becalmed. Time crept by. The sea was a deep, glassy blue. We worked on the ship, dragged ourselves about. The flag hung limp. The rudder hung immobile in the water. The steering lines that had made our hands bleed only a few days ago were cleated now.

Arno saw to it that we didn't lie idle. The hull had to be cleaned. Thousands of small white mussels had attached themselves to it underwater. It looked as if snow had fallen on the ship's belly or as if small white flowers were blooming there. That was the impression the mussels created for the diver who attempted to scrape them off with a chisel-like tool.

It was exhausting work. The diver went overboard, submerged, stayed under for thirty seconds, a minute, maybe a little more, clutched onto a rope with one hand to hold himself under, scraped frantically with the other. The fish that had become our loyal traveling companions during the last few weeks circled around him. Their numbers and size were increasing steadily. Dorados running five to six feet joined innumerable smaller fish in circling the *Tai Ki*. And there were some sharks too.

Their fins rose out of the water for a few seconds at a time, and we watched them circle the *Tai Ki*, disappear, and come back again. Their presence added some spice to our underwater work on the hull. Even a "small" shark about six feet long looks quite formidable at close range.

None of us had had any experience with sharks before, and our theoretical knowledge wasn't of much use to us. We didn't know how to interpret shark behavior and had no idea how a hungry shark acts. We couldn't tell whether the shark gliding by us was in search of a meal or had just eaten, whether it would be aggressive or not. We didn't understand the signals the shark's movements might be giving us and never knew whether it meant to cruise peacefully by or would turn quickly and attack.

Our strategy for dealing with sharks underwater was to rise slowly to the surface, always keeping an eye on the shark, until we could breathe through the snorkel. Then we would lie quietly next to the ship and avoid any rapid movements that might prompt the shark to attack. We had learned still another way of coping with sharks from the Austrian marine biologist Hans Hass. He recommends yelling at them underwater. The sound waves conducted by the water will supposedly frighten a shark and drive him away. We had no way of telling beforehand if this technique was 100 percent reliable, though Hans Hass himself could be cited as living proof that his method works. We prayed devoutly that we would never have to put his advice to the ultimate test. As things turned out, we were obliged to make use of it. We screamed as best we could underwater but didn't manage to scare any sharks away. It has to be said, however, that no sharks ever attacked us either, and advocates for Hans Hass might well feel justified in quoting that fact in support of his theory.

Conscious as we were of our ignorance, not only of sharks, which were more a titillation than a serious threat to us, but of other dangers as well, we had established rigorous safety measures for the entire crew. The sea was alien enough to most of us, but the way we had chosen to traverse it made it more alien and threatening still. It was alien in the sense that a mountain wall, a jungle thicket, or a desert waste is alien. It permitted us no mistakes. A moment of carelessness could exact too high a price.

Swimming alone was forbidden, no matter how calm the sea. No one was allowed to swim more than fifty feet away from the boat. If one crew member was working underwater, another was assigned to keep him and the water around him under surveillance. If there was enough wind to move the *Tai Ki* at all, no matter how slightly, swimmers had to be attached to the boat by safety lines. Entering the water was permitted only from the bow of the boat, never from the stern. If the ship happened to be moving faster than the swimmer estimated, he would still have time to climb back aboard before the ship passed out of his reach. And if he failed to reach the ship itself, he would still have a chance to catch the safety line we always towed behind us, which had a red life buoy tied to it. At least one member of every group of swimmers had to be equipped with a face mask and snorkel.

Arno had more experience in extreme situations than any of the rest of us. He was an expert rock climber, had paddled a kayak in the Arctic Ocean off Alaska, had skied on the highest mountains in Europe and North America, and had sailed the skies in a hang glider. He knew that one false move, one miscalculation, or one second of carelessness could mean death, and no one was more adamant about strict adherence to the safety rules than he.

Wolf's nautical training had taught him a great respect for safety precautions, and he too was rigorous in following them. Ironically enough, it was he who drifted some hundred feet away from the boat in a moment of carelessness. As he started swimming back toward her, a shark came up on him. Instead of lying still, as he should have, he continued swimming. Our rules for dealing with sharks hadn't become second nature to him. He had learned his lessons abstractly but hadn't acted on them in the real world. Until we are able to make lessons of this kind part of our instinctive behavior, we remain novices in dealing with danger.

A school of dolphins is heading straight for us, dozens of them, hundreds of them. I've never seen so many. They are coming at us in a line, playing follow the leader, their motions identical. They come to within fifty feet of the *Tai Ki* without breaking their rhythm or pace. The leader suddenly swings to the left, and we can hardly believe what we see happen. No sooner has the leader turned than all the dolphins behind him make the identical turn. No corps de ballet ever executed the same movement with such precision, yet there is nothing unnatural in what these sea mammals do. For them this precision is a matter of course. Now they are moving away from the ship, following their leader in a gleaming blue-gray phalanx, leaping and swimming as playfully as they had when they approached us.

On the fifth day of the calm, the restlessness of the crew increased. There seemed to be no end to these days of idleness and immobility. Every once in a great while, a puff of wind would ruffle our sail only to let it drop slack again.

Carl had retreated to his cabin and was working on his

charts. We didn't see him for hours on end. Only on rare occasions did we see his disheveled hair and lined, exhausted face emerge from the hatchway. He still hadn't recovered his health completely. Allan was sitting out on the catwalk, doing the dishes. He let his feet dangle overboard, paused in his work now and then, stared absentmindedly out toward the horizon. Wolf was writing in his journal. He had been writing for hours, his back against the spare mast, his notebook resting on his knees. Arno and Hal were at work on the forward deck. I was still in poor physical shape and had been obliged to lie down.

Bob stood in the middle of the cabin. He was humming to himself as he strapped his knife onto the calf of his right leg, pulled on his face mask, and flapped outside in his swimfins. He fell into the water with a satisfied grunt.

Allan had finished his work and was sitting on the helmsman's cabin, where Arno joined him. Bob had disappeared. He was staying under longer than usual, a fact that the two observers took note of but hardly articulated to themselves. Then Bob's head popped up. He exhaled, snorted contentedly, adjusted his face mask, and splashed around in the water. I had gotten up and was standing next to Arno. We watched as the safety line cut through the water next to Bob. The *Tai Ki* was making less than half a knot. The life buoy on the end of the line was almost even with him now. Bob dove again just as the ship picked up speed from a heavier gust. We grew uneasy. Bob still hadn't come up again. The life buoy was several yards away from where he went under. A slight wake began to form behind the rudder; our red, white, and red flag stood out from its mast. Bob surfaced, looked around him, realized with a start that the junk was considerably farther away from him than he had expected. He set out after the life buoy, swimming with strong, rapid strokes. It seemed at first that he would catch up with it easily. But the distance between it and him remained unchanged. Our lethargic, contemplative mood of the last few hours was suddenly dissipated. Bob settled into a fast crawl, his strokes picking up more and more speed, but he came only a few inches closer to the buoy.

The wind held steady; the rigging of the *Tai Ki* creaked in the fresh breeze. Bob was in for a struggle. His pleasure swim had turned into a race for his life. His movements became more hectic. He grabbed for the line, missed, grabbed and missed again, and every time he missed he lost more ground. We began a panicked search for more rope so that we could lengthen the safety line, but we could find none.

We knew and Bob knew that the ship could not turn back if she pulled too far away from him. We couldn't sail her any closer to the wind than seventy degrees. She couldn't tack. If a crew member were too far from the ship and the wind picked up, he was lost.

Bob slashed furiously at the water and finally caught hold of the line. Panting heavily, he let it drag him along. Then he pulled himself in toward the boat, hand over hand. He hauled himself on board, leaned against the helmsman's cabin, too breathless to speak for several minutes. His face was pale. The sea had nearly taken him.

A few days later we are becalmed again. It's early August. Wind velocity: zero. Ship's speed: zero. Barometer: 30. Course: anywhere between 20° and 330°. We have forgotten Bob's adventure, had forgotten it an hour after it happened. We're diving again. A school of dorados, about fifteen of them, is circling the junk. But the harpoons remain idle. Hal is the cook, and we don't want to upset his plans. Up to now he has always been the one whose menus had to be drastically changed at the last minute because of fresh fish.

The expanse of the sea disappears for the swimmer. He sees nothing but deep blue all around him. But this limited perspective that swimming off the bow of the *Tai Ki* offers is a welcome change, particularly in a calm when just about any change, even one for the worse, seems welcome. The monotony is telling on us all. Even chess fails to interest us. Carl can hardly bring himself to inspect the spars. Arno, Bill, and Wolf had done some unsuccessful shark hunting earlier. Arno had even climbed the mast to spot the sharks that had been lurking around the ship. On deck again, he tries to organize work details to make some repairs.

I wrote in my journal:

Despite the restful atmosphere we're living in now, I'm still tense. My circulatory system isn't functioning as it should. During the storm, I was able to cope with my spells of vertigo, but now this circulatory problem is turning up. I'll talk to Carl about it. We discussed back on Taiwan what we would do if anyone should have to leave the ship. Neither Carl nor Arno nor I was ready to accept this possibility, and the whole subject has been ignored during these last six weeks. Now we'll have to deal with it in concrete terms, and I'll have to have a detailed consultation with Bob. I've passed out twice. If my condition gets any worse, I can endanger the entire expedition. It would be easier to get me off now than later.

The *Tai Ki* is drifting — certainly not sailing — toward the north-northwest. The current has taken hold of us, and the farther north we are carried, the better our chances are of picking up good winds and stronger currents. And even if we don't find any wind, it would at least be a gain to profit from better currents.

A Japanese fishing boat crosses our bow, comes in closer, stops, moves ahead again, finally comes to another stop and lies off our starboard bow. We wave. Allan stands on the roof of the helmsman's cabin and with the aid of an empty bottle, he presents a broad pantomime of a beer drinker. He takes the cap off the bottle, guzzles, wipes the foam from his mouth. Would they understand? A number of ships had visited us briefly, veering off their courses to have a look at this peculiar vessel before they sailed quickly on. We seemed to have something downright repulsive about us.

"Maybe they think we're spies from Red China," Bill ventures.

"From the People's Republic of China," Wolf corrects him.

"Oh, shit."

The Japanese fishermen have gotten the message. Frantic and gleeful activity takes over on the *Tai Ki*. Beer! After our wretched chlorine water, beer will taste like nectar.

We trade gifts, eagerly take some proffered cartons on board. The fishing boat toots farewell. We rip open our cartons and find nothing inside but some soft drinks.

"It's illegal for Japanese ships to carry alcohol on board," Carl tells us.

The crew could care less about rules aboard Japanese vessels. We had looked forward to some beer and had come away empty-handed. Everyone agreed we should personally search the next ship from top to bottom. But when would the next ship come along?

Another underwater hunt is on. Bill, Bob, Arno, and Allan dive overboard. Arno is having trouble with his harpoon. The line isn't properly attached to it. He hands me the rope. I'm supposed to hang on. Then he disappears underwater again. I see the hunters' white bodies dive and roll next to the ship. I tie the end of the line to a nearby post and run to get a movie camera. When I come back, I find the rope gone. The knot had come untied; both rope and harpoon have disappeared in the depths. Arno is fuming when he comes back on board. The whole crew becomes embroiled in a debate about attitudes in special situations. There is yelling and anger. Arno, fully justified, accuses me of carelessness. We have all lost sight of whatever pleasure the hunt might have provided.

A little later we argue with Carl about his failings as a leader. Reproaches fly back and forth as we pursue further the theme that we began to discuss back in Kao-hsiung. Arno, Wolf, Bill, and I insist on more rigorous organization. Hal seems content with things as they are. Bob expresses no opinion, and Allan keeps his silence, too. Tighter organization or not, his work as radioman — and that is what concerns him primarily — remains unaffected. We decide to rethink our work schedules, set up new duty rosters. It's been a rough day.

We've been going backward again, toward the west and northwest. I've been cook today and started off by making a total wreck of the pancakes at breakfast. I try to foist them off on the crew as something special, crêpes à la Vienne, but nobody falls for my fancy name. "Crap is right," Arno says. Then at noon I manage to burn the spaghetti. "If you put salt in the tea," Hal says, "I'll nominate you as permanent cook for the rest of the trip."

A full moon shone that night, full moon after a golden sunset. The sea glows like silver on molten lead; silver strands shimmer between sea and sky. The horizon is gone, lost in a faint mist that hides it from view. Sky and sea become one in a hazy veil that the moonlight touches but cannot penetrate. Even the creatures of the deep appear to be silver shadows, all aglow in the glistening water. They seem to give off light themselves, of their own power, but they are nothing more than living mirrors that reflect once more the reflected light of the moon.

Bill and I had rowed out in the dinghy at 1800 to see the ship from another perspective, to see her against the backdrop of the setting sun and flaming clouds. Out there in the dinghy I encountered total silence for the first time in my life. Not a breeze stirred. Not a ripple slapped against our boat. The *Tai Ki* rose and fell silently on the swells of the Pacific. Water, only water, all around us. And a silence so deep that we could hear our hearts beating and the blood rushing in our veins.

Silence. We let the sea's breath carry us. Its motion spoke of infinite patience, of infinity itself. There is no way to describe the repose we experienced. It defies comparison. There is no color, sound, word, or idea that begins to suggest it. Only the experience itself can convey what we felt in that momentary isolation we had sought.

The outline of our junk rises over the swells like some absurd figure a magician had pulled out of thin air. It is a tangle of black lines running in all directions against a backdrop of red and gold clouds in a deep blue sky. It is reminiscent of a Japanese shadow puppet, a complicated, awkward figure yet also a light, airy one.

Our only ties with the *Tai Ki* are occasional sounds that reach us faintly across hundreds of yards of water: the creaks and groans of wood and rigging. It would be easy to forget time, to forget one's own being out here. How we perceive things becomes unimportant. We submit to a tide of forgetfulness, of self-efface-ment. We don't return to the ship for a few hours. Then we have to force ourselves to leave this stillness whose power we have just begun to sense. I have hardly ever acted so much in violation of my innermost desires before.

My journal for August 4:

I spent a sleepless night, searching for rest but finding none. We lie bogged down in the sticky, immobile waters of the Pacific. The ground swells are growing weaker still, and even the illusion of forward progress is taken from us. Not the faintest breeze stirs the surface of the sea. We keep watching the algae alongside the hull, hoping to see it moving past us, but it lies nearly motionless in the oily water. A high-pressure system 100, maybe 200 miles in diameter, maybe much less, holds us captive like a great bell jar lowered over us. We haven't had any wind for over 200 hours. The barometer needle seems to be glued in place. The grea-test variation it registers is from 30.1 to 29.8. During the coolest hours of the night the thermometer drops to 79°. Daytime temperatures hover in the high 80's. The deck is often so hot that we can hardly walk on it with bare feet. A muggy silence hangs in the cabin. We are exhausted from doing nothing. We move slowly, lethargically, as though we were strung on heavy ropes. San Francisco is no more than a name, maybe a picture postcard. It is a distant fleck of color, an unreal place. Europe is a dream.

In my apathy I've nearly forgotten the purpose of our expedition. I try to read Bosch Gimpera, but my eyes merely skim over the letters before me on the page. Nothing reaches my mind. More circulatory trouble, cold sweat, dizziness, unconsciousness. Bob tries another acupuncture treatment but with no positive results.

Inactivity is aggravating an uneasy mood in the crew. Bob's efforts on the guitar evoke neither applause nor irritation. The music tinkles pointlessly in the void. A calm is far more dangerous for morale than a storm. Even the creaking of the mast in the tabernacle becomes a source of vexation. At 1400, the thermometer reads 90°. Ship's speed: zero. Wind velocity: zero. Course: 0 to 60°. Position: 141° 11′ east longitude, 31° 48′ north latitude. Barometer: 30.2. The chances of any wind coming up soon are minimal. Days pass; we fall farther and farther behind in our schedule, and there is nothing we can do about it. Conversation becomes rarer and more subdued than ever.

The first phase of our journey is behind us. We've almost passed the easternmost longitude of Japan. But we should be much farther along our route by now. We'd planned to be approaching the international date line by early August. Where exactly is that mythical line? Does it really exist? Do we really have a concrete destination after all?

There is little variety in our lives, and we take excessive delight in any diversion that presents itself. The early morning watch provided Wolf with some excitement. He was on the forward deck at 0500, standing lookout, when he heard familiar snorting noises coming from the water. We are all used to these sounds by now. Schools of whales and dolphins have visited us time and again, slapping their tails against the water and shooting fountains into the air.

The sun started coming up during Wolf's watch. He heard the snorting come close to the ship, heard a slapping against the hull. Then only a few yards away from him a whale's head emerged from the sea and rose up above the bow of the ship. The whale's tiny eyes looked long and glumly at the *Tai Ki*. Wolf called to Bill to get his movie camera, but the whale disappeared again before Bill could get his gear together. Then the deck began to tremble, and a scraping sound rose up from below the ship. The whale was scratching its back on the belly of the *Tai Ki*. Wolf passed a few nervous minutes as the scraping continued. There was a splashing of water. Wolf ran to the catwalk, took hold of the stays, and dangled out over the side. The whale surfaced once more and took another quick look at the ship. Then it dove and disappeared. The sleeping crew hadn't noticed a thing.

The whale's visit provides us with a topic of conversation at breakfast. Hal has a book written by a Scottish farmer who sold his farm and bought a boat in which he and his family planned to sail around the world. Near the Galápagos Islands, a pod of killer whales attacked his yacht, and within minutes they had so seriously damaged the hull that the boat sank on the spot. The crew took to a rubber life raft and drifted on the Pacific for thirty-seven days before a freighter picked them up. The story made the newspapers everywhere in the world, and the Scotsman wrote a book about his experiences in the life raft. Hal had brought this book along on our voyage because it contained detailed information on survival techniques at sea. After the morning's episode with the whale, this book assumed more than a passing interest for us. In retrospect, we realized that one blow from that massive tail would have been enough to damage the *Tai Ki* seriously. Bill is relatively unconcerned about the danger; what upsets him is the fact that he arrived on the scene just too late to get any pictures. "Fantastic," he grumbles all morning long, "they would have been absolutely fantastic pictures." For our cameraman, nothing has priority over pictures.

"Don't fret about it," Arno says, trying to console him. "They probably wouldn't have turned out anyway in that light."

But Bill continues to mourn his lost opportunity.

August 5. Still no wind. The blackboard we use for current log entries shows another string of zeros written down either in anger or indifference. We could have simply enjoyed this slack time, but none of us — with the exception of Bob and Allan — was able to. We wanted to be on our way. We were weeks behind before we even left Hong Kong. We talk again about what kind of weather we'll run into when we reach the American coast in November. My heart is giving me trouble again. I've got to talk with Bob.

Bob seems to be in the dark himself about my case and won't

even venture a precise diagnosis. It's obvious enough to us both
that the circulatory system is involved, but why is my sense of
balance affected? Bob is also concerned about my loss of weight.
But all he can really offer me is a lot of ominous hypotheses.

Jenny had called our Swedish radio contacts from London
and asked them to pass on to us the intelligence that we were
running behind schedule. That was hardly news for us. But still,
the concern it expressed touched us all, even if we did burst out
laughing when Allan read the radio message to us.

A little later Allan pulls a piece of fishnet attached to a glass
ball out of the water. He is about to throw it back, but Bill urges
him to hang onto it. Glass balls of this kind seem to wash up on
the California coast frequently, and they can bring twenty-five
dollars on the open market. I can't help remarking that he has
just provided another piece of evidence in support of our case: if
the currents of the Pacific will carry glass balls from Asia to America, they can just as well take ships along the same route.

We are still on a longitude with northern Japan. The gates of
the Pacific are still closed to us. But the U.S. radio station on
Guam has broadcast some encouraging news: a low-pressure system is building off Okinawa, only a few hundred miles away.
That could well mean wind for us. The skies cloud over briefly,
and we are hopeful again, though mixed in with the hope is some
fear that we may get not only wind but a typhoon as well.

I have a talk with Carl about his leadership and my state of
health; then Arno takes up these same subjects with him. Arno
wrote of this talk in his journal: "It is no pleasure to be around
when people who have difficulty making contact with others are
forced to open themselves up. I find it difficult myself to respond
in a situation like that."

But the talks Arno and I had with Carl brought obvious improvement. Carl directed and organized work on board, fully assuming his role as captain. He worked energetically himself to-

gether with Wolf. We all noticed an immediate shift in the mood
on board.

My journal:

Having some real work to do is good for the crew's spirit. But still, if we
take account of today's position in terms of yesterday's, we see that the
current and a few friendly puffs of wind have brought us ahead only
fifteen nautical miles in the last twenty-four hours. If we had been able
to anchor a buoy at our position twenty-four hours ago, we would still be
able to see it now; and it's more than likely that we would still be able to
see it after forty-eight hours.

Full of envy, we watch two ships about five miles away pass by us.
They have taken two hours to traverse the distance we have been covering in the last several days. It has been a long time, and time will continue to pass slowly as long as this Pacific Ocean continues to live up to
its name.

Bob is demonstrating still other aspects of his versatility. He's making portraits now, one of me, one of Allan. We have some more whales
around the ship, about a dozen this time.

On August 6 we finally had some wind. After nine days of
calm, we were underway again. From 0600 to 1000 we averaged
a little better than one knot per hour. And today is Bob's birthday,
his thirty-fourth. We hold our second celebration aboard the *Tai
Ki,* complete with bottle of whiskey.

We cleaned up the forward deck in the morning. The last
scraps of rattan are gone now. Everything gleams, and Wolf looks
on our work with great pride and pleasure. We throw the last of
our lemons into the sea, the last of 500 that we loaded on board
back in Hong Kong. Bob performs a great service for Lap Sac: he
cuts the dog's toenails. In the evening we play a game of cards.
This is the second time so far that more than two people do something together during free time. Carl dominates the game and the
conversation. Hal too is in a boisterous mood. Bob stares at his
cards with great concentration. I don't really understand the
game. Carl explained it to me in an offhand manner. He suddenly

seems to feel much more at ease than he has. And Hal seems more comfortable too.

The weather turned cooler in the next few days. Arno and Bill had gone out after dorados again, and Arno managed to catch a huge one before long. He permitted himself to be photographed next to his prize. And, of course, Hal just happened to be cook.

More wind. Between the current and the wind we made about three knots, heading north toward Japan.

I handed out sugar rations this morning. Everybody received his portion for the week in a glass. My skills as cook are not improving. I managed to burn soup today. With a little more effort, I may even be able to ruin tea.

The ship is heeling over in the wind. The waves wash up constantly on the starboard catwalk, but there is nothing threatening about this steady wind. On the contrary, it has breathed some life back into the crew. We're on our way, and we take up our calculations again. How long will it take us to reach California if . . . ?

On the forward deck, all we can see for minutes at a time is the gray sky whenever the *Tai Ki* lies heeled over to port in the wind. Then she rights herself suddenly, swinging like a great bell. Waves smash into her starboard side, sending spray flying onto the cabins and the deck. Then the ship heels over again, and everything seems to be as it was seconds before. Our ship is a safe, steady island. She will remain.

But I will not, not on the *Tai Ki* in any case. This is a bitter pill for me to swallow. I've been holding this fact at bay for several days now. I wouldn't allow myself to give up. Surely my will had to be stronger than my body. I simply couldn't give up. I hadn't been planning this expedition and been dreaming about it for years, only to sneak out of it through the back door, as it were. I couldn't leave my shipmates in the lurch. But the resumed motion of the ship had aggravated my condition. My sense of balance was so severely impaired that I could barely walk a straight line.

And I was suffering constantly from dizziness and blackouts. Bob was spending more and more time with me. I couldn't tell from his impassive face what he was thinking, but his concern was evident in his questions and in his vain attempts to help me. The acupuncture treatment seemed ineffective, and we had discontinued it. Nothing helped. It was all I could do to keep my food down. I fell unconscious time and again. The others had unobtrusively taken over my duties on board. I was hardly aware that they had done so.

Bob consulted with Carl. As ship's doctor, Bob said, he could no longer consent to my remaining on board. Carl told me about this conversation later.

"We're still not too far from shore, and a Japanese boat can pick Kuno up now without much trouble. But if he should have a heart attack when we're thousands of miles from any land, what do we do then? In his condition, he's in danger himself and constitutes a danger for all of us."

"And you don't think there's any chance of his improving?" Carl asked.

"I'd thought so before we put in at Kao-hsiung," Bob replied. "I'd still hoped then that he was just having a hard time getting his sea legs under him. But he should have been over that phase long ago by now. No, his heart and circulatory system aren't up to snuff, and he's running on nothing but sheer willpower. I say he should go before he gets any worse."

"Who's going to break the news to him?" Carl asked.

"Yeah, that won't be any picnic. But I'm pretty sure he knows he's in bad shape, and he knows that he's jeopardizing the rest of us as well as himself if he stays on. I'll tell him."

And he did.

Then Carl, Bob, Arno, and I talked over the need for me to leave the ship. On the night of August 9, Allan sent out a general message asking any ship underway to Yokohama to pick me up if at all possible.

My journal of August 10:

Weather: windy, heavy cloud cover. Wind steady out of the northeast. Hazy, very humid, almost foggy. Barometer: 29.7. Visibility: about 5 miles. Ship's speed: 2 knots. Thanks to wind and current, we've made fairly good headway in the last two days, putting 84 nautical miles behind us.

At breakfast Carl officially announced what everyone knew anyhow: I would be leaving the ship soon. Bob explained why this was necessary. He had already prepared a medical report for me to show to the doctors in Japan.

Sunday, August 11. The sea off Japan lies leaden under a gray sky. The clouds hang low, mingling with fog rising from the water. We can see huge freighters around us, their shapes obscured by the fog even over this short distance.

Quiet reigns on board the *Tai Ki*. Everyone is busy writing letters. The mailman is just about to leave. I'm feeling terribly weak. Bob hands me his medical report, grumbles and curses.

The fog closed in on us about 0500. We can hardly see more than 50 or 100 yards. The temperature is 72. For us that's miserably cold.

It's strange here in this southern climate where we've experienced nothing but sun for days on end to wake up to foghorns. Hal and Bill are standing next to the helmsman's cabin, blowing our foghorn. Ships lying half a mile or maybe only a quarter of a mile off respond.

Inside the junk everything is dank and slippery. Wisps of fog drift through the helmsman's cabin, and from where we stand in the living quarters, only fifteen feet away from the helmsman, his face and figure appear strangely veiled and distorted.

In the course of the morning, the fog lifts, and the sea turns a color we haven't seen before, a deep green, a jade green. The foam on the crests of the waves looks like a whitish deposit in the dark, mineral color.

We hear a whoop from Bill. He had been fooling around with the cabin radio that hadn't been functioning for several days and had picked up the noon news report from an American shortwave station. Nixon was referred to as the "ex-President." When had he resigned? High-level politics had been passing us by.

Then we start receiving Radio Tokyo, and Radio Tokyo is playing some Johann Strauss directed by an Austrian, Willy Boskowsky, whose name we can understand even in the pronunciation the Japanese announcer gives it.

Our proximity to land is obvious. Jet planes fly overhead. We can't see them, but we can hear the familiar drone that has been absent from our lives in recent days. Ships are crossing our bow more and more frequently. We pass through clumps of filth and garbage, watch a child's red shoe drift by. A butterfly floats toward us, wafted along on the music of Strauss.

A plane comes in low over us, circles, and comes in again. At first we assume that it's a commercial plane that just wants to have a look at this peculiar device floating on the water. Then we realize that it's a search plane from the Japanese coast guard. They've pinned down our position now.

No one on the *Tai Ki* can really accept the fact that I'm about to leave. I'm nervous, dripping with sweat, weak. All my gear is packed, but I'm clinging desperately to those last few minutes on board.

Wolf comes to say good-bye, then Arno. If anyone knows how I'm feeling right now, it is he. He hands me a small sack of films and makes a weak stab at a joke. "Here's something to show the folks at home so they'll know we're underway."

I'm given a lot of letters to forward.

I lean against the helmsman's bench, feeling that I hardly belong here anymore.

Hal says his farewells and hands me a small package. "For Mary," he says.

Bill has packed all his films in a special sack. "Here," he says, handing it to me, "and give my regards to Paris."

We're all uneasy. No one knows how much longer we'll have to wait, and no one is ready to accept what is going to happen, what has to happen. Other ships surround the *Tai Ki*, freighters, tankers, fishing boats. The sea is calm. Then we see a white boat heading straight for us. There is an exchange of blinker signals, a waving of flags. Our wait is over. The Japanese coast guard has come to take me off board. Everyone on the *Tai Ki* moves into swift action. Our dinghy is lowered into the water, and in his excitement, Wolf drops the line tied to its bow. Hal snatches up the line before the dinghy can drift away. Carl rushes from his cabin and says nervously to me, "Come on. Let's go."

Brief, nearly wordless farewells are exchanged. I stumble into the dinghy, and Carl rows me over to the Japanese coast guard boat that lies gleaming white some two hundred yards off our starboard bow. On board the Japanese boat, we embrace quickly, then Carl jumps back into the dinghy. I go onto the forward deck of the patrol boat and stand there waving, a smile frozen on my face. The crew of the *Tai Ki* waves back as the engines beneath me begin to howl.

The bow of the patrol boat knifes through the water and tosses up spray. The engines are howling still louder now, and I have to adjust quickly to the unexpected speed of the boat. I cast a last glance back at the *Tai Ki* and at the men standing on the helmsman's cabin, waving to me. I can see them for a few seconds more, then the *Tai Ki* disappears from view, and a doctor leads me into the ship's sick bay.

The men left on the *Tai Ki* avoid each other's gaze.

"Why the hell aren't we getting some decent wind?" Bob grumbles.

"Shit," Bill snorts as the white dot of the Japanese patrol boat disappears over the horizon.

CHAPTER SEVEN

Will There Be a Tomorrow?

WHILE JIRO TASAKI, THE SHIP'S DOCTOR OF THE JAPANESE patrol boat *Awajy*, was examining Kuno Knöbl — Tasaki came up with the same diagnosis Bob Kendrick had: a dysfunction of the circulatory system — Carl rowed back to the *Tai Ki* with a rubber dinghy full of booty: twenty pounds of sugar and five cans of beer. The crew, all of whom had been yearning for beer for weeks now, drank to Kuno's health.

There is no doubt that Kuno's absence leaves a huge gap in the crew. His departure is particularly hard on Wolf.

"Kuno is gone," he wrote in his journal. "It all happened so quickly; in a matter of minutes we were only nine, counting the dog and the rat. Or maybe we're 999 if you count the cockroaches. At any rate, we're not a full crew anymore. I worry about how things will go now without him. Arno and I are acutely aware of his absence because there are now only two instead of three of us who share the same native language and can communicate in it at more meaningful levels." He notes bleakly: "It's a bad sign that one of the originators of the expedition has had to leave the ship. The lack of his mediating presence is already palpable." The final words of this entry reflect the depression he feels: "All of a sudden there is a lot of empty space aboard ship, a vacuum. . . ."

Arno, Bob, and Bill openly express the dismay they feel at

Kuno's departure. Allan says nothing, while Carl emphasizes again — and quite correctly — that there was no other choice. Kuno simply wasn't physically able to continue the voyage, and it would have been irresponsible to let him stay on. While this conversation was going on aboard the *Tai Ki,* Kuno was subjected to another and more thorough examination on the *Awajy.* The doctor noted, in addition to the circulatory problem, a drastic loss of weight — twenty pounds in two months is more than a man of one hundred and fifty pounds can safely lose — disorders of the autonomic nervous system, and vertigo. But the diagnosis does not require hospitalization in Tokyo. Kuno flies directly to Vienna and spends the next ten days under medical observation. The diagnosis the Austrian doctors reach confirms that of their Japanese colleagues.

During the night of August 12, the *Tai Ki* was driven far to the west. If the crew had cared to take to the oars, they could have reached Yokohama with relatively few strokes. They could see lights on the coast of Japan all night. Considering the *Tai Ki*'s limited maneuverability, this proximity to land could have proved dangerous.

The desired winds refuse to blow, and whatever progress the junk makes is due almost exclusively to the current. Land is in sight again, probably the volcanic island of Oshima. The crew busies itself listlessly with small jobs. Arno is making fishhooks out of nails; Hal tinkers with the rattan lines on the mast.

The water is a bit cool for swimming. The crew members are accustomed to the warmer water temperatures of more southerly latitudes. And then, the sea off Japan is badly polluted.

Allan catches a fish by letting a hook hang in the water, then jerking it up as the fish swims over it. He reaps considerable praise from his shipmates for this accomplishment. How did he do it? He must have some kind of sixth sense for fish. And what should his angling technique be called? He didn't catch the fish with a hook in the normal way, and he didn't spear it either. Yet he both hooked it and speared it.

A breath of wind stirs; the sail swells.

"Now we're off for the open sea," Bill says optimistically.

Tuesday, August 13. The sun is shining, and it's clean-up day aboard the *Tai Ki*. All the kitchen gear is moved aside, the floorboards propped up, the interior of the ship scrubbed within an inch of its life. The rat has left ample evidence of his presence; nibbled plastic bags and crusts of bread turn up everywhere.

"No wonder I'm always hungry," Allan says. "That rat is eating up all our rations."

"Shut up," Arno grumbles.

Arno introduces further rationing measures. He divides up what is left of the chocolate and distributes it to the crew in seven equal portions. Everyone receives his share to do with as he pleases. This arrangement proves to be a poor one for Allan. He soon discovers that the rat has gnawed its way into his chocolate and eaten up a lion's rather than a rat's share of it. The rat has clearly been with the ship since she left Hong Kong. Numerous attempts on the rat's life have been made, but it has managed to escape every time. Its skills in evasion are impressive, for it has only a limited area in which to hide. For two months the only signs of its presence were holes chewed in food sacks. Increased hunger seems to be making it bolder now.

Bill's hopeful remark about heading for the open sea was premature. The broad Pacific may be in view, but land is still close by. A fighter plane circles the ship, comes in close over her, rolls, waggles its wings, and disappears. A little later a U.S. Navy ship appears on the horizon, steaming straight for the *Tai Ki*. This ship must have received Allan's message but hadn't learned in the meantime that Kuno had already left the junk. Blinker signals and Morse code pass back and forth. Confusion reigns. The ship comes in closer, and the name *Warden* becomes visible on her stern. More attempts at Morse code. The message still isn't

Overleaf: Going on the assumption that the stowaway rat was nesting in our extra spars, we gave the spars a thorough dunking. But we still had our rat on board afterward. (D)

Left: Maintenance of the sail and lines was part of the daily routine. No one would ever have expected that mountaineering experience would be essential on an ocean voyage, but repair work at the ends of the spars was a task only the surefooted could handle. Arno, our alpinist, was the perfect man for the job. (BM)

Below: At the outset of the journey, fish was a welcome addition to our menu, but before too long some of the crew members could hardly stand to choke down another mouthful of it. Here half of the crew, equipped with snorkels, swimfins, and harpoons, is out after fish. (R)

Left: Harpoon at the ready, Bob keeps a lookout for prey. (KK) A shark (*below*) was circling the ship, and Bob was hoping — in vain, as it turned out — for a clear shot at it. (G)

Above: The sudden appearance of a shark only a few yards away sometimes made underwater hunting a rather tense affair. (D) Even a small shark (*right*) was quite large enough to make a swimmer nervous. (D)

Food was one of the focal points of our life on board. Among the items that appeared on our varied menu were rice dishes (*below*) (R), fish, such as this magnificent dorado (*right*) (R), and homemade bread, a loaf of which Hal displays with justifiable pride. (P)

ight: Pollution in mid-ocean. Some
,500 miles from the nearest land we
shed this lump of oil out of the sea. The
ai Ki often crossed trails of filth that
ankers and freighters had left behind
hem. (KK)

elow: A hot, sticky afternoon in the
abin. Bob is drying dishes while Bill,
ooking rather weary, does his tour of
uty on the pump. (K)

Kuno's departure from the *Tai Ki*. The initiator of the expedition was a member of the crew for nearly two months; then his health failed him. Vertigo, heart trouble, and circulatory complications put a premature end to the great adventure for him. Carl is preparing to row him over to a Japanese coast guard ship. (R)

getting through. Two sailors in life vests stand ready to lower a launch from the deck of the *Warden*. Signal flags go up, but no one on the *Tai Ki* can make out their meaning. Finally the captain shouts across through a megaphone, "Do you need medical help?"

Since radio contact is impossible, the *Tai Ki* runs up a negative signal flag on the mast. This message gets through, and the *Warden* moves off again.

The *Warden*'s visit was reassuring for the crew because it demonstrated again how promptly and generously any call for help would be answered. But the fact that it was impossible to make radio contact with the *Warden* also raises some grave doubts.

"They just didn't have their radio set on," Arno says.

"Hogwash!" Bill replies. "There's something wrong with our radio equipment."

Allan puts in his two cents' worth, saying that he'd pointed out the inadequacies of the radio gear before the expedition even left Hong Kong. "I don't know what we'll do if the stuff fails us in a real emergency," he adds.

Arno's temper is flaring; he points out how much the ship's radio gear cost and says that they are carrying extra radio equipment specifically intended for extreme emergencies. Allan is about to reply, but Arno turns his back on him and cuts off the discussion.

The *Tai Ki* is in the midst of heavy traffic. A fishing fleet passes her on its way out to sea and finds her again in almost the same position the next morning when it returns to port. At night, the lights of Tokyo fill the hazy sky with a red-orange glow. That glow and the planes circling Tokyo airport will soon become all too familiar sights for the crew.

Wednesday, August 14, 1974. Kuno has already spent one day in a Viennese hospital. He flew via Anchorage and the North Pole to Europe and Vienna, covering thousands of miles in only a few hours. In the same period, the *Tai Ki* had traveled hardly a dozen miles.

Fog has descended on the ship, more fog, more dampness. Allan tries to take a bearing by radio, but his equipment isn't cooperating. The humidity seems to have affected it adversely.

More and more fish are circling the junk. She lies on about the thirty-fourth parallel now, and the predominantly gray fish in these waters contrast sharply with the colorful varieties in more southerly latitudes. Arno suffers another attack of fish fever and has soon harpooned a few dorados. Hal is the cook. He is not the least bit inclined to congratulate Arno on his good luck, and several other members of the crew also seem less than enthusiastic about delicacies from the sea. Arno, who often ate nothing but dried fish for days on end in Canada and Alaska, thinks his shipmates over-finicky in their tastes, but he refrains from making any comments.

Wolf leaves his portion of dorado untouched, fetches some chocolate from his personal stock, and chews into it with obvious delight. Hal would like to do the same, but as cook he can't undermine morale by refusing to eat his own food. He hopes in his secret heart that these omnipresent schools of fish will soon disappear. He would give a great deal for a good spaghetti dinner.

Bill is not going to let Arno outdo him as a harpoonist. But to the great relief of the crew he does not insist that his catch appear on the table. Instead, he provides Lap Sac with a change in diet. The dog pulls one of the fish off into a corner and busies himself with it there for quite a while. When Bob goes to see how Lap Sac has fared with his meal, he finds little left of the fish, but the dog doesn't seem to have enjoyed his feast all that much. He lies near his banquet table, looking as green in the face as a dog can. He hasn't been able to keep the fish down. Even dogs on board the *Tai Ki* seem to have delicate stomachs.

Allan's radio contact in Hong Kong sends him a message the crew of the *Tai Ki* has heard all too often: a tropical storm is on its way. At the moment, it is only a few hundred miles from the ship. The crew were suffering under an illusion if they thought themselves finally clear of the typhoon belt. This is the twelfth storm warning the *Tai Ki* has received in eight weeks.

The typhoon is approaching from the southeast, and the first heavy waves strike the ship during the afternoon. Hal is in for some ribbing because the weathermen have given this storm his wife's name, Mary.

Carl first tries to avoid the storm by heading north, but he orders a change in course when he sees that the one he's on will take the ship in too close to shore. Meanwhile the meteorologists in Hong Kong have radioed the junk that she should head for a harbor if at all possible. If at all possible, that is precisely what she won't do.

The seas grow heavier, with waves reaching fifteen to eighteen feet. And there is fog. The *Tai Ki* feels her way ahead in the approaching storm. Foghorns sound around her several times, and on at least two occasions she is on a collision course with other ships. The *Tai Ki* isn't able to execute any intricate maneuvers in these seas, and the oncoming ships are obliged to change their courses. Carl assumes that they picked up the *Tai Ki* on their radar. Allan had wisely mounted radar reflectors on the helmsman's cabin for just such conditions as these.

It remained foggy, and the seas turned still rougher. The waves were coming in from port, and Carl noted in the log that they went as high as thirty feet. "Mary" came dangerously close to the junk. The position of the *Tai Ki* on August 16 was 141° 13′ east longitude and 34° 51′ north latitude. "Mary's" position at the same time was 141° 10′ east longitude, 28° north latitude. She was moving northwest by north at about 7 knots. Wind velocities at the eye of the storm went over 55 knots.

The ship is showing her first signs of storm damage. Two rattan lines on the mast break, and a bamboo spar shatters. The crew remains calm despite its precarious situation. While Carl retires to his cabin, claiming he has some calculations to make and some work to do on his charts, the rest of the crew go into a huddle and talk about "Mary."

The storm becomes more intense still, and past experience seems to be of little help. Arno, who was the most coolheaded of the crew, noted in his journal:

The night was horrible. Sleep was out of the question. All of us were tossed about in the rolling ship. The waves were short yet vicious and seemed to be coming from every direction at once. The stern of the *Tai Ki* smashed down onto them continually with one ear-splitting crash after another until we thought the boat would split apart. I was amazed that she took this punishment. Last night certainly showed how well built she is. . . .

Heavy rain sets in at midnight. The cabin roofs leak, and no one can find a dry place to lay his head. The down sleeping bags soak up water; the rattan mats are drenched. Bill is able to find some relief by spreading his raincoat over himself. A half-hour later he jumps to his feet. Huge drops are falling right in the middle of his face. And he has to pay the price of jumping up too suddenly: he loses his footing and is tossed across the cabin to starboard, crashing into the wall next to Arno.

Lap Sac, who has been tied out on the forward deck, whines interminably under the drenching he's taking. He's not reliably housebroken, and in stress situations he has to stay out of the cabin. Bill stumbles out on deck and tries to comfort the dog. No success. Lap Sac keeps on howling and whining, his complaints blending with the smashing of waves against the hull, the groaning and creaking of mast and superstructures. Bill snorts and heads back inside, snatching at anything he can find for support: the tabernacle, the sail crank, the cabin roof.

A few hours later the storm is as intense as ever. Everyone has jammed himself into some corner or another, trying to keep himself from flying through the cabin with every roll of the ship. There's not much chance of sleep tonight. Wolf suddenly jumps up, tosses his clothes in every direction, tangles his foot in his sleeping bag, kicks at the bag, howls into the night: "I'm gonna go out of my mind! How the hell can anybody sleep in this mess? Sleep, for Christ's sake, I want some sleep!"

He rages on, curses, bellows. His voice cracks. The others, who are sleeping or at least trying to sleep, rise up with a start. But Wolf's fury passes as suddenly as it began. He just had to blow off some steam. Apparently relieved, he lies down on the scattered rags of his sleeping place and falls asleep, oblivious now to the water streaming through the roof and the squirmings of his companions.

The mood of the crew is foul after this sleepless night, and morning brings no relief from the storm and waves. Wolf precipitates a set-to at breakfast when he complains loudly that his portion of dry rolled oats, which he prefers to the cooked oatmeal the others receive, is too small. Allan takes his side against Bob, who is cook for the day. Allan remarks that cooked oatmeal is unfit for human consumption. "Where I come from," he says, "we scare little children with the word 'porridge' the way other people do with the bogey man." But when Wolf wants more rolled oats, Bob refuses him nonetheless. Wolf flies into a rage and stamps off to his sleeping place. At noon he stages a hunger strike to drive his point home, begins to pack some of his things in one container, then in another. Is he trying to suggest that he wants to leave the ship? And if so, when and how?

Wolf writes in his journal:

The meals on this ship are catastrophic. If you don't want the so-called porridge served at breakfast, you have to make do with one and a half tablespoonfuls of rolled oats. The amount of porridge allowed is skimpy enough after a stormy night when you use up a lot of energy just keeping your balance, but if you prefer dry rolled oats instead, the portion you get is downright ridiculous. I'm not going to put up with two or three more months in a state of such extreme starvation that the very thought of a peanut butter sandwich can make me delirious. After passing up breakfast and lunch in a rage, I'm starved by early afternoon, and I have to resort to a half-moldy chocolate bar from my candy ration.

By evening his fury had subsided, and he joined the rest of the crew for supper as if nothing had happened. Everyone inquired after his appetite.

During the afternoon the bilge has to be pumped out. The compartments have more water than usual in them, and the job takes correspondingly longer. And once again there is a dispute about whether compartments four and five are leaking more than they should be or not.

Carl answers brusquely: "There isn't a wooden boat in the world that doesn't leak."

"But why is it that compartments four and five are taking on so much more water than the rest?" Hal asks.

He receives no answer.

But despite storms, heavy seas, and typhoon warnings — Allan received still another during this period — the *Tai Ki* made no headway at all. She didn't lie becalmed. Far from it. She had wind enough, but the wind played with her as if she were a Ping-Pong ball, driving her at a good pace to the southeast, only to reverse itself and drive her back to the northwest again. Day after day the same routine, and every evening the discouraged, exhausted crew would see the lights of the Japanese coast or the glowing sky above Tokyo, distant but all too close just the same.

For Hal this was the most depressing episode of the entire voyage. He could handle a calm with tranquility, but this eternal shuttling back and forth off the coast of Japan got on his nerves. He thought it would make more sense to drop an anchor and do nothing. It was the fruitlessness of the crew's efforts that wore him down.

The further the expedition fell behind on its schedule, the more urgent the need became to make some real progress.

A look at the wind charts from August of the previous year

showed that the desired winds had indeed blown about the middle of the month; but they had not occurred — perhaps because of continental influences at work in this area — where the *Tai Ki* found herself at the moment. They had set in, however, to the south, north, and east of her position. Hal pointed this out to Carl.

"Why don't we head south?" he asked. "We might be able to pick up the right winds there."

Wolf chimed in with Hal. "Then we'd at least put an end to this ridiculous back-and-forth business."

But Carl was reluctant to accept this suggestion, and his objections were by no means unfounded. He feared that the *Tai Ki* might not be able to pick up the current she needed to carry her across the Pacific if she were too far to the south. And then the right winds would have to come up soon.

"We had no choice but to wait for wind," Carl recalled later. "We had come in much closer to Japan than we had planned to, but we never crossed the Kuroshio Current that was to carry us to America. According to the charts, we crossed it four times. But the charts didn't coincide with reality. We didn't encounter the faintest trace of a current. But later on near the international date line we struck onto a west-east current that, according to the charts, had no business being there. That's the way it was on the whole voyage with both weather and currents. Nothing panned out the way it was supposed to."

The winds failed to appear. No current made itself felt. The fog continued to hang over the *Tai Ki*. There was hardly a ray of sun to be seen for days on end. The sea turned calm, and the crew took advantage of the lull to make some necessary repairs. Almost all the bamboo spars were cracked and had to be reinforced. A number of hemp ropes were worn down to nothing and were as good as useless. The crew was obliged to replace them with nylon ropes and toss historical authenticity to the nonexistent winds. A careful examination of the ship showed that she had suffered considerable damage in the recent storms.

Bill decides to climb up the mast and shoot some movie film from that perspective. He runs into trouble and provides the rest of the crew with some comic relief. He gets tangled in the lines halfway up the mast and dangles there helplessly, unable to go up or down. A conference takes place on deck. Arno decides to make novel use of the "toilet seat" — a board that usually hangs by two ropes at the stern of the ship. The seat is rigged into a sling, and Bill is hoisted up the mast on it. He reaches the top and makes his film.

Now it's time for Bill to descend, and new complications with ropes, mast, and sling set in. Bill lowers his camera on a separate line, but apparently the camera felt as queasy about heights as the cameraman. In any case, it suddenly fell, barely missing Wolf's head on the way down, and slapped onto the pliant roof of the cabin. Then it slowly started to slide off, picked up speed, raced for the deck and certain doom, only to fall into Arno's waiting hands. Relief all around. The gods were kind once more.

Another fleet of fishing boats appears, and the usual waves and hellos are exchanged. If there is anything the crew yearns for above all else, it is cold beer. Hal finds the beer carton Carl had transported from the *Awajy* and holds it up for the fishermen to see. They understand. There is more gesturing, and the fishermen keep calling out "Hong Kong — America." Do they want to come on board, or should the *Tai Ki* send a boat over? The dinghy is finally launched. Allan, Bill, and Wolf row over to one of the fishing boats and are given five bottles of deliciously cold beer. When the *Tai Ki*'s emissaries ask for some tuna, which the crew has been unable to catch as yet, a fisherman descends eagerly below deck and returns with an armful of Japanese pornographic magazines that awaken no enthusiasm among the men of the *Tai Ki.*

"We seem to have been misunderstood," Bob observes drily.

Food and drink are more important on the junk than any vicarious sex thrills, and the magazines are politely declined.

A sense of well-being descends on the crew almost instantly once the beer has been consumed. How long will they have to wait for the next bottle of beer? Until they reach America? Or Japan?

The ship is becalmed. Not a breath of air stirs, but despite this everyone's spirits are high. Beer is clearly able to work wonders.

Tuesday, August 20, and the *Tai Ki* is still not making any headway. On the contrary, she is caught in a relatively strong back current, and everyone has the impression that the junk is moving backward, hardly an encouraging feeling for sailors who are waiting for wind.

The calm is telling on the crew's morale again. The *Tai Ki* hasn't made any progress worth mentioning for three weeks. The expected winds from the southeast and northwest still haven't put in their appearance, and all the dissatisfaction the crew members are feeling is directed at Carl, the captain and navigator, who bears the final responsibility for the ship's course. A little wind, a little progress, and those harsh judgments would disappear in an instant.

The water pollution in this area can't be ignored. Patches of garbage float by the *Tai Ki* constantly. Plastic and Lord knows what else swims on the surface, and underwater visibility is greatly reduced.

Bill gets up on the wrong side of the bed: "No wind, no headway, no nothing," he grumbles. If that was meant as a weather prediction, it proves to be a correct one. A slight breeze comes up in the afternoon and creates a sense of motion, but the actual progress the ship makes is hardly worth mentioning.

Two days later the sea seems to be aboil. Fountains shoot up into the air and splash back down on the surface. In the midst of this foaming, rolling stretch of water is a pod of whales. This one is far larger than any that has visited the *Tai Ki* before. Whales had approached the ship in the past, circled it, accompanied it a way on its course, but never before had they totally surrounded it as they did now. There seems to be no end to them.

Water shoots out of their air holes like steam blasting out of locomotive valves, and a fine spray descends on the ship. Suddenly both ship and sea take on an odor that is both strange and at the same time familiar: whale oil.

The crew members are standing on the forward deck and alongside the helmsman's cabin, are staring out at the sea, laughing, fascinated.

"Smells like cod-liver oil," Bob says. "Yeck!"

"It's awfully good for you," Hal says as he wipes the spray from his glasses.

Some of the whales are only a few yards away from the ship. They heave the huge tonnage of their massive bodies out of the water, rise in slow motion like cliffs come alive, then sink back with a gurgling moan, rise again, one after another. They stage a water ballet of the titans, and the men of the *Tai Ki,* who are not a group to be easily impressed, stand watching in openmouthed amazement.

"Walt Disney would pay quite a heap for this," Bill says, winding up his movie camera.

"You could make a fortune with it on Broadway," Bob adds.

The crew kept watching the whales until their dark bodies disappeared on the horizon. A fountain rose glistening in the sun, then another. Nothing more was to be heard. The men saw foam roll, saw the water boil, saw the waves toss and finally subside. All that remained was the faint odor of whale oil clinging to the ship and to the skin and clothing of the crew.

Bob has prepared supper, salad à la Kendrick, cans of diverse meat and vegetables tossed together in a bowl and mixed up with mayonnaise. During the meal, talk centers on what the final destination of the voyage should be. This discussion arose from a previous one about the eternal question of provisions and whether larger portions could be served or not.

Carl thinks the *Tai Ki* can still reach San Francisco by mid-November despite the calm that holds her captive now. From that point on, the trip to Mexico should be unproblematic.

"On that leg of the journey, the winds are eighty-three percent in our direction."

"According to the charts," Bob mumbles skeptically.

"And what do the charts say about where we are now?" Hal asks. "What percentage of favorable winds are we supposed to be having off Japan?"

Carl declines to answer.

Before the expedition has even come clear of Japan, there is disagreement about where it should end. Bill and Wolf push for San Francisco. Wolf wants to get it over with. Hal abstains. The factor of time is unimportant for Bob; he doesn't care when and where the *Tai Ki* ends her voyage. Arno, Carl, and Allan offer no opinion.

Thursday, August 22. A breeze comes up, but it proves to be an unsatisfactory one. It isn't taking the ship in the right direction, and it soon gives out again, leaving her stalled among fairly heavy ground swells.

The compartments below deck are taking on more and more water each day, especially the two right behind the mast. It's obvious that the hull is leaking heavily in that area. Pumping has become a major project, and it continues to be an irksome one because of the seemingly endless supply of wood scraps that keep jamming the pumps and interrupting work every few minutes.

Friday, August 23. Wind at last, and even from the right point on the compass. Carl tells the crew the next day that the *Tai Ki* has covered the incredible distance of 90 nautical miles in twenty-four hours, an all-time record for the past few weeks and one of the best sailing days of the entire journey to date. The ship is underway to the east. Seas and ground swells are heavy, but the crew puts up with them gladly. On August 24, Carl announces that the junk's position is 144° 21′ east longitude, 36° 28′ north latitude. The *Tai Ki* has finally traveled far enough to make the distance worth entering on a chart.

The winds pick up even more and reach gale force. It becomes difficult to steer the ship and hold her on course in the heavy seas and gusty winds that continue for several days. Then Allan receives still another typhoon warning, but there seems to be something odd about this one. Either Allan misunderstood the name of the typhoon, or the message itself was incorrect. The storm coming up is advertised to the crew, erroneously or not, as "Mary." The storm approaches the boat from the west at a speed of thirteen knots and then suddenly disappears. It's possible that the winds that are driving the ship ahead now can be attributed to "Mary II." But the question is idle. The main thing is that the *Tai Ki* is making headway.

Carl and Arno are standing together on deck, discussing a money problem, some bill that should have been paid in Hong Kong, that was in fact paid by a money transfer that had been dispatched but apparently hadn't reached its destination. A radio message had come in, saying that efforts to trace the money were being made. Allan interrupts this discussion to pass on the latest reports about "Mary II." Hal is sitting nearby, splicing some ropes. Bits and pieces of the conversation reach his ears: "Mary — didn't receive the money — refused — hope Mary doesn't come down hard on us." Hal, who is always composed, always calm and cordial, jumps to his feet and leaps at Carl, sinking his fingers into the captain's throat.

"One more word about my wife," Hal screams, "and I'll throw you overboard."

With considerable effort, Carl, Arno, and Allan straighten out the misunderstanding. Hal, much chagrined, apologizes. Arno looks significantly at Carl: what are we in for if Hal, our most stable crew member, is reaching the end of his rope?

Sunday, August 25. Allan measures a wind velocity of 40 mph. The wind is out of the southeast and is driving the junk a bit farther to the north than is desirable, but just moving along under a blue sky and a full sail raises the crew's spirits. At last, the mood on board is good, and everyone breathes a sigh of relief.

Bob takes over the helm from Allan at 0900, and as he lights up a cigarette, his attention is directed from the helm just long enough to let the ship go into a jibe. Fortunately, the sail pulls up amidships and doesn't snap around far enough to smash into the rear stay on the starboard side. Carl, who is busy making breakfast at the time, runs to the helm and lays it hard over to bring the ship back onto her course. As she swings around, the wind throws the sail back to its original position with incredible force. Four spars shatter; a stay on the port side snaps; the sheets have torn loose and are flying about wildly in the wind. At first glance, it seems as if the whole sail is about to disintegrate. At second glance, things don't look quite so bad. The mast isn't damaged, and though some of the rigging has given way, most of it is perfectly intact.

Despite continuing heavy seas and wind, the crew sets about some essential temporary repairs. Some sail is taken in, and work begins. Wolf, Carl, and Hal, secured to the mast by safety lines, attempt some emergency splices on broken ropes. Arno helps them with this chore. The work progresses in a hectic fashion. The long days of calm seem to have taken the edge off the crew; they are not handling this crisis as calmly and competently as they had earlier ones. Three more spars break in the course of the afternoon; two of them had been arduously repaired just before the accident. No one could guess when final repairs could be made. But damaged or not, the *Tai Ki* is making a good four knots per hour. She hasn't done as well since somewhere south of Okinawa.

Arno hooks a line into his safety belt and flops into the water. The boat drags him along in its wake, and its speed keeps dragging him underwater like a water-skier who hangs onto the tow-rope after he's taken a spill. The crew hauls him on board a little later with much grunting and whooping. Then he settles down exhausted but contented in the hammock he has strung up amidships.

Yes, the *Tai Ki* is making headway. But has the crew made any progress as a team? Is it really all that important that the crew develop close cooperation? Is the cohesion within the group so minimal because some of the crew members are interested in the expedition only as a "crossing" or as an "excursion"? Or are these questions nothing more than a reaction to the near disaster with the sail? Perhaps, but it also cannot be denied that much has gone wrong and been done wrong. Bob's carelessness at the rudder is an example. And lots of other examples could be cited, all the false moves that inexperienced sailors had made under storm conditions, seemingly trivial mistakes that did have, or at least could have had, serious consequences. Then there was the eternal haggling about food. But couldn't that be interpreted as a safety valve by which other emotional pressures were released? It was too early to draw any final conclusions. Last but not least was Carl, the ship's captain, who always seemed to act contrary to the crew's expectations. Would it be fair to reproach him with this fact? Or were the general feelings toward Carl nothing more than that often unconscious tendency to find a scapegoat? And in this situation, who made a better scapegoat than the captain, the man responsible for all nautical decisions?

Despite the pleasure he took in the ship's headway, Wolf was far from content. All he could think about was the end of this voyage whose beginning he was eager to forget. He had experienced a number of disappointments. The hopes and expectations he had had at the outset of the expedition had not been fulfilled. Only disappointment remained, disappointment and a paralyzing sense of helplessness that expressed itself in ill temper and an insistence on having his own way. His preoccupation with food, a preoccupation he shared with others on board, showed

how adept he was at making mountains of molehills. His contact
with the rest of the crew was minimal; he felt more animosity
toward his shipmates than anything else; and there was no one
with whom he could share confidence.

Allan was not given to introspection or self-doubt. He found it
unnecessary to expend energy thinking about the ship, the purpose of the expedition, the crew's behavior as a team. He had long
training and experience in loneliness, and he occupied himself
solely with the job at hand, not with what might have to be done
tomorrow or the next day. He kept himself in top physical condition and had taught himself to take sleep when he could get it,
dropping off and waking up again effortlessly. He was out to do
his job right, and in order to do that — here on this ship or anywhere else — he cut back his personal needs to a minimum and
focused on his work. He took part in discussions only when the
demands made on him seemed to approach the impossible. He
would speak briefly and brusquely, sometimes with biting wit, his
blond hair tossing as he accentuated his words with quick, sharp
movements of his head. Then he would turn away and retire into
himself again. Impatience seemed totally alien to him. Inner tranquility and self-discipline were his hallmarks, also the ability to
postpone satisfaction, to wait as long as he had to for whatever it
was he wanted. He was waiting for America now. He wanted to
have a look at it, "because," he said, "I probably won't have another chance." That was about all he communicated of himself.

By way of Sweden Allan received a message from Tom, the
ham radio operator in Kuala Lumpur, that a cold front was moving toward the *Tai Ki*. The drop in temperature came in the night
of August 27, sending the thermometer down to 72°. The warm
summer days of the more southerly latitudes were a thing of the
past now.

The sky is blue; then in the afternoon a dark cloud bank
emerges on the horizon, rushes down on the ship, and cuts off the

sky like a great curtain drawn by invisible hands. The wind picks up, and the temperature drops even more. But only three hours later the front has passed the ship and is speeding on toward the northeast. The border between the front and the surrounding weather conditions is sharply drawn; on one side black clouds; on the other, blue sky. Most meteorological phenomena can be observed with remarkable clarity at sea, but this encounter with the cold front brought that point home even more vividly. The front came toward the ship and left her again like a moving island of rain and dark clouds. Thunderstorms pass through the sky like great sailboats.

The temperature drops even more after the front has passed over the ship, and several crew members are bundled up in sweaters and foul weather gear. Some even resort to long underwear. Kuno was kind enough to leave his on board. The crew is duly grateful, for the golden days in southern seas are gone forever now.

Arno and Hal press to make final repairs on the sail, but Carl thinks the wind is still too strong. When the ship heels over, the sail dips into the water to port. Working on the sail under those conditions is simply too dangerous.

Whole schools of dorados surround the *Tai Ki,* but it is impossible to go after them in this sea and with the ship moving at this speed. Allan tried to harpoon one from the deck, but he can't manage it. The dorados drive multitudes of flying fish into the air. They sail like silver streaks above the waves, and some go astray onto the deck of the *Tai Ki.*

Hal is bent over working at one of the pumps when a magnificent specimen of a flying fish lands on his shoulder.

"Aircraft carrier Hal," Allan remarks.

Bob rushes to snatch up the fish. "A beauty," he mumbles, "a real beauty." He guts the fish and lays it out to dry on the rudder housing. Presumably he wants it as a souvenir, but he's scheduled for disappointment. The next day there's nothing left of the fish but a few scales. The rat feasted on it during the night.

Wednesday, August 28. Carl announces that the *Tai Ki* has passed another milestone. According to the log, she has covered 3,000 nautical miles, but Carl is sure she has traveled much farther. The device she is towing to measure her progress works only when the ship is moving above a certain speed, and even then it is not totally accurate. Carl is allowing for at least 20 percent error in his data and thinks the ship has in fact covered 4,000 nautical miles.

The weather is growing steadily colder, and the winds hold. Carl has finally decided to make the necessary repairs on the sail, and all hands are busily at work. A total of six spars are broken or split. None of the repairs that are made can be considered final; everything remains provisional. Arno and Bill patch one of the spars together well enough so it will hold for a while, no one knows how long. Work continues after supper and into the night. The crew manages to bandage, reinforce, or reconstruct three of the six damaged spars, and the sail can be hoisted three spars higher. The increase in sail area brings an immediately noticeable increase in speed.

Work on the sail continues the next day, and another session at the pumps is necessary because, contrary to everyone's expectations, the ship has taken on a lot of water again, so much that water has even gotten into the food barrels. This is the first time that has happened. Arno examines one of the affected containers and finds the tin cans inside it rusted. After three hours of pumping, the crew can feel how much better the ship handles in the heavy sea. She has regained her equilibrium.

Free time passes in the usual manner. Hal reads, Carl disappears into his cabin to sit over his charts. Bob studies German, as does Bill, who, after a little less than three months' work, is already able to carry on brief conversations with Wolf and Arno.

Arno urges the crew to keep at the repair work on the sail and get the ship into top form.

"We're going to be getting more wind soon," he keeps saying, and he has proved often enough in the past to be a more reliable meteorologist than the ones that make the official forecasts on the radio. Work proceeds at a good pace, and stronger winds do indeed come up, rising to a velocity of 35 mph and sometimes more.

Sunday, September 1, 1974. A bright, cool day. The temperature is 63°, probably cooler in the wind. Fall seems to have chosen the first day of this new month to make its appearance. Carl announces that the *Tai Ki* has passed the 150th meridian east. Only ninety more to go to San Francisco. According to the original schedule, the *Tai Ki* should be heading southeast along the California coast right now. She is, in fact, only about halfway out to the middle of the Pacific.

With the exception of Wolf, the crew members are all warmly dressed. Wolf is still running around in shorts and still swimming in water the temperature of which corresponds to that of the air. Bill goes to the other extreme. He has on every piece of clothing he can find, and over all that he's wearing his bright red rain outfit. He waddles around the ship, looking clumsy as an astronaut in full regalia.

"I'm warm, and that's all I care about," he says whenever anyone makes snide remarks about his appearance.

Wolf has had an unhappy experience with the rat. When he returned to his sleeping place after coming off a watch, he found that the rat had been working at his private stores. And it had known exactly where to gnaw through the plastic bag to get right into the chocolate.

"That beast has an uncanny sixth sense for chocolate," Wolf commented.

Needless to say, there was no trace of the rat, and all attempts to smoke it out were in vain.

Arno's journal:

Toward evening two ships appear on the horizon and head straight for us. The first is a huge Japanese freighter. It comes in close and toots three times on its foghorn to say hello. We toot back and feel good about the friendly exchange. The other boat is an old Liberian tub that has surely seen better days. It comes in close, too; and feeling very cordial, we give it three toots as well. The ship circles us, then comes in so close that we're afraid it's going to run us down. The crew has misunderstood us. They think we need help, and only after almost an hour of hollering, blinking, and flag-raising can we make clear to them that we're O.K. That's taught us a lesson. We'll be a little more careful about our signals from here on.

At supper, talk turns to the ship's position and when she might cross the international date line.

"Let's bet on it," Arno suggests.

"Good," says Carl. "The grand prize is a bottle of whiskey."

Hal is the most optimistic of all. He guesses September 21. Allan picks the twenty-second; Bill, the twenty-third; Arno, the twenty-fourth; Bob, the twenty-fifth; Wolf, the twenty-sixth. Carl makes his choice only after he's consulted his charts. He comes up with September 20.

"I just hope," Bob says, "that we all lose and that it won't take that long."

As it turned out, no one was right, but the errors were all in the wrong direction. The *Tai Ki* didn't pass the invisible line in the middle of the ocean until September 29, but her crew broke out a bottle of whiskey anyhow. "If not as a grand prize," Bob said, "then as a booby prize."

The crew's greatest concern during these days was the ever-increasing amount of water the ship was taking on. Arno and Bill had been spending hours at the pumps, and now compartment three alongside the mast seemed to be leaking as much as compartments four and five. There is much speculation about the cause. Wolf thinks the boxlike construction of the ship is to blame.

"If boards have to be joined together at a ninety-degree angle," he says, "the joint can't be very strong."

"Hogwash!" Arno replies. "Either the caulking has loosened

up between the joints, or the joints themselves have opened up a little."

"There isn't a wooden hull on earth that doesn't take on water," Carl intones again.

Bill's contribution to this talk is a hearty flow of profanity. He isn't particularly interested in the cause. What concerns him is that he has to spend hours bent over the pumps.

Monday, September 2. The wind dropped off during the night, and the sea is calm. This is an ideal opportunity to continue work on the sail. Arno, Allan, and Bob are soon at it, while Hal and Wolf man the pumps. They spend all morning and a few hours after lunch, and even so they manage to finish only compartments four and five. The boat has taken on a massive amount of water. As soon as the water level in the compartments drops far enough to permit inspection, Hal makes a frightening discovery. Tiny fountains are shooting in through fine cracks in the hull.

Hal fetches Carl. The captain goes below deck with Bob, and, armed with flashlights, they set about finding the cause of the leaks. The mystery is soon solved. Carl cuts into some planking in compartment five where the leaks are heaviest and discovers a whitish creature embedded in the wood. It's about the length of a matchstick and as big around as a garden worm.

Bob cuts into the wood and makes a similar find. Now Carl nervously examines still another point in the planking. Here he finds an elaborate junction of several holes and passageways that is not much larger in area than the palm of his hand.

Dripping with sweat, Bob and Carl climb up on deck. Carl announces that shipworms have attacked the hull. This accounts for the large amounts of water the ship has taken on in recent days.

"As far as I can tell, they're just along the waterline at this point," Carl reports. "There seem to be more of them on the starboard side than on the port."

The crew responds with amazement, anxiety, and outrage.

How could this happen? Precautions had been taken against just about everything in the book, and preparations made for every emergency: for storm and calm, for a broken mast, for illness and any conceivable crisis that could befall the crew. But nobody was prepared for this.

"The ship must have been infested with the larvae back on Ap Lei Chau," Carl said. "Or maybe we picked them up in Kaohsiung, but I doubt that."

"But we talked about this possibility till we were blue in the face," Arno shouts. "We treated the ship's hull to prevent it."

"Right," Carl replies. "The hull was painted with tung oil, six coats at that."

"And what good did it do?"

"You can see for yourself." Carl points down at the ship under his feet. The crew members squat silently on deck.

The *Tai Ki* was infested with parasites that have always been a threat to wharfs, docks, and pilings as well as to ships. At the right temperature and in the quiet waters of harbors, the larvae of the shipworm or *teredo navalis* attach themselves to any available wood. From these larvae develop the mollusks themselves, which then bore conical holes into ships' hulls and form networks of passageways. They can reach the length of a foot and are equipped with small pincerlike shells that are used exclusively for boring. The shipworm can also plug up its holes with small calcium deposits.

The shipworm uses a rotating motion of its body to drill into the wood and cut away at it with the shells on its head. Nothing can make wood exposed to salt water completely safe from these parasites. Even the most modern protective coatings, such as paints with poisons mixed into them, cannot guarantee long-term protection.

Carl had, of course, taken this possibility into consideration while the boat was being built. Oscar So had recommended repeated applications of tung oil as the best protection.

"We use tung oil on every new ship we build," Oscar So had declared. "No problem." In the case of the *Tai Ki,* Oscar had gone drastically wrong.

After the initial shock of the discovery had worn off a little, the crew decided to carry out an extensive examination of the ship to see just how bad the infestation was. It was possible that there were only a few small colonies of shipworms. Such were the crew's hopes at that point. Then every effort would be made to patch up the leaks.

Arno's journal for Monday, September 2:

We've finally finished repairing the sail and just in time. We're getting a good strong wind now out of the right direction. But all is not so rosy. Compartment five is a third full of water. Everyone is hard hit by this development. And as far as I can tell, everyone on board senses that the expedition is fast drawing to a conclusion. Water is pouring into compartment six now and into the radio shack, too.

Arno sets about whittling little wooden plugs to drive into the holes. Carl is below deck, trying to find out how extensive the damage is. Allan is at his radio. He relates what has happened and asks advice on how to deal with the teredos.

The answers he receives indicate that his listeners interpreted his bad news as a joke or remained uncomprehending. The crew was instructed to soap down the hull, give the worms some whiskey, or head for shore. This last suggestion was not dismissed out of hand. Indeed, it had already been discussed just after the shipworms were discovered. Go ashore, why not? But what land should the *Tai Ki* try to reach? The junk lay some 1,000 nautical miles from Japan and hundreds of miles from the next island. Should she turn back and go into drydock for repairs? The crew was aware that teredos die within twenty-four hours after exposure to air or fresh water. But if the *Tai Ki* did turn back, the crew members would have to realize that such a step could mean the end of the expedition in Japan because it would be much too late then to make another try at crossing the Pacific.

The crew is unanimous in the decision to go ahead. The international date line lay 1,200 nautical miles ahead, California another 3,000 beyond that. As long as the crew members were unaware of how seriously damaged the ship was, they could still harbor the hope that both ship and crew could hold out for the rest of the voyage.

The next day the wind picks up even more. The sea is rough, and the water in the compartments rises accordingly. One pump isn't enough to keep ahead of the game. Two pumps manned by two men each will have to be at work constantly. Other crew members help by bailing with buckets. Some of the food containers are more than half full of water, and the radio shack is in danger of total inundation.

Carl and Arno begin the long, arduous task of plugging the holes. Neither of them has had any experience with this work, but the next few weeks will provide them with more than enough.

They both try to widen the holes, kill the teredos inside, then seal off the holes. At first they think it most sensible to plug up the most obvious leaks in a large section of planking. But this proves to be a mistake. They find and kill dozens upon dozens of shipworms, but no sooner have they finished one section than water starts pouring in next to the patches they have made. The planking along the waterline looks like a sieve.

Arno's journal of September 4:

This work is enough to drive us to despair. I worked until 2200, trying to plug up the major leaks, but it was hopeless. The planking is so riddled with holes that the wood splinters whenever I drive a plug into it. More water than before comes in. Then I manage to drop my light or hammer. Who knows if those lost tools will ever see the light of day again.

Carl puts on his wet suit and goes overboard to look at the damage on the outside of the hull. He's pale when he comes back on board. Thousands and tens of thousands of shipworms have attacked the hull along the waterline and slightly below it, especially in the midship section. Carl can't even begin to guess how many of the parasites there are.

Wolf's journal of September 4: "Hal and I spent the whole day pumping out compartments five and six, but we didn't come anywhere near getting them dry. Arno, Bill, and Carl are working on the hull. Bill is whittling wooden pegs. . . . By evening, Arno has driven about seventy of them into the planking but all to little avail."

The men of the *Tai Ki* are suddenly confronted with a new danger. The thought that the shipworms might literally chew the ship out from under their feet and sink her was disquieting enough, but a far more frightening prospect was that the excessive amounts of water the *Tai Ki* was taking on would affect her stability and make her subject to capsizing even in a relatively mild storm.

In her present condition, it seemed unlikely that she would be able to weather storms as serious as those she had been through in the past few weeks.

Allan climbs out of a compartment after hours of pumping. He flops down on the deck, panting heavily, hoping for relief from the pumps until tomorrow at least. But before long, the sloshing of water below deck drives him back to work.

Hal and Bill think the only way to stay ahead of the water constantly pouring through the hull is to man the pumps continuously. Neither Carl nor Arno ventures an opinion. Even Lap Sac seems to be affected by the low morale on board. His behavior can only be called abnormal when he responds to Bob's call to dinner by crawling away under a tangle of ropes.

The evening scene in the cabin of the *Tai Ki* is a dismal one. Sea bags rescued from the flooded compartments are lying around in disorderly heaps. Around them and among them, piled helter-skelter, are tin cans, ropes, strips of rattan matting. The filth the pumps have brought to the surface has spread all over the ship. The cabin reeks of rotting foodstuffs, mold, bilge water, sodden clothes.

"A thousand miles from land in a boat that leaks like a sieve. I've been on better picnics," Bill says.

"The understatement of the year," Bob puts in.

Everyone on board is fully aware of how critical the situation is, but the crew remains unanimous in its decision to go ahead as long as the ship holds together. Tomorrow is Carl's birthday. Tomorrow two men will have to pump for hours on end. Maybe there will be a good wind tomorrow. Tomorrow may bring heavy seas, and tomorrow may also bring the expedition of the *Tai Ki* to a quick and terrifying end. But no one is prepared to think that far ahead.

CHAPTER EIGHT

The Time Bomb Ticks On

THE BARRELS OF PROVISIONS IN COMPARTMENT FOUR ARE already more than a foot underwater. In compartment six they're fully submerged, too, and in compartment five the water sloshes over the tops of the barrels whenever the ship rolls heavily. Compartments five and six have been partially emptied of their stores so that the water can be bailed out with buckets. Buckets are more efficient at this point than the pumps, which are constantly clogging up with debris.

Everyone except Carl, who is patching leaks, is at work bailing. One bucket after another is passed up out of the compartments; both pumps are at work, too; and after four hours of work, there are palpable signs of progress. The ship is no longer so sluggish; she rides on waves rather than wallowing in them.

After lunch, the crew removes a food container from compartment four to make room for bailing there as well. It is almost impossible to move around on the deck of the ship. All the hatches are open; barrels, sea bags, and other gear are piled around them. A barrel of canned soups is standing near the mast on the forward deck. Arno sorts through the cans and discovers that most of them are so badly rusted that they have to be tossed overboard.

The drinking water from the tank in compartment six is pumped into the empty tanks in compartments four and five.

Arno and Bill tear the empty tank apart, and the scrapped wood from it winds up lying on deck, too.

The *Tai Ki* is surrounded by a fog so thick it might as well be rain. There is a light breeze, and the temperature drops to 63.

Clothes are drenched, the deck slippery. But despite all this, despite a situation more critical than any the ship has been in to date, spirits are high. Every man is responding to the present danger with a maximum effort. Past irritations seem meaningless now, and even those crew members most directly involved often wonder how the squabbles of recent weeks even arose.

The platitude that extraordinary circumstances elicit extraordinary responses from people seemed to hold true on the *Tai Ki*. The work that had to be done was hard. The ship itself was filthy and cluttered. It seemed impossible that only a few weeks ago this same ship had lain on the dark blue sea of more southerly latitudes, that the crew members could dive into clear, warm water, snorkel, drift on the surface, that they could stretch out on the deck and bake in the sun.

Was the crew finally involved now in the adventure that some of them had sought, the opportunity to grapple with danger face to face? No, this was no great adventure. It was just a period of endless, monotonous, back-breaking work. The scene aboard the *Tai Ki* was one of pure misery. But, paradoxically, the crew was in a state of euphoria. Everyone worked with a will, pitched in, laughed. There was no complaining, and decisions that would have involved long debate only a few days ago were arrived at now in seconds and by means of mere gestures. There was a job to be done, and that was that. Three days after the discovery of the shipworms the crew had finally become a crew. The necessary pumping was done without any palaver about it. The crew worked more intensely and efficiently than before and was able to relax more easily afterwards. For the first time in weeks, Allan whistled as he pedaled away on his generator bike.

209

Thursday, September 5, 1974. This is Carl's birthday. The skipper is forty-four. There is a festive noonday meal and an even more opulent one in the evening. Carl's birthday bottle of whiskey is gradually emptied, and talk turns to other things than the shipworms chewing away at the hull. A tape cassette provides a Beethoven violin concerto as background music. Wolf talks about Rommel's African campaign. Thoughts of war lead the conversation around to the American war in Vietnam and America's role in the Pacific in general. Then lighter topics come up: credit cards, the value of the dollar, the price of whiskey.

Carl thinks everyone should be wearing his safety belt from now on and be constantly hooked onto a safety line. Arno declines to obey this regulation, arguing that he has no desire to be dragged down with the ship when she goes.

That night the boat heels over so steeply that Arno is nearly tossed out of his hammock. It is 0300, and an unusually violent thunderstorm is passing over the ship. Arno pulls himself together, stumbles to Carl's cabin, and wakes the captain. He fights his way to the helmsman's cabin to fetch the anemometer and measure the wind velocity. The rain is so heavy that he can hardly read the anemometer, but he finally makes out that the gusts are reaching 45 mph. The sea is getting rougher, the ship heeling over still farther in the wind. The rigging is stretched to the breaking point. Arno and Carl paw their way across the deck to reef the sail, struggle with it in the wind and rain that drench them through in a matter of minutes.

The *Tai Ki* is making remarkable headway, but she is not handling as well as she should. She has gone sluggish again. Bill wakes up and joins Arno during his watch at the helm, ready to help with steering or anything else that should suddenly need to be done.

The rain continues to fall heavily, and the interior of the cabin is soon drenched. The roof is leaking badly again, but no one will have time anymore to repaint it with tung oil and sawdust. No hands can be spared from the pumps. "We'll just have to get used to these bedtime showers," Bob says fatalistically the next morning at breakfast.

The ship is making five knots, sometimes even six. Those are top speeds for junks, and delighted as the crew may be about moving rapidly along on course, they are not delighted with the by-products of this speed: tears in the sail, split spars, more water in the compartments.

The sail jibes in a gust, and Carl rushes out to bring the wildly flapping rattan under control. Then another gust throws the sail back to its original position, and Carl takes a nasty fall. He had tangled his foot in a line and would have gone overboard if the catwalk hadn't brought him up short. He has a black eye, abrasions, a lump on his head, a twisted ankle. If he had gone overboard, no one would have been able to help him in this sea and at this speed.

But despite his wounds that Bob patches up for him, Carl immediately goes below deck with Arno to renew the battle against the teredos. Carl and Arno are constantly trying out new techniques. They're covering the larger holes with boards taken from the demolished water tank and are continuing to use wooden plugs in the smaller holes. Carl is also resorting to rubber now. He has cut up the remains of an old wet suit and formed small rubber plugs and strips that can be used as a form of caulking in tiny holes and cracks. With this rubber caulking, he is finally able to patch up the section of planking in compartment five that has given him and Arno the most trouble so far. The fountains that had been squirting through the hull day and night there finally dry up.

While Carl and Arno are working on the hull and while Hal, Bill, and Wolf are trying to create some order on deck and in the cabin, Bob is checking through his medical stores and repacking anything that needs it. Praise for Arno comes out in the course of this work.

"As a doctor," Bob says to him, "I can say one thing about this ship: the medical supplies and equipment are first rate."

Arno mumbles a "thank you" and continues with his patching.

"But I do have one complaint to make about all this first-rate gear," Bob adds with a grin.

"What's that?" Arno asks defensively.

"I hardly ever have a chance to use it."

Laughter from all hands as well as the devout wish that Bob's medical supplies will continue to stay packed away in their water-tight containers. Carl, who is wearing a few fresh bandages, doesn't find this conversation particularly amusing.

September 6, 1974. The wind has dropped off and the sea turned calm. The water has a peculiar light green tinge to it, a sign, Carl points out, that it isn't very deep. The *Tai Ki* is in the grip of the cold, northerly current flowing from Japan now, the Ojashio Current, and the crew is experiencing unpleasant side effects: significantly lower temperatures, heavy fog, calms that can last for days at a time. For modern ships, of course, these calms pose no problems; but the *Tai Ki*, dependent on winds and currents, loses more valuable time here.

Once again the question of whether the *Tai Ki* shouldn't end her voyage in southern California comes up for discussion. Opinions remain divided. Arno still favors Central America. No one bothers to ask whether the ship will even be able to hold out that long.

Allan is sitting with Carl on the helmsman's bench, relating to him what advice he has heard by radio from Oscar So on the matter of shipworms. Like most of the suggestions the *Tai Ki* has received on this subject, these too are lacking in relevance. Oscar urges the junk to go ashore on the nearest island. He must have failed to consider that the nearest land, the Midway Islands, is over a thousand miles from the *Tai Ki*'s present position.

"Great," Carl says. "What are we supposed to do, build ourselves an island to land on?"

Oscar maintains that it's essential to bring the boat up on land and treat the hull with a mixture of tung oil, cement, and some other ingredients once the shipworms have died. Unfortunately, Oscar the shipbuilder has no answer to the question of what should be done if the boat can't go ashore and has to remain at sea.

The junk was completely isolated now, and her only tie to the outside world was Allan's radio contact with Nynäshamn. It was somehow comforting for the crew to know that no matter how rough the seas became or how deep into the ship's planking the teredos bored, Allan's radio continued to make contact with Sweden every day at 2400 ship's time.

Hardly is one shift at the pumps over before another begins. Compartments five and six have sprung new leaks. Back to the pumps. Get the water out, and get it out fast. Grinding work that drives even the simplest thoughts from your head and leaves you with barely enough mental energy to count the strokes of the pump, your panting breaths, the seconds, minutes, and hours.

No one thinks far enough ahead to imagine how much water there will be to pump out tomorrow or even a few hours from now. Everyone knows that there will be no end to working at these little yellow pumps. There'll be pumping to do tomorrow, the day after tomorrow, next week. At least everyone is hoping there will still be some pumping to do next week, for as long as the crew is pumping, the *Tai Ki* is still afloat.

But despite all the difficulties they faced, the crew members of the *Tai Ki* were enjoying themselves, strange as that may seem. They derived solid satisfaction from pumping the compartments dry once more, from getting through another day, from plugging another few dozen leaks in the hull. They enjoyed sitting together at meals, talking, enjoying simple pleasures that suddenly assumed great importance for them.

Saturday, September 7, 1974. The *Tai Ki* has been underway a little less than three months. It is cool, only 64°. Winds of 10 mph are coming out of the northwest and shifting to the north.

The junk is making good headway. Bluish gray water slaps against the hull; gusts cut across the surface of the sea. Sometimes there is a lull as if the skies were taking a deep breath only to let go with some more gusts. But there is no danger of a storm. The barometer is steady at 30.2. The ship's barograph, that fascinating instrument that records meteorological history, has gone on strike. The pointer that records the ups and downs of the weather on a rotating drum won't work anymore. It leaves only a barely visible mark in one place, then thick splotches of ink in another. The barograph is hardly an essential instrument for the *Tai Ki,* but the crew had always taken pleasure in being able to read the weather record of the day or week just gone by.

Carl and Arno have been remarkably successful in patching up compartment five. It took on very little water overnight, barely enough to reach the top of the floor timbers. Half an hour's pumping has it cleared of water. The planking remains wet, but it is no longer invisible under a dark, oily flood.

Compartment six is still in poor shape, but there has been some progress even here. The food barrels are no longer inundated. Carl and Arno go back to this compartment to see if they can't conquer the remaining major leaks. The pump detail keeps on pumping.

The sun comes out in the afternoon, peeks shyly through the haze at first, then breaks completely free. Whitecaps shine a brilliant white on the blue water. The darkness of stormy nights is forgotten. The revitalizing force of the sun is most palpable after one has been without it for a long time. Whoever has a free moment goes out on the forward deck to lie or sit in the sun and soak up its rays. The humidity that had plagued the ship disappears. The deck planking and the woven walls of the cabin dry out. Even Lap Sac emerges onto the deck and stretches himself flat.

Sleeping bags, pants, shirts, T-shirts, and handkerchiefs are spread out on the deck or hung on the rigging. The sun's rays were essential for driving moisture out of bedding and clothing;

Waves smashing against the weakened hull complete the work that the shipworms have begun. It is not long before the first leaks open up (*left and below*). (Both G)

A newly patched leak in the ship's interior. Carl and Arno squatted below deck in the compartments for weeks on end, attempting to halt the march of the teredos. (G)

Weapons used in the battle against the shipworms. The knife was used to cut away the wood, the wire to pull the teredo out of its hole, the wooden pestle to drive cement into the leak. The cement itself was made up of glue softened with tung oil and mixed with bamboo wool. For larger holes, special wooden plugs were made. (G)

Left: The struggle against the shipworms was not limited to the ship's interior. The crew members donned their wet suits and went overboard, often in extremely cold seas, to examine the outside of the hull for leaks. An hour of this underwater work was enough to bring on total exhaustion. (G)

Above: Wolf Werner Rausch standing near the mast during a storm. He is wearing a safety belt over his rain gear. In heavy seas, any kind of activity on board was impossible without a safety line, and on more than one occasion the lines were all that saved crew members from death. (D)

Overleaf: With her sail reefed to reduce wind resistance, the junk battles her way across the North Pacific more than a thousand miles away from the nearest land. (D)

First and second page in section: We experienced perfect sailing weather. The junk was making up to twelve knots, and we could hardly believe our good fortune. Then one fateful blow after another smashed down on the *Tai Ki*. She lost her radio contact and began to take on water. We discovered that teredos had attacked the ship. The worms bored their way through the ship's planking and made a sieve of her hull. (D)

Below: A portrait of the enemy. The shipworms looked like huge, thick-bodied maggots equipped with a drill bit. (G)

Right: A sample of the devastation the slimy mollusks wrought as they made their way into the ship's interior. (D)

Storm. The ship can barely be held on her course as one breaker after another crashes into her. The waves rise fifteen, twenty, and thirty feet high. The ship is taking on more water than ever. All hands man the pumps. The crew members put on their wet suits and rain gear to protect themselves as best they can from the cold and dampness. (Both D)

Left: A breaker has smashed a section of the catwalk. (P)
Below: Water in compartment five. Daylight shines up through the darkness. (D) The hull has sprung a major leak at the waterline. (D)

Above right: Again and again the spars snap like matchsticks, and again and again we attempt to repair them. Allan works without a safety belt, supporting himself with no more than a length of rope. (BM)

Below right: Carl and another crew member mount a new bamboo spar. (R)

Left: Breakers smash into the sail. (R)

Below: Damaged rattan matting, now useless for sail repair. A few weeks earlier, when the ship was still in sunnier climes, damage like this could be borne with equanimity. In the present situation, it could mean disaster for the expedition. (BM)

The rudder breaks, and the ship wallows
helplessly. Carl orders his radioman,
Allan, to send out an SOS. (D)
Canvas sea anchors are soon torn to shreds
in the heavy seas. The crew resorts to a
provisions barrel as a makeshift sea
anchor. (D)

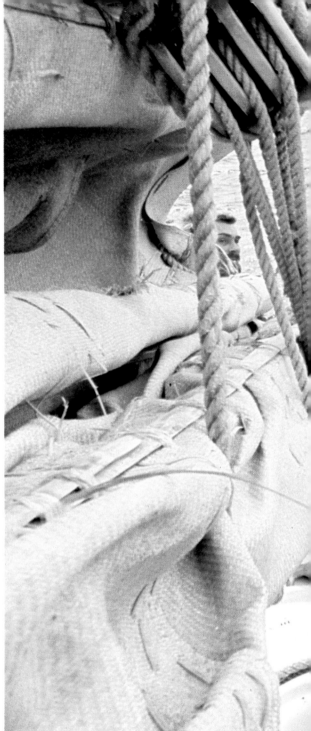

The junk had withstood storms and typhoons for 113 days. We calculated
that she could have reached the coast of North America if she'd been given
only forty days more. But now the *Tai Ki*'s voyage was over, and all we could
cling to at this point was the hope that we would be rescued. . . . (R)

fortunately, they never stayed hidden from the *Tai Ki* for too long at a time. Without them, everything would have turned moldy and finally rotted.

The question of why the shipworms attacked the *Tai Ki* is the topic of conversation at supper. Were sufficient precautions taken? Was the right protective coating used? If not, why not? Carl is obviously pained by this talk. It is easy enough to see, even through the armor of his usual reserve, that he has been shaken badly by the discovery of the teredos.

"The ship got six coats of tung oil. To the best of anyone's knowledge, that should have done the job," he snapped. "And as far as I know, neither the Chinese nor anyone else had any modern paints or pesticides two thousand years ago."

"But they must have had some effective protection against shipworms," Allan objects, "or they couldn't possibly have crossed the Pacific. What did they use back then?"

"I don't know, and nobody else does either," Carl replies. "But we're fairly sure that the ships were built in freshwater harbors along the rivers, and there just aren't any teredos in fresh water."

"Historical authenticity is a lot of bunk," Wolf burst out. "If we're going to be historically authentic, then we'll have to throw our pumps overboard right now."

"Shut your damn trap!" Carl shouts at him. Then he gets up and goes back to work below deck.

Sunday. How many Sundays has the *Tai Ki* spent at sea? Nobody can remember. Carl wants to have a day of rest. The crew has been working hard and deserves a break. Arno disagrees. He thinks more work should be done on the sail at least. It still isn't in good enough shape to satisfy him. Bill, Allan, and Arno set to work repairing another spar. Carl keeps at the patching. The others pump.

"Ridiculous as it sounds," Arno notes in his journal, "the pump detail seems to be the favorite at this point. Everybody would rather pump than patch up the sail, certainly rather pump than do KP."

Monday, September 9, 1974. A light breeze and the monotonous jobs that have become routine by now: pumping, patching leaks, whittling plugs, cutting out rubber caulking, pumping, pumping.

The sea is relatively calm, and that doubtless explains why the ship has taken on so little water. But the pump detail still has to work better than four hours to clear all the compartments.

And no sooner are they done than the wind comes up and sets the *Tai Ki* heeling steeply to starboard. Bob, who has gone into compartment six to look for leaks, climbs back up on deck, groaning about what he has seen. The water is pouring in again. All hopes of a little rest are dashed.

But despite this, Carl maintains that the crew will be able to cope with the leaks and still reach its destination.

Carl fashions ingenious devices for battling shipworms: wooden plugs, rubber patches, gadgets made of copper tubing. This gear is put to use whenever another stream of water is spotted pouring in through the hull. Arno works patiently and persistently.

The amount of food served at mealtimes has ceased to be a sore point. Now that it is possible to estimate fairly accurately how much longer the voyage will last, it becomes clear that the provisions are more than ample. Larger portions can be served, and there is an end to Wolf's constant complaining. The crew members are content at their work and are getting enough to eat. Their morale remains high despite cold and dampness.

The cold is not much of a problem during the day, when constant motion keeps the body warm, but nighttime is a different story. Arno, grown wise through long experience, had told everyone back in Hong Kong what to expect. "Take plenty of warm clothes, lads, all the long underwear you can carry. You'll be needing it." His shipmates had laughed at him then, but no one is laughing anymore.

The rat has eaten up all of the chocolate Allan had hanging in a bag near his sleeping place. There's nothing left but shredded wrappers. Allan curses up a storm; then he trades his pipes and tobacco with Hal for some licorice so that he'll have some kind of candy left for the rest of the trip. The price of the licorice involves a few dollars as well as the pipes and tobacco. The cash part of the debt will be settled after the *Tai Ki* has reached land. Once the voyage was over, these shipboard transactions seemed comic enough to those involved in them. At the time, however, they were carried out in bitter earnest.

It is not surprising that unique laws of commerce developed on the junk. In a situation where normal wishes and desires have to be cut back, seemingly insignificant items take on an exaggerated value. The loss of a piece of string or sheet of paper or a pack of matches could haunt a crew member for days. In this context, the importance that Hal and Allan attached to their transaction is quite understandable.

Fog sets in again and invades the ship. The wind is favorable and sends the boat along at a good speed. But there is no sun; damp cold seeps through the ship. It is impossible to take a position reading. Both sea and sky are gray; it is hard to tell where the one begins and the other ends. There are hardly any waves to speak of, just long swells that raise and lower the *Tai Ki* in a steady rhythm.

As everyone had expected, the ship has taken on more water, but there is neither alarmingly more nor gratifyingly less than on any other day recently. The floor timbers are covered, but three hours on the pumps suffice to clear the compartments. At last the deck can be cleaned up. When the crew had emptied the compartments to make room for pumping and patching, they had dropped everything wherever there happened to be room. Arno and Bob set about creating order. It's a good thing that all the canned goods are marked with paint. The paper labels have all disintegrated by now. Tin cans pass from hand to hand once more.

"I'd like to know how many more times we'll have to toss this stuff around before we finally eat it," Allan grumbles. An unexpected speech from the least voluble member of the crew.

In compartment five, Carl has jammed himself against the wall for stability. A wave lifts the ship; Carl loses his balance, slips, injures his knee cartilage. Bob does what he can, but the captain will be out of commission for the next couple of days. Arno, Hal, and Bob go below deck to keep working at the leaks. The sight of the riddled planking depresses them all, even though the worst leaks seem to be under control. Then a remark from Arno dispels any sense of security. "I can see daylight through the hull," he says. The worms have bored right through in some places.

Arno has developed a new patching material. He pulverizes some woodworker's glue that has turned rock-hard, adds tung oil to it, then mixes in some bamboo wool. The result is a pliable yet rugged and durable material.

September 11, 1974. The sea turns rough toward morning, but the crew is not overly concerned. They have made remarkable headway against the teredos. When the boat smashes down heavily on the waves, she takes on some water, a little reminder to the crew that they can't sit back on their laurels. But on the whole, the situation looks fairly promising.

Bill is curious about his future, and he consults the cards. They don't seem well disposed toward him. Wolf fares much better. Clearly dissatisfied with the results, Bill starts reading a book about fortune-telling with cards. Maybe he thinks more knowledge will help him on the way toward a rosier future.

Allan has bad news at breakfast. He had trouble with his radio last night. He had sent out his usual call at midnight.

"This is OZ-6 QK on board the *Tai Ki* calling . . ."

No response from Nynäshamn.

"The shipworms are still making life hard for us."

Silence.

"This is OZ-6 QK calling . . ."

Silence.

Allan turns his dials nervously: "This is OZ-6 QK calling . . ." Arne in Sweden is probably working at his radio with equally little success. Allan is able to receive disjointed phrases and strange noises but not a single comprehensible sentence. He keeps at it for two hours, then gives up.

He tells the crew at breakfast that the radio is probably beyond repair, but he is going to see what he can do with it. After spending the whole morning working at it, he reports to the crew at noon that the set is in fact irreparable.

"What's wrong with it?" Bill asks.

"Humidity's gotten into it," Allan answers brusquely.

The crew was shaken. First the shipworms, now this! The ship's precious and fragile link with the outside world was broken, and her possibilities for communication were seriously limited. Constant contact could not be maintained by means of the emergency radios. The ship could not supply sufficient electricity to keep these radios in steady operation, and their range, even under the best of weather conditions, was only about a thousand nautical miles.

The *Tai Ki* was not, of course, as dependent on accurate and up-to-the-minute weather reports as she had been in previous weeks. She seemed at last to be clear of the typhoon belt. But typhoons were not the major problem. The ship was not fully seaworthy now. No one could predict how much longer it could hold out. It could sink at any time or, far worse, capsize in heavy seas.

Allan's transmitter and perhaps the transformer as well had certainly suffered water damage. Allan had been able to exchange a few ragged words with Nynäshamn. He indicated that he was having trouble with his equipment, and he hoped he had been understood.

"I hope so, too," Arno said. "We don't want them going through all sorts of unnecessary motions."

"Such as?" Hal asked.

"They might think that we're sinking or in some serious trouble. . . ."

"Aren't we?" Bill asked.

The same question was going through everyone's mind.

Wolf tries to lighten things up. "Kuno would be pleased. Now that the radio's out, we're much more authentic than we were."

No one laughs.

In Europe, news of the *Tai Ki*'s radio breakdown travels quickly. Arne Andersson contacts Leo in Austria, then reaches for the telephone to call Kuno.

"I imagine Allan will have the thing functioning again soon," Arne adds encouragingly.

Arne is wrong, but no one in Sweden or Austria panics. If the *Tai Ki* were in serious trouble, she could always fall back on her emergency radios. This assumption proved correct. But this new misfortune that is plaguing the expedition still causes concern. The *Tai Ki* seems to be having more than her share of bad luck. But there is nothing anyone can do but sit back and hope for the best.

On the junk, the first shock that Allan's announcement caused quickly dissipates. The crew members are soon able to joke about their broken-down radio, and in comparison with the teredos, it certainly appears as the lesser of two evils.

All this time the *Tai Ki* has been making good progress on an easterly course. She has had an ideal wind for the last few days and is scudding through fog at better than four knots.

"As long as we keep moving along at this speed," Bill says, "I don't give a damn about fog, shipworms, or anything else." And the others all agree.

Although Carl has not been able to take the ship's position for several days now, she must be nearing the 170th meridian. Only ten to go to the international date line. No one expects to win the bet made some ten days ago because the whole crew thinks the *Tai Ki* will pass the date line well before September 20.

There is, as usual, water in the compartments, quite a lot in five. But the crew of the *Tai Ki* has dealt with far worse floods. Arno and Bill man the pumps and have the compartment dry in an hour.

Arno works on the leaks again in the afternoon. He crawls around in the belly of the ship, drills, chisels, hammers, reams holes out and seals them up. He's working alone. Carl can't help because his knee is still not cooperating.

During the night, Allan receives a clear signal from Sweden. The first question he hears is whether the *Tai Ki* is having radio trouble. Allan's hands are usually busy at the dials, but they lie still in his lap now. There is no adjustment he can make that will let him transmit a reply.

Arno's journal of September 13, 1974:

Cloudy, foggy, miserable. The temperature has dropped below 60° for the first time, and we're getting increasingly heavy winds from the northeast. They're forcing us to take a southeasterly course. I worked all morning below deck with Carl. After lunch he went to take a nap and slept the whole afternoon. He still isn't fully recovered from his injuries.

We've decided to try to raise some coastal radio station and notify it of our position and situation. Allan sets to work, and a little after 2000 he manages to put an end to the *Tai Ki*'s total isolation. He has reached the U.S. Coast Guard in Kodiak, Alaska, and he asks the radioman there to pass on word of the *Tai Ki* to the Marine Department in Hong Kong.

It is unclear whether Kodiak can do this or not. The first thing the station does is notify the Pacific Rescue Service of the *Tai Ki*'s plight. Allan arranges to contact Kodiak again the next day.

It took quite a while for Allan's message to reach Hong Kong. Danny, Allan's contact there, passed the message on to Sweden; and it wasn't until September 23, ten days after Allan contacted

Kodiak, that Kuno finally heard by way of Nynäshamn what had happened aboard the *Tai Ki*.

A storm is rising. Gusts tear at the sail. The damaged spars creak. The ship slaps down hard on the gray-green waves that rush at her, attacking her and being repulsed again and again.

Dark cloud banks form above a light fog. The sun is obscured, and under this gray sky, the foam on the waves looks a dirty white. Spray drives into the cabins, spatters on the rattan matting, and runs down on the deck.

The rolling of the ship makes sleep almost impossible. Arno gets up to inspect the ship. Everything seems in order. In the morning, Bob and Allan are the first out of their sleeping bags. They're the first pump detail of the day. They stretch, still exhausted after a night that provided them with little rest. The weather continues wet and cold.

The junk is heeling steeply to port. The crew members dig in their heels, hang on with their hands. They can't even think about standing up straight. Bob, Wolf, and Bill curse and rage. Arno remains silent.

Allan reaches for the hatchway to compartment five. As he raises the heavy wooden lid, a hollow thumping rises up from below, a thundering that couldn't be heard before above the roar of the storm. Allan's lean face stiffens; the muscles along his jaw stand out. He stares silently into the compartment. Arno, Bob, and Hal join him. No one speaks. The compartment is more than a third full. It has never taken on this much water before.

Arno rushes over to compartment four and tears the hatch open. The same story. The provision containers are barely visible. The lids of the barrels are floating around in the compartment and smashing against the hull with every roll of the ship. The water often sloshes up as high as the top of the drinking-water tanks. It'll be a sad day when bilge water gets into the ship's drinking water.

The *Tai Ki* is wallowing. More and more water keeps pouring in over the deck and through the hull. Three kerosene lamps fall into compartment four and break. Other odds and ends bob around in the dirty water. The crew is on edge.

Bob's journal:

We'll have to pump and bail all day today. We form a bucket brigade, and the two pumps set to work. We work for hour after hour, but there seems to be no end to the water. We finally have compartment five dry. Arno jumps down into it and starts repairing leaks. The water level in compartments four and six gradually drops until they, too, are dry. Things don't seem so bad for a while. Then Arno yells to us that he's found a new bunch of leaks.

Hal's journal:

We grind up hardened glue and mix it with tung oil, then hand the paste on to Arno, who keeps squeezing it into leaks. Carl is fishing tin cans out of the water in compartment four. Bill and Allan are pumping and bailing. And all this is going on in the middle of a storm.

Wolf's journal:

Spray is flying over the cabin from windward, and the lee side of the junk is heeled over into the water up to the catwalk. A great deal of our energy is expended in just moving around the ship and keeping our balance in these seas. If we forget to hang on tight for just one second, we can take some nasty falls. I'm cook today. Dealing with pots and tin cans under these conditions is bad enough, but coping with the stove at the same time makes things even worse. There's spilled food and gravy everywhere.

The crew has not realized until today that the *Tai Ki* is running a race with time. But now no one is worrying anymore about whether she should land in this harbor or in that one. The *Tai Ki* will be lucky if she makes it to the nearest possible harbor. "All I hope," Arno writes in his journal, "is that we can at least make it to somewhere on the American coast. I'll be satisfied with that. And if I wanted more, I wouldn't be able to write it down, because my hands are too stiff and sore."

There is no time for worry, certainly no time for heroism. The only reflection anyone can afford is something like: "I hope everything turns out all right."

Sunday, September 15, 1974. Wolf's journal:

I wish I were anywhere else but on this ship. This is sheer torture. The storm refuses to let up. Indeed, it seems to be getting worse, and we've been in it for 48 hours now already. The waves are playing football with us. They tower over us; the air is dank and full of salt.

Arno's journal:

Another miserable night and another day of storm. The winds vary from 20 to 40 mph. The waves are massive. We're trying to relieve some of the pressure on the hull by not sailing as close to the wind as we were. We've found that some of the planks are pulling apart, and that's why we're taking on more water than before. We have to find a course that puts as little strain on the ship as possible. If such a course can be found in this weather.

A morning and afternoon pass. Arno spends the entire day below deck, and in the afternoon Carl starts caulking cracks in the planking in compartment four. Both he and Arno stick to their work until 2200. The compartments seem to be tight. But how long will they stay that way?

The crew members crawl exhausted into their sleeping bags, but there is no more chance of sleep tonight than there was last. "We should probably tie ourselves to the mast," Bill grumbles after he has been tossed across the cabin.

"Great idea," Bob says. "Then if we tip over we can at least be sure that you'll stay underwater."

"You get drenched one way or another," Bill replies, and he

tries in vain to go to sleep. The violence of the ship's movements is particularly palpable when the crew tries to rest. Work diverts attention from them during the day, but at night the rolling and tossing are the focus of the crew's existence.

Rain sets in, and as the storm grows worse, the rain becomes heavier and heavier. Wolf and Bill have devised a special lean-to for themselves, but when the rain starts pouring down, even this extra protection is of no use. Rainwater dribbles into their faces, and spray forces its way into the cabin from the side. Bill and Wolf try to make improvements on their lean-to but soon give up and let the water pour down on them.

Arno sits on the helmsman's bench, bundled up in his rain gear. The rudder lines are cutting into his wrists. He would like to sleep, too. There's nothing he would like more. The storm has been raging for over sixty hours now. The men stretched out before him are exhausted. They react like robots, are hardly capable of thought anymore, are almost too weak to suffer. This storm that has attacked the *Tai Ki* just before the 170th meridian is one of the heaviest the ship has experienced. The typhoons of the first weeks hardly exceeded it in violence.

Monday, September 16, 1974. The storm is over. The sun is peering through the clouds, and the temperature has risen. The sky is streaked with varying shades of gray, blue, and yellow. The crew regards some cloud banks on the horizon with suspicion, fearing that a new storm is brewing.

Inspection of the compartments shows, to everyone's astonishment, that the ship has taken on very little water. The storm seems to have curtailed the teredos' appetite somewhat. After four hours of pumping, the ship is dry.

The crew washes up, scrubs the ship down. Then they wash their clothes for the first time in days. Shirts and pants flutter from the rigging. Arno goes below to work on the patching. Bill, Hal, and Carl join him later, and by evening the ship is tighter than it has been for a long time.

Carl is pleased with his day's work and returns to his cabin, where he is greeted by a fusillade of squeaks. The rat is sitting on his chart table. It darts off, and for a while the captain puts worries about the ship, the crew, and the teredos aside to concentrate on the hunt. The reward on the rat's head is a bottle of whiskey, and Carl is out to win that prize. The trap that had been used to catch rats in Hong Kong before the ship sailed is useless. The rats that had been caught in it apparently drenched it so thoroughly with urine that no amount of scrubbing and sunshine can eradicate this warning signal. Carl sets about constructing a special trap for our stowaway. More bets among the crew. Will he catch the rat or won't he?

When Hal and Wolf emerge from compartment six, the one that causes most concern because all the dry staples like flour, sugar, and salt are stored there, they find Allan, armed with a long stick, squatting in front of the food box next to the stove. "The rat's in there," he says.

In an instant, the whole crew is assembled, knives, tin cans, and other projectiles in hand. Carl shines his flashlight into the box. No rat.

"That rat is an expert in guerrilla warfare," Bill says.

But the rat's campaign comes to an end the next morning. Carl has caught it in his trap, and he transfers it to the cagelike trap the rat had refused to enter. The captain proudly shows off his captive and then puts a sign on the cage that reads: "Pericles." The ninth official crew member has been christened. Lap Sac sniffs at his new shipmate suspiciously.

The rat has given up any efforts to escape and squats glumly in its cage. If anyone comes too close, it throws itself furiously against the wire mesh.

The crew votes to keep the rat alive. When the voyage is over, Jenny Croppers of the BBC will receive Pericles as a gift.

With the exception of number six, the compartments are holding their own against worms and water. Some of the pressure is off, but despite this, Bob, Hal, and Wolf are detailed to man the pumps. Experience has shown that it's unwise to let water collect over two days at a time. Arno and Carl are working below deck.

"The one thing on my mind," Arno wrote in his journal, "is the battle against the shipworms. It's doubtful that we'll win against them, and the ship is already badly damaged. The places the worms have attacked in force look like the end of the world. But only a few of the crew members are aware of this. Or are they just refusing to accept reality?

"It's possible that we may have to abandon ship. If we do, I hope we'll be able to do it fairly close to shore and not way out here in the open sea."

Wednesday, September 18, 1974. The *Tai Ki* left Hong Kong three months ago. Her position now is about 170° east longitude, 40° north latitude. With half the distance to San Francisco behind her, she still has about three thousand miles to go.

Last night, Carl had said at the triumphal banquet held to celebrate the capture of the rat that the *Tai Ki* would probably be underway for another fifteen weeks. At the time, the crew had been shocked by that estimate. But now only the moment has any importance for them. Compartment six has taken on more water than expected, much more. Arno had discovered more holes in it when he went below to get Carl's prize from the ship's stores.

Water is gurgling happily into the ship. The pumps and the bucket brigade are at work again, and the sense of relative security the crew had enjoyed for a few hours is gone, leaving one of urgency and danger in its place.

The junk presses on through the waves. Her situation is grotesque. She could not be any farther from land than she is right now. Vast distances lie between her and the nearest island; still greater distances separate her from the nearest continent. Her main link of communication with the outside world has been cut off.

The men of the *Tai Ki* hope for winds that will drive them forward, but they also fear those winds, for they know that the stronger the wind becomes, the faster the compartments will fill. But they are willing to pay any price for the sake of moving ahead. They sail on in a ship whose planking grows weaker day by day. They do battle with sea and storm, racing against time and against the small white mollusks that persistently gnaw away at the hull of their ship.

Who would win this race, the *Tai Ki* or the teredos? No one could tell. All the men of the *Tai Ki* could do was grit their teeth and man the pumps.

CHAPTER NINE

No Place Is Farther from Land

THERE ISN'T ANY CLEARLY MARKED ROAD TO PARADISE. YOU can't buy a ticket that will take you there. The idea that men can do anything they put their minds to is an illusion. Reality will always see to it that they don't wander too long in the world of their dreams.

We built the *Tai Ki* to realize a particular idea, a special dream. She would take us on a scientific adventure, take us back into the past so that we could make that past come alive again. And at the same time we hoped to make a small contribution to the understanding of the past, hoped to bring into sharp focus one small section in the huge, indistinct canvas of human history.

We had a picture of the path that would take us to the fulfillment of our dream. Free of civilization's constraints, we would drift across the Pacific for weeks and months on end, would face the unknown joyfully, courageously. Such was the dream. And the reality? The reality was glorious, invigorating, inspiring. It was also cold, wet, uncomfortable, and strenuous; it was full of deprivation and enervating boredom; it was wretched and dangerous. But the danger the *Tai Ki* faced was not a danger that brought out the best in men, one that they could face up to and conquer. No, the enemy the *Tai Ki* faced was a secretive, insidious one. A slow death came down on the ship, spread through

229

its body like a cancerous growth. The teredos chipped away at the wood of the hull and at the morale of the crew. There was no way to halt the march of the white, slimy creatures. The crew knew how that march could be stopped, but in mid-Pacific their knowledge was useless.

But the men of the *Tai Ki* had to do something. They pumped and bailed and pumped some more. And when they couldn't pump another stroke, they fell on their backs, as Arno did, with their legs spread and their hands behind their heads, closed their eyes, got their wind back.

Or they took refuge in pain, as Carl did, lay down, pressed hands against their foreheads, tried to forget, tried to avoid reality, gave themselves up to loneliness and wordless misery. The dream was long since at an end. This was a nightmare, an endless fall into a void, a waking to terror.

The men sit together, but each one stares off into a different corner. The distance between them grows.

The rain continued steady and uninterrupted, night and day. In the morning, pummeled by the constant heaving of the ship, the crew crawled out of their dank sleeping bags, stretched their aching limbs and muscles. They risked a look at the sky. There's got to be a hole somewhere in those clouds; this rain will have to stop sometime. The waves smashed against the hull, poured over the railing, swept across the deck. The crew stared out at the sea and waited for the storm to abate. Wind howled down on the junk. Someone measured its force with the anemometer, saw how fast it was moving and how fast it was driving the junk forward. He hoped — and feared — that the wind would hold. Or did he hope and fear that it would not?

Water poured into the ship, and the crew pumped and bailed and staggered about on board. Bob laughed with his lips pressed tightly together. Wolf raged against the fates, hollered and screamed. Arno kept silent and worked twice as hard as he had worked before. Carl, drained and exhausted by the nerve-racking work on the hull, retired to his cabin, took refuge in charts and sextant and in calculating on paper the course the *Tai Ki* would take in the coming days.

What had become of the dream? How did work here on board differ from the work everyone thought he had left behind? Was the short, slippery path from the helmsman's bench to the hatchways and the pumps any less repulsive than a path that leads through a cold, foggy November morning, across greasy, muddy earth, and down littered streets to a factory bench?

There was nothing novel in the unending chores of tending to the sheets, the rigging, and the shattered spars. Only in rare moments did the danger the ship was in make itself felt vividly enough to make any noticeable difference between the work a man did here and the daily rounds of his life at home, his endless hours squatting behind a desk or standing at a workbench, that daily routine that the crew of the *Tai Ki* had hoped to escape.

Wolf's stamping about in the cabin is his way of protesting against the circumstances in which he finds himself, his way — and perhaps the only way available to him now — of expressing his disappointment. Arno expresses his protest by his silence. Carl expresses his by a tranquility that is not born of self-confidence but of worry, perhaps of fear. In any case, it is a shield that protects him from a truth he has recognized or at least begun to suspect.

The others responded in ways peculiar to them: Allan with a calmness grounded in indifference and therefore with a calmness much stronger than Carl's. Bob with anger and fatalism. Hal with quiet nervousness and forced efforts to make the best of things. For Bill, accomplishment meant everything. He sought success; he wanted it and needed it, and nothing was more appalling to him than the imminent prospect of failure. Behind his cool, professional facade, he too was hiding disappointment and despair over circumstances beyond his control.

Thursday, September 19. The barometer is rising. The weather turns warmer, even though the morning is well along before a fog that enveloped the junk finally burns off. The compartments undergo inspection: four is O.K., five is O.K., but six has taken on more water than ever before. The crew has to take out the ballast stones. Piles of stones rise in the cabin and create chaos there once more.

Arno and Bill man the pumps. After two hours, the water level has sunk far enough to let Carl and Arno go below to inspect the wood.

"There's a hole in her belly," Carl says as he emerges from the hatch.

"Is the planking pulling apart?" Hal asks nervously, prepared to hear the worst.

"Hard to say. It could be that the teredos are down there, too."

Up till now, the assumption had been that most of the leaks were concentrated along the waterline. But the crew was in for a new revelation. Arno had patched several holes, but the water seemed to be pouring in at the same steady rate. The compartment would soon be full again.

Arno climbs into his wet suit. He'll examine the ship from the outside. Maybe he'll be able to find out where the new leaks are. He picks up some cement and bamboo wool, jumps into the water, adjusts his face mask, and takes a look around. A shark is lying in the water less than six feet away.

The shark remains motionless and stares at the diver with its dull eyes. It is almost ten feet long, large enough to tear Arno to shreds. Diver and shark hang in the water for minutes on end. Arno stays cool, tries yelling at the shark. No reaction. How is it Hans Hass does that? Arno — and the crew with him — waits, then waits some more. Then the shark turns and swims away.

Arno sets about his work. What he sees underwater sends shivers up and down his spine. "That scared me a lot more than the shark did," he says.

In a particularly weak section of the hull, Carl shoves a wire right through the planking, and Arno can grab onto the other end outside. Working from both sides, they try to patch up the worst leaks.

Arno's journal:

This ship is so riddled with holes that I don't know where to begin patching. How can this sieve possibly take us across another few thousand miles of ocean? Bill comes underwater with me and takes some pictures with his underwater camera. I don't have time for stuff like that. After better than an hour's work I get cold and go back on board to help Carl inside. He's still working on the same place where he started when I went to work outside, and the water is still pouring in through holes all around him.

Gray skies, invisible horizon, drizzling rain. Hal has baked a delicious bread. By the time Carl and Arno quit work at 2000 and Bob and Bill stop pumping, the junk has crossed the 170th meridian. There is hardly any wind, and the sea is calm. A gentle current keeps the ship moving along its course. Carl and Arno weren't able to fix the leak in the bottom of the hull.

Friday, September 20. Course: 30° to 40°. There's very little wind, but the junk is making some headway nonetheless. A long discussion begins at breakfast. It has nothing to do with the ship or the expedition or with what has to be done. It's about pipes, about the wood from which pipes are carved, about other materials that can be used for pipes — Carl collects porcelain pipes — about their value, their individual features, the cleaning of pipes, the different kinds of tobacco. If these scruffy-bearded men weren't sitting around in tattered clothes, sitting cross-legged on a filthy deck with plastic cups of instant coffee in their hands, if Lap Sac weren't snuffling at the rat's cage, if water weren't slapping against the ship's hull, both from inside and out, then this could well be a breakfast scene in a gentlemen's club. Carl indulges in long discourses about Danish pipes. Bob and Wolf chime in and encourage him. Arno finally puts an end to the conversation. He clambers over the ballast stones and drives the crew out to work. Everybody knows that the ship has taken on more water. The crew will have to get at the pumps and buckets.

Compartments four and five are fairly tight. It's six that is in

233

bad shape. It's clear now that the shipworms are at work on the ship's bottom as well as along the waterline.

Some of the worms have bored right through the planking, and Arno can pull them out of the wood. Bill takes movies. "We want to be able to show people what it really was like," he says. More food containers have to be shoved around and emptied.

Wolf's journal:

The deck of the ship, cluttered with stores from below, is a depressing sight, and our situation is equally depressing. We're running a race against the shipworms, and it looks as though we're going to lose. For all we know, they haven't even begun to mount their major campaign yet. And then there's the rust that has already destroyed a lot of our tinned food and will probably destroy a lot more before we're through. And there's the sea that threatens the very existence of this rickety ship whenever the waves become heavy. But if there is no wind and we don't make any progress, then the danger is that our "steamer" will fall apart and sink before she can reach shore. No one on board expects the ship to hold out too much longer.

It's amazing to see the determination with which Carl and Arno fight back against the teredos. They've become real experts, developing a special cement and special tools for widening and then closing up the holes. The rest of us can't do much more than provide assistance by lugging stones around, clearing the compartments, and pumping away. The worst thing about our situation is its dead-end quality. There's just no way out of it. Our destination is incredibly far away, and there's no way we can bring it nearer any more than we can effectively prevent the collapse of our ship.

Arno's journal:

The ballast stones take up too much room on deck. We have to find some other way to deal with them, so we build a box that can be taken down into the compartments. If we have to fix holes under the stones, we pile the stones into this box to keep them out of the way. It's absurd to drag those stones up on deck, then drag them back down again every time we have work to do on the bottom of the ship.

I must have eaten something yesterday that upset my stomach.

Maybe it was those gulps of salt water I swallowed while I was fooling around with that damned shark. The pain was pretty bad, and I didn't get any sleep last night.

Bill's journal:

I don't know if we're going to make it or not. I think we are; or, more accurately, I want to think we are. The scenes of these last few days would do very nicely in a horror film. We're being eaten up the way you can get eaten up by ants in the Amazon jungle. The only difference between that and our situation is that shipworms don't work as fast as ants. At least I've heard that ants work faster. I don't know whether that's a pleasanter way to go or not. A slow death is supposed to be more painful than a quick one. I have too little experience in dying to make a judgment.

Saturday, September 21. The first day of fall. The wind is picking up, but the seas are not rough. The efforts of the last few days have not been in vain and they demonstrate that the crew can effectively delay the ship's demise. Arno has apparently located the main leak in compartment six and sealed it off, for the time being in any case. The ship has taken on very little water, and Arno's patches on holes that go right through the planking, sometimes reaching a diameter of about a quarter of an inch, seem to be holding fast.

"Hey, there's something wrong here," Bob said as he started pumping out compartment four. "There's hardly any water at all in here."

And when he started on compartment five, he remarked, "What a pleasant surprise!"

"Don't get too cocky," Arno called up from the depths of six, where he had been working for hours, bathed in sweat and bilge water.

Another Sunday, September 22. The weather may have been performing erratically everywhere else in the world in the year

235

1974, but where the *Tai Ki* lay now — the crew could still not take a clear position reading — the climate was behaving according to the book. Both air and water had turned cool.

Arno wrote in his journal:

We're beginning to notice that fall is here. The temperature is cooler than we're used to, and when there's even a little sunshine, everyone leaps at the chance to warm himself and dry his clothes. We're enjoying a day of rest. No one wants to give up that custom, and the regular rhythm of work days and a "Sabbath" seems to hold true on board the *Tai Ki* as well as elsewhere in the world. I'm not sure we should be allowing ourselves this luxury.

The water in the compartments is under control. There's water below deck, but it remains at a "normal" level. But then what is "normal" on this ship? Four hours of pumping? Or six? Are compartments half full of water normal, or does the cutoff line of normality come at one third? What under normal circumstances would be considered abnormal has become the norm here. Storms, for example, certainly cannot be considered unusual or abnormal. The experience of raging waves and a pitching ship, an experience that many of the crew had never had before, has become routine. The crew of the *Tai Ki* has been through thirty days of storm on this voyage. One out of three days at sea has been spent under malevolent skies.

The dampness and cold have become routine, too. And the creatures of the sea are now simply part of the normal environment. Before we left Hong Kong, even the thought of a shark could inspire a lust for the hunt. Now sharks are taken for granted, though they are not taken lightly. Sickness, shattered spars, tattered sail — all those things have entered the realm of the ordinary. The only thing that still remains outside that realm in the minds of the crew is the deadly disease that has attacked the ship's hull.

Two-man teams work at the pumps. In an hour, the compartments are dry, if the word dry can be used in this context at all. Then a Sunday atmosphere settles over the ship. The usual hectic action subsides. The men can busy themselves with things for which they usually don't have time or energy to spare. They put their personal gear in order and settle down for siestas. And they pick up their much-neglected studies. Bill returns to his German vocabulary lists, as does Bob, who is also working on Spanish and Morse code. Hal joins Bob in his Spanish lessons. Arno is cramming English vocabulary. Carl spends most of his free time tinkering. What he does is usually hidden from the rest of the crew. He busies himself alone in compartment seven. He cleans and polishes his nautical instruments, whittles, sews, weaves. It often seems as if his activities serve no other purpose than to fill time. Or are his projects a kind of self-communion, a dialogue with his hands and with himself? In any case, where other men speak, he keeps his hands busy.

Books are the main source of entertainment: light and heavy reading, detective stories and serious literature. Besides learning Spanish, Hal memorizes poems and does some reading about occultism. Bill continues to occupy himself with fortune-telling and mystical realms. "He's been influenced by *The Exorcist,*" Wolf comments.

Games have lost their interest. Every once in a while Arno and Bill manage to play some backgammon. Only rarely do Bill and Wolf play chess anymore, and no one has suggested a round of cards for weeks. During the repair work on compartment six, somebody turned up two Monopoly sets. There wasn't much of them left, just a few sodden houses and hotels, some washed-out paper money, an ownership certificate for some property on Oxford Street in London, and a penalty card that read "Drunken driving. Fine: $25."

What good is any of this stuff? The wet, bedraggled slips of paper are thrown overboard.

Little communication takes place on board the *Tai Ki*. There is talk but little communication. Concrete questions like "Where is the marlinespike?" are asked, but no one raises more fundamental ones. Everyone seems to know what he needs to know, have what he needs to have. Announcements are made, and that is that. Discussions rarely occur. Every individual seems preoccupied with himself.

The danger the junk is in is clear to everyone, but no one speaks about it. Whatever conversation does take place centers on the world beyond the Pacific and the *Tai Ki,* as if that world were almost within reach.

There is no discussion of emergency plans. On a sheet of paper hung up in his cabin, Carl has made some scant notes on what should be done in case of disaster: Bill is responsible for films and cameras, Bob for medical supplies, Allan for radio equipment. The rest of the crew members will stand by near the life rafts. Nothing more has been said or written about the big question of "What do we do if . . . ?"

Monday, September 23. Dank cold. Wind out of the north. The temperature is about 55°. The crew is freezing. Everyone stumbles about in layer upon layer of clothing dampened by sea air and the sweat that work at the pumps sets streaming from the pores.

More water below, nothing unusual, but enough to require a few hours of pumping. Hardly any wind, seas nearly calm. More talk at lunch about who will win the international date line lottery.

This is the first time for several days that Carl can take a reading of the ship's position. She lies at 174° 6' east longitude, 42° 46' north latitude. Carl announces a few hours later, "We have only two hundred and fifty nautical miles to go to the date line." The crew does some more heavy guessing on how long it will take now. The general opinion is another two days if all goes well.

"There are two thousand, seven hundred and ninety-five

miles between us and the entrance to San Francisco harbor," Carl tells the crew. Does that mean Carl has definitely decided to land at San Francisco? No one in the crew can say for sure. If the junk can maintain an average speed of 1.5 knots, she'll need another 77 days to San Francisco. That means she would arrive early in December. If she averages 2 knots, the rest of the voyage will take 58 days. If her speed is 2.5 knots, she'll be in San Francisco in 46 days. No one even dares dream of the average overall speed the crew had hoped to make before they set out: 3.5 knots per hour.

In a few days, the log blackboard in the helmsman's cabin will display a large "W" for west in place of the "E" for east that it has carried so far. The 180th meridian has a symbolic meaning for everyone on board, even though the ship has long since passed the halfway mark of her journey from Hong Kong to San Francisco. The crossing of the date line will mean the ship has passed into another hemisphere. The crew will have officially returned to the Western world.

"We won't be climbing up the east side of the globe anymore," Bill says. "We'll be sliding down the west side."

Allan has picked up a message from Nynäshamn. The message he sent via the coast guard station in Kodiak finally reached Europe. The Swedes confirmed receiving it. So everyone in Europe knew now where the *Tai Ki* was or knew where she had been two weeks ago, knew she was making headway then and that the crew was well. The Swedes could not know whether their message would reach the junk or not. They could only hope it would. They were still unable to raise the *Tai Ki* on their radios. No other ship had reported seeing her. No one else had made radio contact with her.

Tuesday, September 24. Favorable winds. Position: 176° 29' east longitude, 42° 7' north latitude. Cold. Exhaustion. Work at the pumps, sometimes twice a day.

Arno harpoons a fish from the deck of the ship, hits it right in the head. Everyone, including Arno, is astonished by his sharp aim and steady hand.

Arno's journal:

We'll be able to keep that fish around for a few days. The temperature is 54, and this ship has become a floating deep-freeze. In this climate, we're much more eager to crawl into our warm (but not always dry) sleeping bags than we were before. The days are shorter by a few hours. The sun travels across the sky farther to the south, and its warmth leaves us earlier in the day....

Wednesday, September 25. Wind, a heavy cloud cover. The *Tai Ki* is making reasonable headway. The pumps are in action, not so much to clear the compartments as to drain them enough to permit more patching. Carl and Arno will fix more leaks today only to see new leaks open up tomorrow. This endless task drains the strength, tears at the nerves. Exhaustion and lethargy reign on board.

Thursday, September 26. Will there be two September 26's? Carl thinks that's a possibility. It looks as though the man who picked the latest date in the lottery will be the winner. The great pessimist — or the great realist — will walk away with the prize. But more important than that is simply the fact that this symbolic line will be left behind, this symbolic step accomplished.

Compartments four and six are leaking heavily again. More provisions in four have been spoiled, particularly tinned goods that have been rusted by the salt water. The crew throws them overboard along with some soaked egg powder, flour, and macaroni from compartment six. Arno's eternal warning — "Go easy on the food! We don't know how much longer we'll be underway" — takes on a new meaning under the present circumstances, but it is no less valid than it was before.

But despite the loss of provisions, the crew members are unable to restrain their appetites. Everyone is starved, and many seem to have a need to stow away as much as possible at every meal. Perhaps everyone feels that each meal may well be the last the crew will have a chance to eat on board ship.

The last set of rattan ropes on board is used to replace the bindings that hold the sail to the mast. Hal wraps the bindings with rattan matting to prevent them from wearing through too quickly. "This is a voyage between fear and hope, despair and confidence, expectation and disappointment," Wolf writes in his journal today. "We live constantly torn between these poles."

Friday, September 27. Erratic wind. Cold. Position: 179° 10′ east longitude, 40° 19′ north latitude. No one will win the date line lottery.

Bill writes: "We're moving toward the date line at a pace that makes a snail look like a jet plane. This ship is sailing through molasses, not water."

Arno and Bob repack the stores in compartment six. In the course of their work, they come upon another sack of ruined egg powder that smells like carrion. But as compensation for that loss, they turn up several sacks of beans that had been shoved back into a corner.

Leakage is "normal," and the crew puts in four to five hours at the pumps while Carl and Arno continue patching below deck.

Saturday, September 28. The crew sits down to breakfast, convinced that today is the day the *Tai Ki* will cross the international date line. But then the wind — and with it the junk's progress — drops off quickly. Today won't be the day after all.

The sail has to be reefed for more repairs. Hal, Carl, and Arno set to work. In the afternoon, the sun comes out for the first time in days. Everyone dives into the water for a bath. At 60° the water is still just barely tolerable. Clothes and sleeping bags flutter in the wind, and on the south side of the ship, the crew members search among piles of boards, ballast stones, and gear for a few square feet where they can stretch out and soak up some warmth, a rare commodity these days.

Carl takes the ship's position repeatedly, calculates and re-calculates, but even with his best mathematical efforts he can't make the date line come any closer than it is. The *Tai Ki*'s position is 179° 42′ east longitude, 39° 55′ north latitude. Everyone has lost in the lottery, even the worst pessimists in the crew.

Sunday, September 29 (I). The night brings a rapid change in weather. The barometer dropped from 30.2 to 29.8 during the day, and the crew was forewarned. The wind rises to gale force and develops gusts worthy of a typhoon. The sail is reefed in the course of the night, the watches reinforced. The storm seems to be coming from every point on the compass.

At 0800, Carl announces that, according to his latest calculation, the ship has crossed the 180th meridian. This news does not prompt any jubilation, and why should it? The compartments have taken on a lot of water, as they inevitably do whenever the seas are heavy. Four and six have held out fairly well, but five seems to have imbibed whatever water four and six didn't want. And there is a new development: compartment three, the one in front of the mast, is flooded, too.

Bob's journal: "We've finally crossed the date line. We can hardly say we've arrived anywhere, but we've at least gotten somewhere. If this grand event had taken place much earlier, we — or at least I — might have been able to work up some enthusiasm about it. But now we simply acknowledge the fact and let it go at that."

Bill's journal: "It's a pleasant enough day, but I can't say I have any strong feelings about crossing the date line. So we've covered some distance and are a little farther along on our way to America. I'd like to think the last half will be easier than the first, but I can't believe it."

Allan's journal: "The announcement that we'd passed the date line didn't hold much meaning for me. I certainly didn't feel any great pleasure. The only thing I felt pleasure about was that we had a good wind and were making good time. That's what gave me pleasure that day."

Wolf's journal: "We've crossed the 180th meridian. Now we're on our way into the Western world. The countdown has begun. May the winds be kind to us. We've gained a day, and we've set the clocks ahead an hour. This is progress we can feel. We've moved into a new dimension of time that may well bring us a change in luck."

Hal doesn't consider the crossing of the date line worth mentioning. "Heavy winds and swells. We reefed the sail, had to tack it later, a dangerous business in this weather."

All quiet on the western front. Wind, cold, heavy seas, cloudy skies, the horizon rising and falling in the diffuse light. The constantly shifting wind makes a tack essential. Mounting it was not a simple task.

The sail is reefed so that the force will be reduced if it should happen to jibe. But this necessitates bending a lift to the aft tip of the sail to let it clear the roof of the cabin. Once that is done and the tack is in place, the sail can jibe without smashing too heavily into the starboard stays. Once the tangle of lines is straightened out, the sail can again be raised five spars high.

Arno climbs up the mast and leaps about like an acrobat, disentangling the lines. Bill films his daring feats. Then Carl emerges from below deck and joins Arno on the mast as Bill's camera continues to hum.

The *Tai Ki* is making good progress, five knots and sometimes more. But the result is, of course, that water starts pouring through the hull again. The planking is so porous now that there is no hope of sealing it off quickly and effectively.

At supper, the crew discusses whether the crossing of the date line should be celebrated.

ARNO: "There's still a lot of water in six."

CARL: "I know. Should we keep on working?"

ARNO: "Well . . ."

ALLAN: "I wouldn't bother."

CARL: "Why not?"

ALLAN: "Now that we're in the Western Hemisphere and so

close to the American coast, we can swim to shore in a pinch."
Carl jumps up and descends into compartment six. Allan, whose
attempt at humor has enraged Carl, shakes his head. Bob quietly
withdraws from the group.

WOLF: "We better start pumping again. The less water there
is in the ship, the faster it goes."

Another joke? Irritated glances fall on Wolf, who tries to clear
up the misunderstanding.

"No, I'm serious. I wasn't kidding."

No one replies. No celebration takes place.

September 29 (II). The same date as yesterday and another
Sunday at the crew's disposal. Two Sundays one right after the
other have to be a good omen.

The wind remains steady, and the *Tai Ki* must be several sea
miles into the Western Hemisphere by now. The sky is cloudy,
and Carl is unable to take a sextant reading. Hal is sick and
spends the entire day laid out on his sleeping mat. Bob and Allan
man the pumps. Wolf takes over Hal's duties as cook. Bill mixes
cement and hands it on to Carl and Arno, who keep plugging
holes and finding new ones to plug.

The strong wind out of the west and northwest abates somewhat in the course of this second Sunday, but it may well be that
the wind of about 15 mph that remains is a fairer one yet for the
Tai Ki. It leaves the sea relatively calm, sends the ship along at a
respectable three knots, and gives the impression that it means to
blow steadily for a good long while. It gives the crew hope that the
voyage may yet come to a happy end sometime in the foreseeable
future. But hopes of that kind remain hopes, nothing more. "If"
continues to be the word most frequently used on board.

That evening, a bottle of champagne emerges from the deep-
est depths of compartment seven. Carl had saved it for celebrat-
ing the crossing of the date line. Toasts are proposed and drunk in
plastic "wineglasses."

CARL: "Here's to the international date line."

BILL: "To San Francisco!"

Allan smiles to himself.

No one can quite manage a festive mood, and the celebration on the deck of the *Tai Ki* soon comes to an end.

Monday, September 30. A day like any other day, despite the fact that it was preceded by two September 29's. That, of course, is a fiction. Two days passed, regardless of what numbers anyone chose to give them. There's no catching up with time and certainly no getting ahead of it.

The condition of compartments five and six is "normal" today, but four has taken on twice as much water as usual. Several teredos seem to have bored all the way through the planking there. Hal and Wolf man the pumps all day, and Carl finds a large hole in the narrow slot between the bulkhead and the water tank, a hole a good half inch in diameter in the bottom of the ship. Water bubbles up through it as though a spring had started to flow in the belly of the *Tai Ki*.

Compartment three has water in it, too. Wolf pumps for two hours before he has it more or less dry. The ballast stones will have to be removed here in the next few days and the holes plugged.

Tuesday, October 1. The fifth month of the *Tai Ki* expedition begins today with storm, rain, cloudy skies, high waves, and water below deck. It begins with exhaustion and a fit of ill temper.

Carl complains at breakfast that his cabin has sprung a leak, that the water woke him, and that he couldn't go back to sleep again. He complains so bitterly that one could almost have the impression he was blaming the crew for his misfortune or taking the sea itself to task for the disrespect it showed the captain of this ship. A journal, a notebook of Allan's, some films and signal rockets, and a number of other things are drenched and ruined. Under other circumstances, this tirade might have inspired

245

laughter. But given the mood the crew is in, it evokes only irritation.

The sea turns rougher, and the ship's anemometer measures gusts of 55 mph. The waves rise to twenty-five feet and higher. Everything is dripping wet, and the same jobs have to be performed once again. The crew's physical and psychic reserves are nearly at an end. A lethargy sets in that renewed activity can conceal but not dispel. It is present in every motion, every word, every thought.

Wolf's journal:

Plugging up that one big hole that Carl found in compartment five is not going to save this ship. The shipworms are everywhere, chewing out new passageways and popping up in unexpected places. And those that aren't chewing are surely copulating and reproducing madly. The presence of gurgling little fountains at every conceivable point in the hull has long since disproved the theory that the teredos had attacked the ship only at the waterline.

Storm. Anything that isn't tied down and anyone who doesn't hold on tight will be tossed from one side of the ship to the other. Bob claims that the dog's behavior is a sure sign the storm will become more severe still. Lap Sac is a "sea dog" if there ever was one, and his instincts can be trusted. He doesn't dare go out on the forward deck anymore; all he does is cautiously stick his nose out from under the canvas curtain behind the mast, then retreat again under the deck planking.

Waves smash over the deck. Water pours through the leaky roof into the cabin. Water sloshes around below deck. Water smashes against the hull. Water splashes over the bow.

Wednesday, October 2. The wind has dropped, and the *Tai Ki* can lay on her full sail. She is making good time again, but despite this, there is tension in the crew. Exhaustion has driven each crew member so deeply into himself that he can't emerge enough to meet another halfway. The loose unifying bond that

The U.S. Coast Guard received Allan's SOS and initiated a rescue action that ran like clockwork from beginning to end. Two Coast Guard search planes, we learned by radio, were sent out to find us. Jubilation broke out on board when we heard the sound of a plane's engines. Soon after, we saw the search plane as it spotted us and began to circle the ship. (D)

It had become impossible to keep the compartments dry with the hand pumps, and the Coast Guard plane dropped a motorized pump by parachute. The chute hung up in the mast (*above*) (BM), and it was no easy task to lower the dangling pump to the deck (*below*) (K). The parachute remained stranded on the mast, and it puffed out in the wind like a torn spinnaker.

Right: Lap Sac's final portrait. We had no assurance at all that we would be found; and if we were not, the rubber life rafts would be our only means of survival. The danger that Lap Sac's nails might puncture the air chambers of the rafts was too great, and we had to put our faithful shipmate to sleep. (BM)

Below: The rescuers arrive. The container ship *Washington Mail* steams toward the *Tai Ki* while a Coast Guard plane circles overhead. (D)

The final minutes. The *Washington Mail* has moved in close (*above*) (P), but she cannot lower her lifeboats in the heavy seas. The massive ocean-going ship carefully maneuvers into position (*previous page*) (WM), and only after a number of attempts can the *Tai Ki* be lashed alongside her (*right*). (WM) Then the crew of the *Tai Ki* and all the portable equipment on board her are taken off in feverish haste.

Left: Captain Greenwell of the *Washington Mail.* When he first received word of the *Tai Ki*'s plight, he was almost 400 miles away from the foundering junk, but he steamed to her aid without a moment's hesitation. (D)

Farewell to the *Tai Ki*. This picture, taken from the deck of the *Washington Mail*, is the last ever made of the expedition ship. The wreck will drift in the trackless ocean, continuing its voyage for days and weeks until further storms finally smash it to pieces or — somewhere, sometime — wash it up on the American coast. (D)

had held the crew together is coming apart, and there is no one on board who can halt that process. Arno tries to close the breach in the crew's unity by calling constant attention to necessary work that has to be done. Hal tries by working. Wolf tries by loudly pointing out everyone else's errors. Carl remains silent.

Arno's journal: "We plugged up a large hole under water tank number six today. I'll be curious to see how much water the compartment has in it tomorrow. After six hours of pumping, I won't have any trouble falling asleep . . . thank God." Would Arno ever have thought or written that even a few weeks ago? Hardly.

The faces of the crew have changed, and the men behind those faces have changed, too. Bill, the big American who could do without food for a couple of days running two months ago and who thought he should "lose a little weight," has grown gaunt. His face is angular now, his expression harder. And his cool eyes have turned positively cold.

In Hong Kong, Bob had been a gruff, muscular Englishman with a bounce to his walk. Now, with his beard and straggly hair, he looks like a disheveled hermit. He still laughs his brusque laugh, but not quite so often.

Arno shows the signs of what he has been through more than anyone. His beard cannot hide the deep lines that have formed in his cheeks and around his mouth. He has aged, and he is tired. Exhaustion has left dark folds under his eyes.

Wolf's glance is less confident than it was. All joy seems to have been driven out of him, certainly any joy he took in the sea. He has apparently not found the path he was seeking. Or he has left it. Perhaps he has lost it.

Allan and Carl are the least altered of the crew, even in their appearance. Have they remained least affected by the voyage because of their peculiar relationships to reality? Allan expects little from reality and therefore cannot be disappointed by it. Carl remains unshaken by reality because he shuts out those aspects of it that might disturb him.

247

Hal seems to have grown stronger. Or is it simply that he has pulled the mantle of his knowledge and education so tightly around him that nothing suggestive of change could show through? Objectivity and calmness remained his hallmarks, even in the thick of this storm.

But everyone in the crew, with the exception of Arno, remained closed to his shipmates. Arno had struggled to build a community on board the *Tai Ki,* and he suffered most from the fact that he had failed.

How much solidarity really existed in this crew? How far could each man trust the one next to him? How much could the crew members depend on each other in a tight situation, in that situation that no one mentioned but that everyone thought about? This crucial question hung unanswered in the air.

A renewed discussion takes place about whether the *Tai Ki* should make radio contact with a U.S. Coast Guard station again. Arno and Allan are in favor, but Carl objects. He is afraid the *Tai Ki*'s messages could be misinterpreted and lead to unwanted reactions. Allan feels that he should maintain regular radio contact with a coast guard station and keep it constantly informed of the ship's position. No decision is reached.

Wolf's journal:

Compartment three: full. Four: not so bad. Five: the temporary patch in the big hole in the bottom of the ship broke open during the night. There was so much water that the pump could hardly make a dent in it. The problem now is that the shipworms have started breaking through in places that Carl and Arno can get to only with great difficulty. There are a lot of leaks like that, and there are some that can't be reached at all.

Every aspect of this trip has fallen under the influence of an evil star: we have neither a second of time nor a square inch of space we can call our own. We live in filth, are constantly drenched by salt spray, are always cold. It has been raining all afternoon, often heavily. On days like this I have little hope that this voyage will end well. What I want most of all is that it end soon.

I hold the flashlight for Arno in compartment six while he plugs up leaks. If I turn the light out, we can see little dots of light all over the hull wall. It looks like a miniature planetarium. Behind that surface, Arno tells me, the shipworms are at work, perforating the ship. We have to head for America or nowhere. We have no choice.

The nervous strain is tremendous. Our margin of error has been cut away to nothing. We can't afford any mistakes, can't afford any more damage to the hull, the rigging, the mast, And we can't allow ourselves any slack either. Let's hope we can survive and win this race against time and the elements. Our victory will come hard, if we can manage to win it at all.

Thursday, October 3. The mood aboard ship corresponds to the weather. It is gray in rain or fog, bright when the sun shines. And the ship's speed determines how much courage, energy, and élan the crew will have available at any given time. Their physical and mental state is totally dependent on weather and ship's speed; they are subject to forces they cannot control at all. Today the sun is shining again at last; every chore goes more easily, and every aching muscle ceases to ache.

There is, as always, water in the compartments. Three is full. Four, five, and six look somewhat better, but what can "better" mean under these circumstances? The water level may be two or three inches lower than it was yesterday. That isn't much in the way of comfort.

Repeated observation has made one thing clear; if the *Tai Ki* has to sail through heavy seas or close to the wind, water pours through her hull, but if she sails in relatively calm seas or before the wind and if her starboard side does not lie too deep in the water, she will not leak much at all.

In the evening, Carl finally decides that the ship should make contact with the U.S. Coast Guard again. Allan sets to work immediately, and after a few minutes he is in touch with the radioman on Kodiak. The coast guard man expresses his relief at hearing from the *Tai Ki* again. The last radio contact had been on September 13, and the coast guard was growing uneasy.

Allan gives the ship's position: 174° 27′ west longitude, 41° 0′ 2″ north latitude. The coast guard man confirms. Allan reports that all is well on board and arranges to make contact again in a few days.

This is the ship's first contact with the outside world in three weeks. The crew's reaction demonstrates how much that world out there on the other side of the horizon means to the men of the *Tai Ki*. Everyone on board, without exception, is relieved, happier. The possibility of communication with others has been granted them again. They will be able to get in touch if they have to. They won't just disappear without a sound, unseen and unheard. There is a world out there after all.

Friday, October 4. The wind is ideal. The junk has put 100 nautical miles behind her today: 98, to be exact. The sky is blue; the sun is shining. The ship is making a steady 4 to 4.5 knots and has traveled far to the east in the last few days. The sun comes up red in the morning at 0600 now. Not long ago it didn't rise until 0700.

Optimism flourishes on board. The men laugh and joke with each other, act as if they were just about to sail into San Francisco. Carl says he has his drydock all picked out.

"As soon as I'm on shore," Bill says, "I'm gonna go on one elegant binge."

"My spirits rise and fall with the wind velocity out of the west," Allan says. "My spirits are high today."

On a day like this, even the fact that the hull is in worse condition than ever doesn't depress the crew as it usually would. The water level in all the compartments is higher than it was yesterday. Bob and Allan are working at the pumps. Arno is hanging upside down in compartment three, plugging up leaks. His efforts seem hopeless. For every hole he patches, another opens up. In case the comparison with Sisyphus has slipped anyone's mind, a Greek visitor appears to remind the crew of it. The visitor is the *Master Petros,* a large freighter out of Piraeus. The ship approaches the *Tai Ki* and circles her, even though the *Tai Ki* is doing her best to remain unobtrusive.

A voice calls over through the megaphone: "Do you need help?"

Carl raises the signal flags "N" and "O": No!

The *Master Petros* steams on toward the east.

Saturday, October 5. The moon seems closer to the sea than the clouds scudding by it. There is a halo around it, supposedly a sign of a storm, but none blows up. The *Tai Ki* has hardly any wind in her sails. Only the barely perceptible current is propelling her forward.

The condition of the ship again gives cause for alarm. More and more compartments are springing leaks: more and more water is pouring in, so much water that the crew can hardly pump and bail it out anymore. What happens when they can't keep ahead of the flood, when there is just too much for them to handle?

Allan, who had almost always seemed confident up to now that the crew could sail the *Tai Ki* to the ends of the earth as long as they stuck to the pumps, begins to talk about abandoning ship. He mentions this possibility to Carl, and Carl too admits for the first time that a situation could arise in which the ship would have to be abandoned. But when exactly and under what circumstances?

Foundering presents no great danger. The crew could foresee that in ample time and prepare for it. They would be able to reach the outside world; they could contact the coast guard, then take to their life rafts. The real danger is a sudden turn for the worse in the weather, for a ship unresponsive to the rudder, full of water, and totally unstable is a ship ready to capsize in a matter of seconds.

Capsize! A word no one wants to hear but a word that haunts the crew. Everyone knows just how real the possibility is. The *Tai*

Ki, wallowing about with several thousand gallons in her belly, is hardly seaworthy. And if she should capsize, the disaster would be instantaneous. No one would have a chance to launch the life rafts, snatch up his gear, or even save himself.

The high hopes the crew had felt only a few hours ago are dashed now. The teredos have been at work in still another compartment; number two has taken on water. The crew members set to work clearing it out, bringing barrels of supplies on deck to make room below for the pump and the repair work. The barrels are heaved up on deck, shoved around; some are tossed into the sea. Rations are divided among the crew.

Food, food. Everyone is eating much more than he normally would. This increased need for food is partially a result of fresh air and hard work. But it is also clear that every meal may be the last chance the crew will have to eat their fill. Then, too, Arno's strict rationing, which had been maintained up to now, is no longer in effect. No one is thinking in terms of several months at sea. The future is a matter of days, perhaps one more month at best. No one wants to look too far ahead. And then there is the very real question of who will get to the canned goods first: the crew or the rust?

Position: 173° 2′ west longitude, 40° 56′ north latitude. The *Tai Ki* has been in touch with civilization again for a few days now. The cabin radio, which had been useless for many weeks, has started to work again. The reception is poor, but the set is pulling in Canadian and American stations on the West Coast. They haven't much to offer. There has been an earthquake somewhere. Sports news. Fashions. A bank robbery somewhere else. Music.

Carl offers some new calculations at supper: "If we maintain our present speed, we'll reach San Francisco in forty-six days."

Forty-six days. Such a short time but one that looks like an eternity now. A month ago this announcement would have elicited whoops of joy. But at this point? There is hardly any reaction from the crew.

Allan has contacted Kodiak by radio again. He inquires about approaches to the port of San Francisco. An argument with Carl follows. Carl insists it is the captain's business to make inquiries of that kind. Carl will speak with the coast guard himself next time. Allan shrugs his shoulders.

Sunday, October 6. Arno's journal:

Sunday as a day of rest is a thing of the past. We can't afford it anymore. Bob and Allan have to keep on pumping. Carl and I climb down into "the cellar" to search for holes and patch them with cement.

In the afternoon we clear out the barrels in compartments five and six. Bill helps with this chore. Hal and Allan and Bob man the pumps, not with the greatest enthusiasm. While they are at it, they discover still more leaks in compartment six. I spent the whole morning cementing holes in that compartment. These worms are insatiable.

We are discussing a new system for the watches. The idea is Bob's. I am very much against it, because it would throw us into total confusion. I suggest a modification of the old system. Some change seems necessary because Carl is complaining constantly that he gets too little sleep. He takes no part in this discussion that concerns him more than anyone else.

Two groups have formed. Bob, Hal, and Allan are in one; Bill, Wolf, and I in the other. Carl keeps to himself. I am able to convince the others to adopt my plan for the watches. Then Bill, Wolf, and I discuss possible arrangements with the coast guard. We should, I think, establish a schedule by which we call in at regular intervals or the coast guard calls us. If anything should go wrong, the coast guard should at least know about it and start a search action for us. I'll talk to Carl about this.

A strong wind all day. The sails are full. The change in weather the moon had forecast takes place, sending the barometer down. The *Tai Ki* is making good headway, but at the same time the increased speed also means more water pouring through the ship's hull.

BOB to Allan: "Well, what does our skipper from Denmark have to say?"

ALLAN: "Who?"

BOB: "You."

ALLAN: "About what?"

BOB: "About the whole show."

ALLAN: "It's one hell of a mess. We can't hold out much longer. If the worms do get us, you can bet it won't be in calm weather. It'll be on some dark and stormy night."

BOB: "Right. . . ."

ALLAN: "The worst thing that could happen to us would be to capsize. We'll have to stay in constant contact with the coast guard from now on so they'll be able to find us or at least always know where we are. The people in Kodiak suggested that themselves. . . . Nynäshamn has given them a full report on our situation."

BOB: "And why haven't you established contact with them?"

ALLAN: "Carl is against it. But as far as I'm concerned, this boat isn't seaworthy anymore."

Everyone else is worried about a sudden emergency, too; but still nothing is said about it; no preparations are made; no questions are asked. Is everyone basically optimistic, or are the crew members repressing reality, or is reality in fact much different from what it seems to be? Has the gnawing of the worms, the endless pumping and bailing, the staggering around on the cluttered deck, and the continual patching of leaks dulled and exhausted the crew, or is it just time — three and a half months at sea — that has nibbled away at their spirits?

Monday, October 7. Position: 170° 4' west longitude, 40° 31' north latitude. The *Tai Ki* has left the first ten degrees of west longitude behind. Position readings will fall in the 160's for a good while now. The weather is cold and damp, and the wind continues to blow strong. The barometer is high, 30.4. The sky is clear; visibility is good. Seas are moderately heavy. Blue sky, blue water. Scraps of white clouds overhead, torn by the wind; whitecaps somersaulting across the sea.

Breakfast is the scene of what will be the last argument about food. Arno distributes coffee to the crew. Each man gets six cans that will have to last him until the voyage is over. Wolf suggests that they divide up the remaining sugar and tea in the same way.

He gets into an argument with Carl. Tempers flare, then silence sets in again. Why bother? Everyone knows where the others stand, or thinks he does.

The old routine. Man the pumps, clear out the compartments, shove around tin cans and barrels. Arno stirs up a new batch of cement and descends into the compartments. Carl disappears into the darkness, too. The pumping goes on and on. Water everywhere. The scene has long since lost its novelty. Bob climbs down into a compartment to help Carl.

Bill is the cook. He decides to come up with a treat. He bakes cinnamon buns. Suddenly the whole ship begins to smell like Christmas.

"It was the greatest event of the trip, a real holiday feast. Cinnamon buns! Imagine, cinnamon buns! Fantastic!" Hal said later.

Arno and Carl have elevated the struggle against the teredos to a fine art. The first thing they did was make special tools for the job. One of these is a knife with a bent blade that they use to enlarge the hole. Once that is done, the shipworm is usually driven out of his lair by water pressure. Then they stick a long piece of wire into the channel to clear the hole of debris and kill any other teredos that might be in it. Now, of course, the water bubbles up in earnest, but Arno has his special cement ready, and he presses it into the leak with a stick whittled to fit the hole. If all goes well, one more leak is sealed off. But sometimes Arno comes on a whole colony of shipworms in the process of patching one hole. Then entire sections of planking have to be repaired. In the process, he encounters passageways that come to the surface of the wood and then disappear again. These evasive tunnels gobble up huge amounts of cement. Water streams in. The whole enterprise often seems hopeless, and the amount of work required nearly endless.

As long as the leaks are easy to reach, the repair work is not in itself difficult, even though it takes a great deal of time. But when the leaks occur in the bottom of the hull, under the water tanks, under the food barrels, or in remote, barely accessible corners, the job is no longer simple; and these are the leaks that let in the most water. Carl and Arno bend over, working more by touch than by sight. When the ship rolls, they are drenched by the bilge, tossed against the planking, stabbed by the wooden pegs that stick up through the hull and frame. For weeks on end Carl and Arno have been crouching down there hour after hour every day.

Carl has incorporated a number of refinements into his battle against the shipworms. In addition to making his special tools — drills of different sizes, wires, handles — he has sewed himself a canvas apron with pockets in it to accommodate the tools. He has devoted almost as much time to the design and care of his equipment as he has to the actual struggle against the teredos. Arno is much less fastidious. He stuffs his tools into his pockets or hangs them around his neck on strings, then sets to work.

Lighting presents a problem. Almost all the lanterns are useless. Arno tried to replace their broken chimneys with jelly glasses, but the lanterns prove unsuitable for working below deck. Carl and Arno have to rely on the ship's two flashlights. Hardly anything on board receives such loving care as those flashlights, but they develop eccentricities anyhow.

That evening Carl announces that the *Tai Ki* has covered quite a bit more than half the way from Yokohama to San Francisco. Everyone gets a whiskey. A toast is proposed: May the time be not too distant when we shall drink our whiskey with ice and soda.

Then Carl says that from now on the *Tai Ki* will make radio contact with the U.S. Coast Guard every Tuesday. Allan will give the ship's position. If the coast guard does not receive this regular message and if no other messages from the *Tai Ki* are received for seventy-two hours after the appointed time, a search action will be initiated.

In the meantime, Kuno has received word from New York

that a California newspaper carried a complete report on the sinking of the *Tai Ki*. He has had no word from the crew, no sign of life. What has happened? Frantic telephone calls with Sweden, with the coast guard in San Francisco, Kodiak, and Los Angeles. He notifies the crew members' relatives. He has nothing certain to communicate but feels he has to prepare them for bad news. He passes the night plagued by fear, anxiety, and a sense of helplessness. Neither San Francisco nor Los Angeles has received any word of the *Tai Ki*. Then, hours later, a message comes through from Kodiak: the *Tai Ki,* identification number Oe-20-60, is O.K. and not in any danger. Someone in New York got his story wrong.

During these same hours, a gale is developing rapidly in the Pacific. Wind velocity reaches 40 mph. The seas grow heavier. The wind tears at the sails, shreds the rattan matting. Wolf staggers out on deck and tries to reef the sail. With Arno's help, he gets it under control.

Some gusts reach hurricane force. Waves tower over the *Tai Ki*. The crew members face another wretched night. Most of them will go without sleep. The ship rolls in the heavy seas. The storm bellows, takes a breather, roars again. Another gust whistles through the rigging. What will the ship look like tomorrow? How much water has she taken on? How many hours will we have to pump? Bob growls and curses.

At about this same time another ship is crossing the date line. She is the S.S. *Washington Mail*, a 720-foot container ship traveling from Japan to Seattle. The ship's 22,500-horsepower engines are driving her through the water at 17 knots. First Mate Larry Dale is standing on the bridge, looking out over the calm sea. In four and a half days he will be in Seattle. The *Washington Mail* will lie in port for a few days, then cross the Pacific to Japan again. Ordinarily she takes ten days for the crossing. Under ideal conditions, she can make it in nine.

Larry Dale takes a deep breath, lets it out wearily. In four days and a few hours the crew of the *Washington Mail* will be home. Then they will turn around and sail back again. They have been underway constantly for six months now, back and forth across the broad waters of the Pacific. Captain George Greenwell left the bridge an hour ago and retired to his cabin. In two hours he will be back.

For the coast guard of the Pacific Area this night is beginning like any other. Steve Pitro, the duty officer in Seattle, comes into the office at 2100. There is nothing new, nothing of any importance to attend to. He sighs and leafs through the day's log.

At Headquarters, Pacific Area Operations Division, on Sansome Street in San Francisco, Commander Bacon casts a last glance at the messages that have come in during the day. A low-pressure system between 120° and 130° west longitude and at 15° north latitude has been reported. A storm is building at 160° west longitude, 45° north latitude. There is another storm near the Queen Charlotte Islands off the Canadian coast. No emergencies at sea. All is quiet. Commander Bacon leaves his office, nodding to the NCO on duty as he goes out.

At 17th Coast Guard Headquarters in Juneau, Alaska, Lieutenant Olszewski and Lieutenant Commander Cannon are sitting in a canteen that reeks of plastic and are sipping coffee from paper cups they have fetched from a machine. The two pilots are on standby duty. They are far from eager to climb into their planes and take off for a night flight along the Pacific coast. Patrol flights are routine for them, but like all routines, this one too is wearying, exhausting, enervating.

In the coast guard station on Kodiak in the Gulf of Alaska, the NCO on duty leafs through the reports his predecessor has left on the steel desk for him: ships' positions, weather, and a schedule for radio contact with some crazy junk that is floating around in the middle of the Pacific and apparently running into a little trouble. The NCO lights a cigarette, tosses the ring notebook with the reports in it back on the desk, and tramps into the radio shack.

Tuesday, October 8. On the *Tai Ki,* Bill and Bob have managed to reef the sail some more. The wind has become even stronger, and they have made the decision to reef without waking Carl, who seems to be sleeping soundly in his cabin. Arno comes to help them. He can't sleep. Then he goes aft to take his watch at the rudder. Wolf stumbles out later to relieve him.

What has been noted on the coast guard maps as a relatively harmless storm descends on the crew of the *Tai Ki* with considerable pugnacity. At 0800, when the traditional cry of "Breakfast, *Frühstück,* breakfast!" wakes the crew members and brings them crawling out of their beds after a nearly sleepless night, the wind out of the southeast has reached a gale force of 45 mph. The seas are growing heavier. October 8 promises to be a busy day. Between 0000 and 0800, the barometer has dropped almost half an inch.

"Respectable, respectable," Allan grumbles as he slurps chlorine-scented instant coffee out of a plastic cup.

Arno's journal:

The day's work is divided up, as it is every day. Bill is in charge of the kitchen. Hal and Wolf will man the pumps, assisted by Bob and Allan. After breakfast, I'll crawl into compartment four to plug up some holes. Carl claims we don't even have to bother looking into compartment five. Everything is O.K. there. It's true that we have less water in the boat than we expected after last night.

I'm so preoccupied with my work that I hardly notice the wind increasing and the seas becoming heavier. With time you get used to just about anything. I climb topside and see Carl at the rudder. He's having trouble with it and can hardly manage to steer the boat at all. . . .

The wind velocity has increased even more, and gusts of hurricane force smash down on the *Tai Ki.* Bob claims that the waves are already over thirty feet. Hal says they're over forty. Spray is thrown against the cabins and squirts through the walls into the ship. Everything is wet. Bob is tossed against the wall near hatch number six and throws the pump down in a rage. Bill squats in front of the stove, cursing and trying in vain to start a fire.

The towering waves begin to flood the forward deck and smash against the roof of the cabin. The noise is deafening: the howling of the storm, the crashing of the waves, the pounding of the bow against the turbulent seas. The port gunwale is continually under water.

Allan stumbles to the helmsman's bench, where Carl is sitting with his legs spread wide for stability. Allan tries to measure the wind velocity. He opens one of the rattan doors and sticks the anemometer out. He doesn't want to believe what he sees. The little red pointer races up the scale and comes up short at the far end. The wind exceeds the capacity of our anemometer. It is over 80 mph, considerably over. The "click" that Allan seems to perceive with his eyes makes that clear. The pointer strikes the limit of the scale and bounces back like a spring.

Work on board ceases. It is impossible to move about any longer, much less accomplish anything. Some of the crew put on their life jackets; safety belts are secured. The men try to jam themselves into corners in the cabin so they won't be tossed about inside the ship.

Water pummels the *Tai Ki*. A few of the emergency oars were torn loose during the night and have disappeared into the sea. Now part of the catwalk on the bow shatters. Then there is another crunching sound. A board has been broken out of the rudder housing. The water has chopped through it like an axe. The after catwalk on the port side is starting to crumble now, too. It won't last out the day.

Visibility grows increasingly poor. Fog seems to envelop the ship, but it is not fog. It is water, a fine saltwater spray tossed up and atomized by the wind. Breathing is difficult. Another deafening crash is heard, and still another plank in the rudder housing is reduced to splinters. The storm has become a full-fledged hurricane.

It is 1300. Carl has been on the dripping helmsman's bench for hours now. His muscles are cramped, his limbs stiff, but he does not want to be relieved. The storm is so fierce, the sea so heavy, that he does not want to give up the rudder to anyone else. At 1330 he gives the order to lower the port leeboard, hoping to give the ship additional steerageway. Arno and Wolf set to work. Arno dangles over the side on a thin nylon line. The waves tear at him as he clings to the planking with his fingernails. He is unable to lower the leeboard more than half its length. And it proves to be of no use. The *Tai Ki* continues to lose steerageway. She takes the heavy seas broadside. Nothing can be done. The ship soon has no steerageway at all, and wind and sea are growing heavier still. The pumps have been abandoned long since. The crew can only sit back and wait for the storm to subside. Bob takes his camera and, accompanied by Arno, goes out on the forward deck. Tumbling about like acrobats, they take pictures of the boiling sea.

1445. Bill fights his way to the stern, where Carl is doing battle with rudder and sea. Bill stands by, ready to help if he should be needed. There is a sudden snapping sound, as if a steel guitar string had broken. Bill experiences a moment of panic, yells to Carl. The storm nearly swallows his words.

"Is anything wrong?"

Carl responds with a reassuring gesture. Nothing serious. Probably just another smashed plank in the rudder housing. But before Bill has had a chance to calm himself fully, Carl shrieks at the top of his lungs: "Arno!"

Arno tumbles toward the stern, bumps into Hal, who has jammed himself in near the mast, rams a shoulder into Bill, finally reaches Carl.

"What's up?"

Carl points at the rudder lines, then pulls on them. They run free in the pulleys. There's not an ounce of pressure on them.

The rudder is broken. The massive trunk of billian wood has snapped in two. The hurricane and the waves cracked it as easily

261

as a man can snap a matchstick between his fingers. The broad blade of the rudder is hanging on its chains below the helmsman's cabin. The remains of the shaft stab out into thin air.

Now the *Tai Ki* is completely at the mercy of the waves. They spin and turn her at will. The crew rushes out on deck. Wolf and Arno lower two sea anchors to port; Bob and Allan do the same to starboard. Bill and Hal reef the sail completely now. In the meantime Carl has freed the ship of its broken rudder. The blade bobs up once off the stern, then disappears in the foam and raging waves.

As Bob and Allan are setting the second sea anchor on the starboard side, the *Tai Ki* rises up on the crest of a high wave. A gust of wind, perceptible as a gust even in this storm, tears at the rigging. Several spars are splintered, but the crew hears nothing. The roar of the hurricane swallows every other sound.

The *Tai Ki* seems to lie at rest on the crest of this wave. She hangs there for fractions of a second that seem like minutes. Then, as if spun about by some ghostly hand, the ship turns 180 degrees. Suddenly everyone is looking in the opposite direction he was facing just an instant before. But this fact is hardly perceptible, for the violence of the sea is the same on all sides.

The sea anchors are torn from their lines. The water pressure has snapped the ropes as if they had been threads. The crew lowers two baskets into the water as sea anchors, but these too disappear in a matter of minutes. Arno improvises still another sea anchor from an empty barrel. This time heavier ropes are used, but the anchor has little effect. It rides too high in the water and cannot hold the ship steady.

Now Carl orders Allan to contact the coast guard on Kodiak and give the *Tai Ki*'s position. Allan tumbles into his radio shack and sends 169° west longitude, 40° 30′ north latitude. He cannot raise Kodiak. Despite the cold, the wind, the water pouring in on him, he drips sweat as he sits at his radio and tries to make contact. Nothing. He decides to wait until dark before he tries again. He will notify the coast guard of the *Tai Ki*'s position and ask that rescue operations begin if she does not call in again within twenty-four hours.

Arno goes to Carl, who is sitting calmly on the helmsman's bench, playing with the soaked, blackened hemp of the steering lines. The captain of the expedition opines that the crew will have to install the spare rudder now.

"Impossible in this weather," Arno replies.

"Well, then we'll just have to wait till it gets better."

But when will it get better? How long will this storm last?

Although the crew members had anticipated situations like this with considerable anxiety, they are remarkably calm now that the ship's condition is critical. Everyone knows what the facts are, and all the facts are bad. Everyone knows that the *Tai Ki* can capsize rapidly and without warning. But despite this knowledge, the crew's attitude is one of composure.

Bill, Arno, and Hal put on their wet suits. They go out on the forward deck and sit down. There is nothing more they can do.

Arno writes in his journal: ". . . and here we are just sitting around, all in rather good spirits. We don't have time to be afraid, although we actually would have time for it right now. I feel confident we'll come through all right. After all, we're well equipped; and wood floats."

Not everyone is as sanguine as Arno, but the entire crew braces itself calmly and stoically for whatever is coming. The hurricane has not diminished in force. The red pointer on the anemometer still races to the far end of the scale and bounces back. Breakers are still crashing down on the ship. This is clearly the most violent storm the *Tai Ki* has encountered on her voyage.

Hal suddenly jumps up from the hatch near the life rafts.

"I just heard something!" he yells at Arno.

Arno stands up. He hears a muffled, rushing sound from below deck.

"Come on," he says.

He and Hal race, tumble, and crawl into the cabin. Hal yanks on the hatch of compartment five. Arno takes hold with him. They heave together, and the hatch flies open. They see daylight. Daylight rises up to them through the darkness of the compartment and illuminates the dim cabin. A gaping hole has opened in the hull. A patch of light a yard square shimmers up through the water that has risen to the hatchway and is now sloshing over it.

"Carl!" Hal yells.

Carl comes to the hatchway, steadies himself by hanging onto the cabin roof, peers into the hatch. He stares, seems paralyzed for seconds on end, forgetting, wanting to forget. Then he turns away quickly and says softly, perhaps too softly, to Allan, "Mayday! Put out an SOS!"

Time: 1615.

Allan rushes for the radio shack and sends out his SOS to Kodiak. There is no response, and the men of the *Tai Ki* have no idea whether their call for help has been heard or not.

No one can say for sure what caused the break in the hull. The water tank that had broken loose and was floating around in the compartment might have smashed into the hull hard enough to shatter the planking. Or a piece of billian broken off the catwalk might have crashed through the hull from the outside. Or the hull may have been so weakened by the shipworms that it simply gave way under the water pressure. There is no telling now which of these factors caused the break or whether all three had a part in it.

Carl sums up the ship's situation tersely. "The ship can't stay afloat much longer. Water is pouring into her, and she's losing her balance. There's real danger of capsizing now."

The crew members assemble their essential gear in frantic haste. In what seems a matter of minutes, the cabin looks the way it did just before the departure from Hong Kong when everyone had just brought his gear on board. Sea bags, cameras, and aluminum suitcases are piled everywhere with smaller bags and life jackets thrown on top of them. Lap Sac weaves in and out among the luggage, whimpering as he makes his rounds.

Kodiak and Juneau had received the *Tai Ki*'s call for help, and at 1627 Juneau transmitted the following message to all ships in the vicinity of the *Tai Ki:* "Urgent, urgent, urgent. The junk *Tai Ki* is in danger of sinking. Her position is 169° west longitude, 40° 30' north latitude. All ships in the area are requested to give what help they can and report any action taken to Juneau or the next closest coast guard station."

This message with the priority of "urgent," which is one stage lower than the SOS Allan had sent, reached the radio room of the *Washington Mail* via Adak in the western Aleutians at 1700. Captain Greenwell sent his response to the coast guard station in Juneau: "My position is 174° 51' west longitude, 44° 14' north latitude. I am about eighteen hours away from the *Tai Ki.* Can I be of any help?"

Juneau's answer was prompt and brief: "Sail for the *Tai Ki* at top speed, and many thanks."

Before the radioman on the *Washington Mail* had even sent out his reply, Captain Greenwell had come quickly to the conclusion that his ship was the only one that could reach the foundering junk in time. He immediately changed his course and ordered an increase in speed from 17 to 22 knots. At this point, the *Washington Mail* was about 350 nautical miles away from the *Tai Ki.* It could well be that Greenwell's decision made the difference between life and death for the crew. He reacted instantly to the "urgent" message, although he was by no means obliged to do so. Only an SOS would have made it mandatory for him to undertake a rescue action.

On the *Tai Ki,* the crew has no idea that help is already on the way. Allan's radio maintains its silence. Uncertainty reigns aboard the junk as she is tossed about in a raging sea. How much longer can the ship take this beating? Everyone is afraid the junk will capsize suddenly, everyone except Carl and Arno, who will later look back with some astonishment on their unshaking faith in the *Tai Ki*'s buoyancy.

Everyone but Carl puts on his wet suit and life jacket, and the crew assemble rations for the life rafts. Along with the danger of capsizing, the crew also have to reckon with the possibility that large breaks may occur in compartments four and six.

Allan finally makes contact with the coast guard in Juneau. The message he hears comes in faintly, but it comes in: help is on the way.

Lieutenant Olszewski and Lieutenant Commander Cannon are taking off from Juneau. They will be circling the *Tai Ki* in a few hours, and at the Navy base of Adak, another plane is standing by. Kodiak has put the coast guard cutter *Boutwell* on alert. Equipped with a helicopter on board, she is ready to sail at a moment's notice. A second coast guard cutter, the *Jarvis,* which is cruising on the Bering Sea, has picked up the *Tai Ki*'s SOS. She, too, is put on standby alert.

The two search planes will attempt to locate the *Tai Ki* and then guide the *Washington Mail* to her. If this plan fails, additional ships and planes can join the rescue action. The coast guard's rapidly but carefully thought out rescue action begins to move like clockwork.

Night falls on the *Tai Ki,* and everyone hopes this will be the last night he spends on board. The crew members have snatched what they could for an evening meal, possibly their last meal for a long time.

At 2000, Allan receives a radio message: the coast guard has pinpointed the *Tai Ki*'s position, and a search plane should be reaching her at 0100. The *Washington Mail* is approaching from the northwest and is expected to arrive around 1000 the following morning.

2200. The wind dies down somewhat, but occasional gusts are still of hurricane force. The ship is still being tossed about unmercifully by the heavy seas. Breakers continue to smash down on her; planking cracks; the hull trembles. The pumps are still at work in compartments four and six. This helps the ship maintain her buoyancy. Even as a wreck, the *Tai Ki* remains amazingly stable and takes the waves with an ease that almost inspires a sense of confidence and safety in the crew. Everyone knows that help is on the way. It's just a matter of hanging on for a few more hours now.

The crew members take what rest they can. They wait. Some popular song or other is coming out of the cabin radio. And the dog dies. Bob had mixed a heavy dose of sleeping powder into Lap Sac's supper. Bob did this at a point when no one could know if help would come or not and when the crew had to be ready to take to the life rafts. The dog would have been a serious danger under those circumstances. He could have clawed or chewed holes in the rubber life rafts and left the crew swimming for their lives. Lap Sac was the *Tai Ki*'s first casualty. The ship was the only world he had known, these 350 square feet of wood with the sea beyond them, a world inhabited by bearded, long-legged creatures that greeted him with curses or, as Bob and Allan did, with gentle hands. Lap Sac had staggered across the cabin and died next to the sleeping mat of his master, Bob Kendrick. The next morning, the crew wrapped Lap Sac's body in canvas, weighted it down with stone, and sent the small Chinese dog that had set out to sail halfway around the world to his seaman's grave.

Worry and anxiety plague the crew. Will help reach us in time? Bill and Arno are sitting together. These two men who were near enemies before the ship sailed from Kao-hsiung have become fast friends. They empty a bottle of port wine together, and Bill says with a grin, "Just like the good old days back in the Red Carpet." His allusion is to the little restaurant in Hong Kong where the crew always ate together before they set out on this voyage that was ending far differently than anyone had imagined it would.

Allan receives another message from the coast guard at 2230. Two search planes have been dispatched at different times so that the second can relieve the first when it has to go back to refuel. The crew is hopeful, but hope cannot completely dispel the fear they feel, alone in the midst of a stormy sea.

Wednesday, October 9. 0015. The crew hears a plane approaching from the west-northwest; then the plane's running lights come into view. Allan makes radio contact, and Carl fires a signal rocket. Arno and Hal set up a blinker so that the plane can always make out the *Tai Ki*'s position. A blinding light flashes out intermittently over the water.

The *Tai Ki* is no longer alone, but now she is threatened by another internal danger. The water tank that is floating around loose in compartment five is smashing against the bulkhead that separates compartments four and five. It could easily break through. The crew reinforces the bulkhead, but water begins to leak into compartment four anyhow. The pumps are called into service again. The *Tai Ki* puts out a sonar buoy. This device will enable the search planes to pinpoint her position at any time, even if visibility should be cut off.

The seas abate somewhat. The men can sleep a bit, briefly, restlessly. Then morning dawns, clear and sunny, a morning that will probably be the last for the *Tai Ki,* the last of a voyage that should have lasted longer. The storm has left heavy swells in its wake. The crew will learn later that they had passed through a "mini-typhoon." Meteorologists became aware of this type of storm only recently. For reasons no one has yet been able to determine, these storms rise suddenly, then disappear again just as suddenly after traveling a few hundred miles. They are rarely more than 250 miles in diameter, but peak wind velocities near the eye often exceed 120 mph. The *Tai Ki* passed through the eye of this storm. She had weathered twelve typhoons, but the thirteenth was one too many for her.

Just as this number thirteen calls up associations of farfetched sailors' yarns, so too does another event that took place on the *Tai Ki*'s last day.

The rat Pericles had been with the *Tai Ki* for the whole voyage, spending the last few weeks of it as a captive but a captive that Carl had fed and tended carefully. Pericles had been through just as many storms as the crew had. But on this particular morning, when it became clear that the crew would abandon ship, the rat began to stagger about in its cage, then fell over dead. Pericles too had been a ship's mascot in his own right, and he chose to take his leave of life before the ship met her end. He was one rat that failed to leave a sinking ship.

A last breakfast on board. The crew members cast melancholy glances at all the rations they had refrained from eating but that would now be lost to the sea.

0900. Radio message from Lieutenant Commander Cannon: "Do you need a pump?"

"Yes!"

"O.K., you'll get one."

Arno's journal:

The plane makes four passes over the *Tai Ki*, then drops a smoke marker. Question over the radio: "Where do you want the pump? On the forward deck or at the stern?"

We don't take this question very seriously, but we answer it anyhow: "On the forward deck."

"O.K.," the pilot responds.

Then the plane makes two more passes very low over our heads. A parachute is falling dead center onto the forward deck. It would have been a bull's-eye if the parachute hadn't tangled in the mast.

The parachute provides a few more minutes of risky activity for the crew. It's no easy job on a violently rocking ship to cut a pump out of the air and bring a flapping parachute under control. Carl finally manages to cut through the parachute lines, and the pump comes thudding down on the deck. It is put into service instantly. Compartment four is soon dry, but it isn't long before it fills up again.

Allan receives another radio message: a ship is approaching the *Tai Ki* from the south and should reach her about 1300. Whether this is the *Washington Mail* or not is left unclear.

The crew does some more packing. The ship's provisions will be abandoned with her. Last nibbles of chocolate and licorice, those carefully guarded treasures, are passed around recklessly now. The men of the *Tai Ki* may be shipwrecked, but rescue is close at hand.

1015. A message comes in from the *Washington Mail.* She'll arrive in an hour and a quarter. At the same time, Captain Greenwell wires the coast guard in Juneau: "Approaching the *Tai Ki,* will take on survivors."

Carl and Captain Greenwell confer by radio about how the rescue should be effected. Final decisions are put off until the *Washington Mail* has actually come up alongside the junk. The crew will attempt to rescue as much of the ship's gear as possible.

At 1115, the container ship appears on the horizon. There is no jubilation on the *Tai Ki.* Everyone is glad that the struggle is over, glad to have survived. But it is not easy to abandon this ship.

The last phase of the rescue action begins. The operation will not be as simple as everyone concerned wishes it could be. The *Washington Mail* cannot lower her lifeboats in this heavy a sea. And then the junk is moving along at a surprisingly fast speed. The glowing red parachute still tangled in her mast is acting like a spinnaker. Captain Greenwell has to put his ship to windward of the *Tai Ki* to come up alongside her at all.

After half an hour of maneuvering, the two ships are side by side, 30,000 tons next to 30.

"We weren't any bigger than a container on the *Washington Mail,* and we were smaller than one of her lifeboats," Hal reported later. The mast of the *Tai Ki* didn't even reach up to the deck of the steamer, where curious crewmen peered over the railing to watch the rescue.

The *Washington Mail* lowers some lines to the nutshell bobbing alongside her. The first line is made fast on the *Tai Ki,* then winched taut. It snaps. Two more lines will break before the junk is lashed, bow and stern, to the larger ship and lies relatively stable in the water.

Then the first man from the *Tai Ki* goes aboard the freighter. His gear follows, then another crewman, then still another. Hal, Bob, Allan, Wolf, Arno — he takes time to cut down the red, white, and red Austrian flag and the pennant of the Adventurers' Club before he leaves the ship. Bill, a professional cameraman to the bitter end, stays on board the junk to film the rescue; then he too goes aboard the *Washington Mail.* Carl, the captain, is the last to leave the *Tai Ki.*

The lines to the *Tai Ki* go slack; the junk drifts away; the freighter's screws bite into the water. In half an hour the *Tai Ki* has been lost from view.

Captain Greenwell reports to Commander Kellogg of the coast guard in Juneau that the rescue has been completed successfully. Kellogg was in charge of coordinating the entire action; for him and his command, the episode may have been routine. For the crew of the *Tai Ki* it was a small miracle.

On the *Washington Mail,* preparations had been made to accommodate the unexpected company, and the visitors are escorted to their quarters.

The time is 1220. The crewmen of the *Tai Ki* have trouble keeping their balance. They're not accustomed to having solid ground under their feet. The *Washington Mail* is hardly a piece of terra firma: she is in motion; the seas are high around her with waves of about twenty feet; and the wind is still blowing at a respectable 30 mph. But the huge ship is relatively unaffected by these forces. A man can raise a glass to his lips without danger of

271

the drink slopping into his lap. But at the moment, the behavior of drinks in glasses doesn't concern the crewmen of the *Tai Ki*. They are enjoying slugs of aquavit from a bottle that some thoughtful sailors have offered them.

The cabins are painted white and light green. There are showers, beds with clean linen on them. Captain Greenwell extends an invitation to cocktails in two hours. A wood-paneled sitting room with thick carpets and heavily upholstered armchairs. Carl, Arno, Allan, everyone from the *Tai Ki* has spruced himself up, dug his shore clothes out of his sea bag and found them usable though wrinkled and smelling of the sea. The men from the junk feel awkward in these clothes and in their new situation. Civilization has reclaimed them, but they don't quite know yet what to make of it. So little time has passed since they were sitting in the cabin of the *Tai Ki,* hoping for rescue, pushing fear away, counting the hours that separated them from safety. Now they find themselves in an elegant sitting room. All at once they are heroes of the day. They have been thrust into the limelight, temporarily anyhow, before their legs, accustomed to the rolling of the junk, have even had a chance to adjust to the steady deck of the *Washington Mail.* They make conversation, nod politely to all sides. And then that inevitable duty of the famous falls incumbent upon them: they are asked to give autographs; and, hesitantly, they give them, doubtful that they have achieved anything that makes their signatures valuable. Between rounds of drinks their thoughts wander to that structure of wood, bamboo, and rattan that is drifting aimlessly on the sea now and that was their home for four months. The crewmen of the *Tai Ki* are glad that they won't have to witness her death. Whenever they think of her in the future, they will have a picture of her disappearing over the horizon with a bright red parachute still tangled in her rigging.

Monday, October 14. The *Washington Mail* pulls into Seattle harbor at 0500. Kuno Knöbl and his Austrian publisher, Fritz

Molden, who have flown to Seattle to meet the crew, are standing on the dock.

The expedition is over. The crew will remain together for two more days; then everyone will go his own way.

Hal heads for Vancouver, where he had lived for several years. Then he will return to Mary in Hong Kong. Hong Kong — how remote that city seems now.

Bob and Allan decide to spend a month hitchhiking through the United States. They both want to be back in Europe by December, Bob to prepare for a new job in England, Allan to return to the life and work he had left before the expedition.

Arno will visit friends in Alaska. Then he wants to go to Mexico to take some more pictures, especially of the Tajin pyramid, the huge step pyramid that is so reminiscent of the ones at Angkor. Bill is flying to Santa Barbara to see his mother; then he'll go on to New York to edit films of the expedition.

Carl is the only one of us who will remain on the West Coast. He has a plane ticket from Seattle to Los Angeles, from Los Angeles to San Francisco, from San Francisco back to Los Angeles. He's going to visit the coast guard stations along the way. He intends to stay on the West Coast and wait for a while. The currents just might bring his ship to shore here. He has taken a hotel room in Los Angeles that affords him a view of the sea. He can look out onto the beach and the Pacific, onto the waves that rush toward him out of the blue void. He will wait.

Afterword

IN 1882, THE AMERICAN CHARLES BROOKS PUBLISHED A rather strange book. For nearly forty years, he had kept a record of all the ships originating in Asian ports that were wrecked in the Pacific and then washed up on the American coast. The "landing sites" extended from Alaska to Acapulco, and Brooks listed more than fifty wrecks.

The purpose of Brooks's work was to prove that the currents of the Pacific were such that even unmanned ships would necessarily be driven from Asia to America.

That America could in fact have been reached by ship in prehistoric times has still not been proved beyond the shadow of a doubt because the members of the *Tai Ki* expedition were obliged to leave their ship two thousand nautical miles off the West Coast of North America. Similar attempts to cross the Pacific had been made in this century before the *Tai Ki* expedition. More than twenty men have died in these efforts, but further attempts will be made.

We owe a large debt of thanks to all who assisted us. The late Dr. Robert Heine-Geldern must surely stand at the head of this list that also includes Dr. Gordon Ekholm, Dr. Betty Meggers, Dr. Clifford Evans, Dr. Pedro Bosch Gimpera, who died on the same day the crew of the *Tai Ki* landed in Seattle, Dr. Alexander von

Wuthenau, Dr. Ignacio Bernal, Almut Rottenbacher, Dr. Cyrus Gordon, the Smithsonian Institution in Washington, the National Geographic Society, the University of the Americas in Mexico City, the California Academy of Sciences, and the California Historical Society.

We are also grateful to Arne Andersson, Erik Rothstein, Alf Svensson, Kjell Andersson, Axel Westgard, and Lennart Durèn of the amateur radio club in Nynäshamn, Sweden; to the Austrian amateur radioman Leo Mis; the American radioman "Danny" in Hong Kong; the British Marine Department and the Royal Observatory in Hong Kong; the Japanese coast guard; and the United States Coast Guard, particularly the stations in Kodiak and Juneau and Commander R. B. Bacon, Chief, Search and Rescue Branch, Pacific Area Command. Our special thanks go to Captain George Greenwell of the *Washington Mail* and to his crew.

Further thanks are due to those who assisted in the making of this book: my father, Herbert Knöbl, who helped in the production of the maps and illustrations, and Dr. Günther Treffer, my editor at the Verlag Fritz Molden.

And finally I would like to thank everyone who provided material assistance to the expedition: the Julius Meinl GmbH, the firm "Felix Austria," and Austrian Airlines, especially its director, Dr. Anton Heschgl.

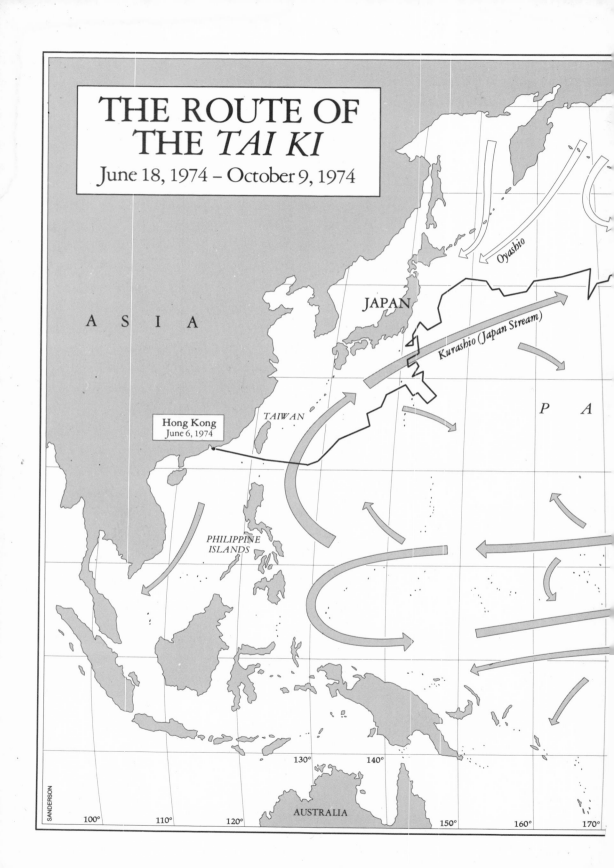

THE ROUTE OF THE *TAI KI*

June 18, 1974 – October 9, 1974